Black Genesis

GALE GENEALOGY AND LOCAL HISTORY SERIES

Series Editor: J. Carlyle Parker, Head of Public Services and Assistant Library Director, California State College, Stanislaus; and Founder and Librarian Volunteer, Modesto California Branch Genealogical Library of the Genealogical Department of the Church of Jesus Christ of Latter-day Saints, Salt Lake City, Utah

Also in this series:

General Editor: Paul Wasserman, Professor and former Dean, School of Library and Information Services, University of Maryland

Managing Editor: Denise Allard Adzigian, Gale Research Company

Black Genesis

Volume 1 in the Gale Genealogy and Local History Series

James Rose

Codirector
Ethnic Genealogy Center
Queens College
Flushing, New York

Alice Eichholz

Assistant Professor
Department of Special Programs
Queens College
Flushing, New York

Gale Research Company
Book Tower, Detroit, Michigan 48226

Library of Congress Cataloging in Publication Data

Rose, James, 1941-
    Black genesis.

    (Gale genealogy and local history series; v. 1)
    Includes indexes.
1. Afro-Americans—Genealogy—Handbooks, manuals, etc.
2. United States—Genealogy—Handbooks, manuals, etc.
I. Eichholz, Alice, 1942-   joint author. II. Title.
CS21.R57   929'.1   77-74819
ISBN 0-8103-1400-2

To

The Principles of the Kinte Library Project

and

Alex Haley, for Inspiration

VITAE

James M. Rose received his Master's at Queens College of the City University of New York. He has published articles in CONNECTICUT ANCESTRY and THE NEW YORK GENEALOGICAL AND BIOGRAPHICAL MAGAZINE. He is codirector of the Ethnic Genealogy Center at Queens College of The City University of New York, and is a teacher of African History at Woodlands High School in Hartsdale, New York.

Alice Eichholz is an assistant professor at Queens College in the Department of Special Programs. She received her M.Ed. from Wayne State University and Ph.D. from New York University. Presently she is codirector of the Ethnic Genealogy Center at Queens College and research associate for The Institute for Psychohistory. In addition to her publication on black genealogy she has published two books on her family--the Linvilles.

CONTENTS

Contents

Contents

Appendixes

Indexes

LIST OF ILLUSTRATIONS

ACKNOWLEDGMENTS

BLACK GENESIS began when Jim Rose was training at the Kinte Library Project funded by the Carnegie Corporation. In the process he spent many hours at the Rockefeller Library at Brown University. While teaching at Queens College he and Alice Eichholz started a research team with the intent of establishing a genealogical research center. The compiling and editing of BLACK GENESIS could not have been completed without the support of Queens College and acting president Nathaniel Siegel. We are grateful for the assistance of Wentworth Ofuatey-Kodjoe, Africana Studies; Dean Anisia Quinones, Department of Special Programs; the Queens College Alumni Association; the Word Processing Center staff; and the industrious work of the many students in the Ethnic Genealogy Center, formerly called the Black Genealogical Research Center.

Research assistance was offered by Arthur Konop of St. Francis College; Dr. Leo Hershkowitz, Queens College Historical Documents Collection; Cynthia Plato, Georgia Department of Archives; Mrs. Gross, Rockefeller Library, Brown University; Frank Bradley and Timothy F. Beard, New York Public Library; and many librarians at historical societies and libraries, who understood the concept we have tried to develop. In addition we are grateful for the support offered by James Dyer and Gloria Primm Brown at the Carnegie Corporation, as well as R.R. Bowker and Company for permission to include some of the material compiled by William Schatz at the Race Relations Information Center in their book DIRECTORY OF AFRO-AMERICAN RESOURCES.

Special acknowledgment is given to Len Jeffries, City College; Courtney Brown, Human Rights Commission; Michael Wrezin, Queens College; and Jimmy Walker of the National Archives, for guidance and helpful advice.

Throughout the several years when the material was being compiled and edited, we were privileged to have the constant moral support of Manuel and Mildred Rose, James Manuel Rose, Jr., Mary Rose, Nicholas Rose, and Brian A. Schwartz. Without them, our energies would have been exhausted long ago.

Finally, but most important, we are deeply indebted to Roger Scanland of the Genealogical Department in Salt Lake City; Mordine Mallory, Queens College

Acknowledgments

Department of Special Programs Librarian; and J. Carlyle Parker, Gale Research series editor. Without their vision, insight, and persistent help we would not have been able to make this work available to the public.

James M. Rose

Alice Eichholz

Part I

BACKGROUND

Chapter 1

INTRODUCTION

Genealogical research begins with an inquiring interest and availability of primary resources. Previous to BLACK GENESIS and ROOTS there was little attempt to spur the interest of thousands of black Americans in researching history through ancestry. In addition, many thought that the primary resources available for white family research were not available for researching black family ancestry. Nothing could be further from the truth.

This volume is an attempt to create an interest in black family ancestry in order to retrieve a large part of history and ancestry which has, all too frequently, been overlooked, ignored, and sometimes obliterated. Three tasks for a restoration of this aspect of history are suggested here: (1) helping the novice in black family ancestry to begin searching for his or her own roots in Western soil; (2) encouraging the development of black genealogical research by suggesting and illustrating areas where records need to be diligently uncovered and published; and (3) suggesting ways genealogical materials can be used to reexamine history.

HELPING THE NOVICE

Very little has been published which deals with black genealogical research (see chapter 2, "General References"). However, there are a few examples of individual black family ancestries in print. These include the histories of the Lansdown family, the Bustil family from Philadelphia, the Varick family in New York, William Steward and Theophilus Gould Steward's GOULDTOWN: A VERY REMARKABLE SETTLEMENT OF ANCIENT DATE (Philadelphia: J.B. Lippincott Co., 1913), and Pauli Murray's PROUD SHOES (1956. Reprint. Spartanburg, S.C.: Reprint Co., 1973). These genealogies, along with that of the Jackson family included later in this introduction, will give a good idea of what can be uncovered and documented in black family ancestry.

The basic principle for genealogical research is to start with the present and work backward one generation at a time. The following are suggested steps for the beginner:

3

1. Read a general reference book. There are many such books which should be consulted, and which are listed in chapter 2 under Genealogical Guide Books. Gilbert H. Doane's SEARCH-ING FOR YOUR ANCESTORS is one of the better ones. This volume does not duplicate similar references, but rather begins where they stop.

2. Conduct interviews with older members of your family. The purpose is to gather as much family data as possible, including dates and places of births, deaths, and marriages. Document your sources of information. Oral history gathered in interviews is a very important aspect of black family research in particular. Chapter 3, "Oral History" describes how to do this part of the research. Other local sources can fill in the gaps in data when necessary. Three pamphlets published by the Department of Health, Education and Welfare are excellent references at a nominal price:

DHEW-HRA 75-1142 WHERE TO WRITE FOR BIRTH AND DEATH RECORDS. $.35.

DHEW-HRA 74-1144 WHERE TO WRITE FOR MARRIAGE RECORDS. $.35.

DHEW-HRA 75-1145 WHERE TO WRITE FOR DIVORCE RECORDS. $.35.

They can be obtained from the Superintendent of Documents, Government Printing Office, Washington, D.C. 20402.

3. Find your ancestors in the Federal Census Schedules. The 1880 census has a Soundex indexing system for all those families who had children under ten years of age. Each person in the household is listed by name, sex, age, place of birth, and place of parents' birth. The 1900 census has a Soundex for all persons. A local library can help you obtain information from the Soundex at the National Archives in Washington, D.C., or in the Federal Records Center in your area. There are census records available from 1790 to 1900, however only those blacks who had obtained their freedom previous to 1865 will be listed in the 1850 and 1860 censuses, and only heads of households of free black families are listed in 1790, 1800, 1820, 1830, 1840 censuses. See chapter 4, "National Archives and Federal Records" for a complete explanation.

4. Check county records (i.e., wills, deeds, court proceedings, etc.), military records, church records, and miscellaneous records for family information. This is where BLACK GENESIS can be particularly helpful. Chapter 5 covers military records available for blacks. Next, chapter 6 briefly outlines the migrating patterns of blacks--patterns which differed from those of white Americans. That chapter is followed by a discussion of records involving slavery and how they can be used to document and trace black family ancestry. The last part of BLACK GENESIS consists of a survey of some states which had large black populations before 1900 and can be considered "nucleus" states for the development of the black family in the United States. For each state, representative data needed for documenting family research are given, in addition to

further suggestions for research in that state. By looking under
the states where a family lived, you will get a general understanding of the kinds of records which can provide specific information on blacks. It is important to understand that the survey of
states does not include the multitude of state and county records
which are general genealogical resources for everyone, and which
have not been indexed or organized specifically for black genealogical research. If a resource is not mentioned here it does not
mean that it does not exist.

UNEARTHING THE RECORDS

Most genealogists, historians, and black Americans are unfamiliar with the enormous scope of records from the last 350 years of both slave and free blacks in
the United States. As this volume illustrates, the records are both massive and
relatively unused because there has been no concerted effort to find and publish them. The survey of state and county records illustrates the types of records and scope of information available, but these records are by no means
the extent of what can be discovered.

Genealogical resource books are written mainly for those who want to trace
European ancestry. Consequently, publications such as will abstracts, vital
statistics, and gravestone inscriptions often do not include blacks. For example,
persons identified as "negar" or "negrine" were excluded in a recently published
work. In addition, published census indexes often leave out "color" designations which are included in the original census returns. Abstracts of wills, such
as New York City Surrogate's Court Wills, do not include names of black slaves
mentioned in the original wills. Consequently, in order to trace black families,
the original source must always be used.

This is a very time-consuming, expensive process for an individual. It is hoped
that research and publishing teams will be formed to do for every state's records
what has been briefly done in BLACK GENESIS for the records of Maryland,
Louisiana, Georgia, and Virginia.

Roger Scanland, a staff member of the Genealogical Department of the Church
of Jesus Christ of Latter-day Saints in Salt Lake City, Utah, has suggested the
following long- and short-term projects. They begin to illustrate the tremendous task necessary in retrieving black genealogical records.

1. An alphabetical, nationwide index of all slaves over 100 years old who
   were listed in the 1860 census. These are virtually the only slaves listed
   by name in any population schedules. (See Nebraska and Utah sections
   for exceptions.) Although free blacks had been listed in the census since
   1790, slaves were not usually listed by name. The 1860 census lists ages
   and place of birth (in many cases, Africa) of the slaves over 100.
2. While information regarding free blacks is now available in print for the
   1790 and 1830 censuses, similar projects should be undertaken for the

1800, 1810, 1820, 1840, and 1850 census returns.

3. Revolutionary War records for blacks are now available in print. Other National Archives pension and war records need to be retrieved and printed from the War of 1812, Indian wars, war with Mexico, Civil War, both Union and Confederate, and the war with Spain. (See chapter 5, "War Records.")

4. Vital records of blacks found in family Bibles and diaries need to be located and indexed. Previously, most family Bible records printed in genealogical magazines omitted slave entries. The Genealogical Department (see appendix B for list of branch libraries) has on microfilm many Bible records gathered by the Daughters of the American Revolution; however, searching these records would be a tedious task.

5. All genealogical material in the Freedman's Bureau records needs to be published. They are presently being microfilmed at the National Archives in Washington, D.C. (See chapter 4, "National Archives and Federal Records.")

6. Slave traders records should be found, indexed, and published.

7. A search for slave-aid-society records needs to be undertaken.

8. In addition to archives of integrated congregations, black religious archives should be surveyed for genealogical material and such material should be published.

9. The obituaries and other genealogical records in all black newspapers and magazines, especially those published by black churches, should be sought out and indexed. And black genealogical information from all newspapers should be indexed.

10. A nationwide, alphabetical computerized index of all slave owners in the 1850 and 1860 U.S. Slave Schedules should be published.

11. The 1890 special census of Civil War veterans should be published, indicating all blacks.

12. The manumission records available for all counties in all states should be published. Many such records are available on microfilm through the Genealogical Department. But others are hidden in deeds and miscellaneous papers in town halls and courthouses.

13. Marriage records of blacks should be published for all states which kept segregated records as well as those where licenses identify blacks.

14. All court records involving blacks should be found and published, especially for those states keeping segregated records.

15. A bibliography of "Who's Who" books pertaining to blacks should be published.

16. A list of sextons' records of black cemeteries could be located through a national organization of such sextons.

17. Extant records of black funeral homes could be published with the help of the association of black funeral home directors.

18. Black cemetery inscriptions should be copied and published.

19. Alumni and matriculation lists of black colleges and universities should be published along with black public school records.

20. Plantation records and diaries available on microfilm and microfiche and in manuscripts need to be located, indexed, and published.

21. Mortality schedules for the 1850, 1860, 1870, 1880 Federal Census Schedules should be indexed to include all slaves and free blacks. (See

chapter 4, p. 26 for explanation.)

One research project is presently being completed by the Ethnic Genealogy Center at Queens College and will be published by Gale Research Company. It is an index of all free blacks listed in the New York State Federal Census from 1790 to 1850. This project is only a small contribution to the vast amount of work that is still left to be done in every state. But there are more than just names, dates, and places to be found. The quality of life, character, and experience still needs to be understood as part of our story.

REEXAMINING HISTORY

It is very difficult for someone not knowledgeable in genealogy to understand what "family trees" have to do with "history." For many years genealogy was a science conducted by those who were privileged with time and money. For a similar number of years "history" has been thought of as dates, places, and wars.

But, genealogy and history have much to offer each other in understanding the life and times of our past. These sciences can be used to understand ourselves and our relationships to each other. Genealogy is primarily a quest for identity, not in terms of names or status (although it has been used that way sometimes), but as a basis for finding oneself through understanding the psychological, social, political, and economic forces which influenced one's parents, grandparents, great-grandparents, and family life in general.

To understand what was happening in and to your family during those dates, at those places, and through those wars is to breathe life into history. The past is prologue. If you watch the excitement in a young person when he or she realizes that everything did not begin and end at 147th and Lenox, that older people are a rich source of family information, that what happened in previous generations has a profound effect on them, then you will understand the joy of making history live. There are several ways genealogical tools and techniques can be used to uncover this part of history. The following examples of Joshua Hempstead and Richard Linville's records are two illustrations.

Joshua Hempstead was a prominent resident in New London, Connecticut, in the early 1700s. He was a widower who lived in a moderately sized frame house that still stands on the corner of Truman and Hempstead avenues. He wrote an extensive diary between 1711 and 1758 which conveyed the names, places, dates, activities, economics, weather, and politics during that period. Although an index of all surnames was developed when the diary was published, it did not include an index of those people (black slaves) who were mentioned only by first name. By going through the diary and retrieving all information about Adam, one of those slaves, and the people he interacted with, and comparing that information with court and church records of the New London area, a remarkable tapestry of life among blacks and between blacks and whites is woven. While that tapestry and the genealogy represented therein has been re-created for the whites, without the retrieval of the information surrounding Adam the following family ancestry would not have been known.

THE JACKSON FAMILY

John Jackson married Joan, the daughter of Maria, a deaf and dumb slave belonging to James Rogers. John and Joan Jackson had eight children:

(1) Peter Jackson was born between December 1693 and June 1710. Peter grew up in the household of John Rogers, son of James, and after Rogers's death in 1721 he resided with Rogers's son John, Jr. In 1732, the heirs of Samuel Beebe attempted to claim Peter, valued at 110 pounds, but their suit was unsuccessful.[2] Peter Jackson was evidently released from any obligation to service between 1732 and 1735, because in November 1735 he was sued for a debt of fifteen shillings, undoubtedly indicating that he was a free man.[3] Peter Jackson married Hagar, a slave of the widow Elizabeth Winthrop of New London. Hagar died August 21, 1734.[4] The Lois Jackson who was baptized as an adult in the New London First Congregational Church on May 17, 1741, may have been Peter's second wife. Peter and Hagar Jackson had two children: (i) Eunice, born February 1729/30, died March 19, 1745; (ii) Rose, born March 18, 1732/3, died April 14, 1741.[5]

(2) Abner Jackson was born between December 1693 and June 1710. Like his brother, Peter, he remained in the households of John Rogers and his son, John, Jr. He, too, was claimed by Samuel Beebe's heirs in their unsuccessful suit of 1732.[6] After John Rogers, Jr.'s death, Abner apparently lived with John's son James, and then with the latter's son, James of Mamacock. Abner died in New London on June 20, 1801.[7]

(3) Hannah Jackson was born between December 1693 and June 1710. On December 9, 1723, John Rogers, Jr. agreed to free Hannah at the end of a ten-year period of service.[8] Hannah, with her brothers Peter and Abner, was the subject of the Beebe family's unsuccessful claim in 1732.[9] She was presumably emancipated by Rogers in 1733.

(4) Adam Jackson was born in 1710. Adam Jackson's life, along with the lives of many other blacks whose families have been traced into the 1800s, is the subject of a forthcoming book, TAPESTRY, by James M. Rose and Barbara Brown. The story of his life had been hidden in the Hempstead diary.

(5) Miriam Jackson, born before 1710, grew up with her brother Adam in the household of Samuel Fox of New London. Miriam married Cuff, another of Samuel Fox's slaves, on June 10, 1726.[10] Before his death in 1727, Fox sold Miriam to his son, Samuel, Jr. Young Samuel sold her to Nathaniel Lathrop of Norwich prior to 1728. Samuel Beebe and his heirs made at least three attempts in the courts to claim Miriam: (1) from Samuel Fox in 1726, (2) from

Lathrop in 1728, and (3) again from Lathrop in 1732.[11]

(6) John Jackson was born about 1709 and came into the possession of Samuel Beebe in 1711. Beebe sold him to John Livingston, who in turn sold him to Winslow Tracy of Norwich. John Jackson instituted a suit in 1718, claiming that his son John had every right to freedom, his mother having been declared a free woman by the Massachusetts courts in the previous year. The Connecticut court found in favor of Tracy, and John remained a slave.[12] Apparently John eventually returned to the Beebe household from the Tracy household, for the records show that in July of 1731 he ran away from his master, Samuel Beebe of Newport, Rhode Island, while the two were on a trip to New London. John was caught and tried as a runaway slave in Saybrook. He claimed that he was a free man, being the son of Joan Jackson. Beebe, however, won the case.[13]

(7) Ruth Jackson was sold by Samuel Beebe to John Livingston on June 13, 1711. At that time Ruth was six months old and there is no further record of her.[14]

(8) Jeremiah Jackson was sold by John Livingston on January 1, 1714, to John Stone of Framingham, Massachusetts. He was a year old at the time and the fact that he was not mentioned in Joan's suit against Stone in 1716 indicates that he died young.[15]

Wills are another rich source for discovering black ancestors. But each will must be viewed in the perspective of the cultural, economic, and social occurrences surrounding the time the will was written. One will, written by Richard Linville in Polk County, Oregon, on February 25, 1847, states: "As it is my intention to live with my son Harrison Linville and he will probably be burdened with my property and myself in my declining years, I hereby will and bequeath to him and his heirs or legal representatives at my demise all rights I may have to my two slaves called Maria and Johnson now in Oregon."

While there is a wealth of literature surrounding the 1846 emigration to Oregon, there has been little mention of blacks or slaves being part of that journey. But Richard Linville, his wife, three of their children, and many grandchildren were the first settlers to take the Applegate Trail to Oregon in the late summer and fall of 1846. It is obvious from Richard's will, written shortly after their settlement in Oregon during the winter of 1846–47, that both Maria and Johnson had been on the journey. That fact is brought to light only by understanding the circumstances of the time and the words "now in Oregon"--implying their recent emigration with the family. Since slavery was supposedly illegal in Oregon and no slave census was taken in 1850, the knowledge of these two people would have been lost had not a family member doing research recognized the importance of this historical discrepancy.

How many other blacks have been disregarded in the recounting of history, but can be found through concerted genealogical research?

CONCLUSION

It is an enormous task--helping the novice to develop research teams for un-
earthing and publishing the records to understand more completely our history.
But it is one which reaches to the roots in each of us. We cannot unlock the
doors to the future without an understanding of the past as it was in fact, not
in fantasy or half-fact. This volume is a small part of that enormous task.
But hopefully it can be a substantial base for unlocking those doors to the
future.

1. New London County Court, June 1710, Files.

2. New London County Court, February 1732, File 64.

3. New London County Court, November 1735, File 127.

4. DIARY OF JOSHUA HEMPSTEAD (New London County Historical Society:
New London, Conn., 1970).

5. Births of Eunice and Rose in New London Vital Records; their deaths in the
HEMPSTEAD DIARY.

6. New London County Court, February 1732, File 64.

7. Inventory of John Rogers of New London, 1753, in New London Probate
District, File 4543, C.S.L.; Abner's death in Holt Record of Deaths in New
London at the Historical Society.

8. New London, Land Records, VIII, 186.

9. New London County Court, February 1732, File 64.

10. New London, First Congregational Church Records.

11. New London County Court, November 1726, February 1728, File 51, June
1728; New London County Supreme Court Records, March 1728, February 1732,
File 63, September 1732, File 20.

12. New London County Court, November 1718; November 1719, Files.

13. New London County Court, November 1731, File 228.

14. New London, Land Records, VII, 119.

15. New London County Court, November 1717, Files.

Chapter 2
GENERAL REFERENCES

The resources listed in this chapter are of major importance to black genealogical research.

GENEALOGICAL GUIDE BOOKS

American Society of Genealogists. GENEALOGICAL RESEARCH METHODS AND SOURCES. 2 vols. Washington, D.C.: 1960-71.

> Excellent manual on research techniques basic to all genealogical research.

DIRECTORY OF HISTORICAL SOCIETIES AND AGENCIES IN THE UNITED STATES AND CANADA. Nashville: American Association for State and Local History. Biennial.

> Local historical societies often have a wealth of records which can be helpful. This is a complete guide to the societies, including addresses and hours of operation. Often a historical society will have records on blacks which have not been centralized in that state. Moreover, a local historian can provide many leads.

Doane, Gilbert S. SEARCHING FOR YOUR ANCESTORS: THE HOW AND WHY OF GENEALOGY. 4th ed. New York: Bantam Books, 1974.

> One of the best beginning books for black genealogy. Provides fundamental knowledge in basic genealogical techniques and is very easy and interesting to read.

Everton, George B. THE HANDY BOOK FOR GENEALOGY. 6th ed. Logan, Utah: Everton Publishers, 1975.

> A good guide of research libraries, county divisions, and basic

genealogical information available in various states. It is constantly being revised and improved.

Greenwood, Val D. THE RESEARCHER'S GUIDE TO AMERICAN GENEALOGY. Baltimore: Genealogical Publishing Co., 1973.

Not as personal as Doane's book, but an excellent guide on research techniques.

Hale, Richard W., Jr. GUIDE TO PHOTOCOPIED HISTORICAL MATERIALS IN THE UNITED STATES AND CANADA. Ithaca, N.Y.: Cornell University Press, 1961.

This gives information on where census, government, state, county, town, city, church, personal, business, ship, and other records can be found.

Kirkham, E. Kay. A SURVEY OF AMERICAN CHURCH RECORDS. Salt Lake City: Deseret Book Co., 1971.

During the seventeenth through the middle of the nineteenth centuries, blacks did not usually have separate churches and in many cases they were baptized, married, or buried in white churches. Often they were full members. Consequently, it is necessary to know the location of these records.

Newberry Library, Chicago. THE GENEALOGICAL INDEX. Boston: G.K. Hall, 1960.

A very complete index of all published family genealogies owned by the Newberry Library in Chicago up to 1918. It is helpful if you need to find out whether a genealogy has been completed on the white family who owned or employed your ancestor.

Peterson, Clarence Stewart. CONSOLIDATED BIBLIOGRAPHY OF COUNTY HISTORIES IN FIFTY STATES IN 1961. Baltimore: Genealogical Publishing Co., 1973.

County histories often have considerable genealogical value in addition to describing the quality of life in specific localities during different historical periods. Many county histories can be purchased or borrowed in microfilm form. See Research Libraries section, below, this chapter.

Spear, Dorothy N. BIBLIOGRAPHY OF AMERICAN DIRECTORIES THROUGH 1860. Worcester, Mass.: American Antiquarian Society, 1961.

Lists city and business directories for 1,646 communities, through 1860. Most of the directories listed are available on microfiche at the Brooklyn Public Library, New York City 42nd Street Library,

Columbia University, San Francisco Public Library, California State University at Northridge, and some other large libraries throughout the United States.

Stemmons, J.D. THE UNITED STATES CENSUS COMPENDIUM. Logan, Utah: Everton Publishers, 1973.

An excellent survey of census records. Genealogical forms and materials may also be purchased through Everton Publishers.

ARTICLES ON BLACK GENEALOGY

Haley, Alex. "My Furthest-Back Person--'The African.'" NEW YORK TIMES MAGAZINE, 16 July 1972, pp. 13-16.

Fascinating description of some of the processes Haley used in uncovering his ancestry.

McGue, D.G. "John Taylor--Slave-Born Colorado Pioneer." COLORADO MAGAZINE, September 1941, pp. 161-68.

An interesting account, if one can ignore the attempt to reproduce black pronunciations.

Murrell, Peggy J. "Black Genealogy: Despite Many Problems, More Negroes Search for Their Family Pasts." WALL STREET JOURNAL, 9 March 1972, p. 1. Reprinted under title "Tracing Roots of the Black Family Tree." ST. LOUIS POST-DISPATCH, 14 March 1972, section 4A.

Not as informative as it could be, but interesting.

Roderick, Thomas H. "Negro Genealogy." AMERICAN GENEALOGIST 47 (1971): 88-91.

A brief article which attempts to define the research.

Whiteman, Maxwell. "Black Genealogy." REFERENCE QUARTERLY 11 (1972): 311-19.

Short but informative.

BLACK GENEALOGICAL REFERENCES

Bacote, Samuel William, ed. WHO'S WHO AMONG COLORED BAPTISTS OF THE UNITED STATES. Kansas City, Mo.: Franklin Hudson Publishing Co., 1913.

Includes some genealogical information in biographies.

Bentley, George R. A HISTORY OF THE FREEDMEN'S BUREAU. Philadelphia: Octagon Books, 1970.

A good guide and evaluation of the Bureau of Refugees, Freedmen, and Abandoned Lands (Freedmen's Bureau) and its records, which will lead researchers to many marriage, birth, and other vital statistics of blacks included in these records. An explanation of the records can be found on pages 266-67. (See also the section on the bureau in chapter 4, p. 27.)

Berlin, Ira. SLAVES WITHOUT MASTERS. New York: Pantheon Books, 1974.

This is an excellent resource for information on blacks during slavery. The book also has a bibliography, which contains some excellent black genealogical resources both for publication and individual family research. For example, the Free Negro Register from Chatham County, Georgia.

Brewer, James H. THE CONFEDERATE NEGRO. Durham, N.C.: Duke University Press, 1969.

This is an excellent resource for information on blacks who worked for the Confederacy during the Civil War.

Brignano, Russell Carl. BLACK AMERICANS IN AUTOBIOGRAPHY: AN ANNOTATED BIBLIOGRAPHY OF AUTOBIOGRAPHIES AND AUTOBIOGRAPHICAL BOOKS WRITTEN SINCE THE CIVIL WAR. Durham, N.C.: Duke University Press, 1974.

A 118-page listing of such books. Slave narratives are included.

Catterall, Helen Honor Turncliff, ed. JUDICIAL CASES CONCERNING AMERICAN SLAVERY AND THE NEGRO. Carnegie Institution of Washington, publication no. 374. Papers of the Division of Historical Research, 5 vols. 1926-37. Reprint. New York: Negro University Press, 1968; Octagon Press, 1968. Washington, D.C.: Carnegie Publications, 1926-37.

These volumes contain many thousands of court records on blacks, with hundreds of manumission records.

Chaunu, Huguette. SEVILLE ET L'ATLANTIQUE, 1504-1650. 7 vols. Ecole Pratique des Hautes Etudes. 6. section. Centre de Recherches Historiques, Ports, Routes, Trafics, 6. Paris: A. Colin, 1955.

This work contains extensive slave shipping lists of ships coming to the Spanish Indies. It has, unfortunately, not been translated from the original French.

Dillard, Joey Lee. BLACK NAMES: CONTRIBUTIONS TO THE SOCIOLOGY LANGUAGE. The Hague: Mouton, 1976.

Discussion of the etymology of black names. Bibliography included.

Disciples of Christ Historical Society. PRELIMINARY GUIDE TO BLACK MATERIALS IN THE DISCIPLES OF CHRIST HISTORICAL SOCIETY. Nashville: 1971.

This 32-page bibliography is also available on microfilm through the branch library program of the Genealogical Department of the Church of Jesus Christ of Latter-day Saints. (Order no. 873, 670).

Donnan, Elizabeth, ed. DOCUMENTS ILLUSTRATIVE OF THE HISTORY OF THE SLAVE TRADE IN AMERICA. 4 vols. Carnegie Institution of Washington, publication no. 409. Reprint. New York: Octagon Books, 1965.

An extensive work which contains many slave ship manifests.

Everly, Elaine C. "Marriage Records of Freedmen." PROLOGUE 5 (1973): 150-54.

Information on locating marriage statistics in the Freedmen's Bureau records.

Federal Writers' Project. SLAVE NARRATIVES: A HISTORY OF SLAVERY IN THE UNITED STATES FROM INTERVIEWS WITH FORMER SLAVES. Typewritten records prepared by the Federal Writers' Project, 1936-38, assembled by the Library of Congress project. Works Progress Administration for the District of Columbia. Washington, D.C.: 1941.

The WPA conducted these interviews during the 1930s with 2,000 former slaves. They contain an abundance of information about the lives and families of the people interviewed. It is only in microfilm or typescript form and has been indexed for genealogical material.

Jackson, Margaret Y. "An Investigation of Biographies and Autobiographies of American Slaves Published between 1820-1960: Based upon the Cornell Special Slavery Collection." Ph.D. dissertation, Cornell University, 1953.

A fascinating collection of materials on slave narratives.

THE NATIONAL UNION CATALOG OF MANUSCRIPT COLLECTIONS: BASED ON REPORTS FROM AMERICAN REPOSITORIES OF MANUSCRIPTS. Ann Arbor, Mich.: J.W. Edwards, 1959-61.

The NATIONAL UNION CATALOG entries contain descriptions of the manuscript collection cited and include information concerning the availability of microfilm, the calendar or catalog of its collection, and controls or restrictions concerning its use.

Newman, Deborah L., comp. LIST OF FREE BLACK HEADS OF FAMILIES IN
THE FIRST CENSUS OF THE UNITED STATES, 1790. National Archives and
Records Service, Special List no. 34. Washington, D.C.: 1973.

> See chapter 4, below, pp. 24-26, for a description of informa-
> tion found within the Federal Census Schedules.

Nichols, Charles Harold. MANY THOUSANDS GONE: THE EX-SLAVES'
ACCOUNTS OF THEIR BONDAGE AND FREEDOM. Bloomington: Indiana
University Press, 1969.

> A guide to slave narratives and an excellent source for oral
> history.

North Carolina. University. Library. Southern Historical Collection. THE
SOUTHERN HISTORICAL COLLECTION: A GUIDE TO MANUSCRIPTS. By
Susan Sokol Blosser and Clyde Norman Wilson, Jr. Chapel Hill: 1970.

> This is an exceedingly valuable guide to the family papers, slave
> records, plantation records, land grants, and court records housed
> in the Southern Historical Collection at the University of North
> Carolina. Thousands of birth and death records of slaves are con-
> tained in these records. (See Research Libraries, below, this
> chapter, for a brief indication of holdings related to slavery.)

Porter, Dorothy B. THE NEGRO IN THE UNITED STATES: A SELECTED
BIBLIOGRAPHY. Washington, D.C.: Library of Congress, 1970.

> An excellent bibliography.

Postell, William Dosite. THE HEALTH OF SLAVES ON SOUTHERN PLANTA-
TIONS. Louisiana State University Studies, Social Science Series, no. 1.
1951. Reprint. Gloucester, Mass.: Peter Smith, 1970.

> Contains explanations of some common terms used to describe
> slave deaths. Especially good for terms no longer in use. Also
> contains an excellent bibliography of plantation records.

Pucket, Newbell Niles. BLACK NAMES IN AMERICA: ORIGINS AND
USAGE. Edited by Murray Heller. Boston: G.K. Hall, 1975.

> Here there is an explanation of early names. One can get an
> idea of origins of black names and the time in which they were
> popularly used. Chapter 5 is a dictionary of African origins,
> explaining where particular African names probably originated.
> If you are able to trace back to an African name, this book
> may help determine the appropriate geographic and ethnic group
> in Africa.

Race Relations Information Center. DIRECTORY OF AFRO-AMERICAN RE-

SOURCES. Edited by Walter Schatz. New York: R.R. Bowker Co., 1970.

Excellent for additional sources available for black genealogical research. This book is classified by states and lists records of historical societies, personal papers, libraries, insurance associations, etc. Many of these sources should be published for easy access for research, especially family records containing lists of slave births, deaths, and emancipations.

Reuter, Edward Byron. THE MULATTO IN THE UNITED STATES: INCLUDING A STUDY OF THE ROLE OF MIXED-BLOOD RACES THROUGHOUT THE WORLD. 1918. Reprint. New York: Johnson Reprint, 1970.

Contains names of hundreds of so-called mulattoes in the early twentieth century.

Richings, G.F. EVIDENCES OF PROGRESS AMONG COLORED PEOPLE. 1900. Reprint. Chicago: Afro-Am Press, 1969.

The twelfth edition (1905) of this book is also presently available through University Microfilms in Ann Arbor, Michigan, and contains good biographies of many blacks who lived in the nineteenth century.

Simmons, William J. MEN OF MARK. 1887. Reprint. New York: Arno Press, 1968.

Lists prominent blacks of the nineteenth century and gives a fairly good biography of them.

U.S. Bureau of the Census. CENTURY OF POPULATION GROWTH. 1909. Reprint. New York: Johnson Reprint Co., 1967; Baltimore: Genealogical Publishing Co., 1970.

This is an excellent source for black population statistics. It also has a surname index which could lead you to the white family whose surname your ancestors might have used.

U.S. National Archives and Records Service. BLACK STUDIES: SELECT CATALOGUE OF NATIONAL ARCHIVES AND RECORDS SERVICE MICROFILM PUBLICATIONS. Washington, D.C.: General Services Administration, 1973.

An essential guide to the record groups housed at the National Archives and now available on microfilm. See chapter 4, below, for a description of the records.

U.S. Pension Bureau. LIST OF PENSIONERS ON THE ROLL, JANUARY 1, 1883. 5 vols. 1883. Reprint. Baltimore: Genealogical Publishing Co., 1970.

If the name of a soldier is listed here or in PENSION ROLL OF

1835 (next entry), the National Archives in Washington, D.C. will photocopy the genealogical records of the soldier for a fee of $3.00. If the soldier is not listed, see chapter 5, "War Records," for additional help.

U.S. War Department. PENSION ROLL OF 1835. 4 vols. 1835. Reprint. Baltimore: Genealogical Publishing Co. 1968.

See note above.

Welling, James Clarke. "Slavery in the Territories." In AMERICAN HISTORICAL ASSOCIATION: ANNUAL REPORT . . . FOR THE YEAR 1891, pp. 131-60. Washington, D.C.: 1892.

For the genealogist who is looking for information on blacks in the various territories, this book is essential. It will help to establish the exact arrival times of groups of blacks in the various states of the frontier.

West, Earl H. A BIBLIOGRAPHY OF DOCTORAL RESEARCH ON THE NEGRO, 1933-1966. Washington, D.C.: Xerox, 1969.

Good bibliography on materials available through University Microfilms in Ann Arbor, Michigan.

Woodson, Carter Godwin, ed. FREE NEGRO HEADS OF FAMILIES IN THE UNITED STATES IN 1830. Washington, D.C.: Association for the Study of Negro Life and History, 1925.

This book, along with Woodson's book cited below, should be referred to before you approach other census records. You may be lucky and find an ancestor here. (Both books are superior extractions of materials from the federal census.) Much more work like Woodson's needs to be undertaken.

_____. FREE NEGRO OWNERS OF SLAVES IN THE UNITED STATES IN 1830, TOGETHER WITH ABSENTEE OWNERSHIP OF SLAVES IN THE UNITED STATES IN 1830. 1924. Reprint. New York: Negro University Press, 1968.

See annotation above.

Work, Monroe Nathan. A BIBLIOGRAPHY OF THE NEGRO IN AFRICA AND AMERICA. 1928. Reprint. New York: Argosy-Antiquarian, 1965; Octagon Books, 1965.

Provides an excellent bibliography of original works on blacks that can be scanned for hidden black genealogical materials.

NEWSPAPERS

Newspapers are useful genealogical resources that can assist genealogists to find ancestors. However, information found therein must be verified, and they are difficult to use because of the lack of indexing. Nevertheless, birth, death, marriage, arrest, conviction, accident, and social notices that are about one's family can be well worth the search time. The following reference materials can be of assistance in locating black newspapers and early American newspapers relating to slavery and abolition.

Abajian, James de T. BLACKS IN SELECTED NEWSPAPERS, CENSUSES AND OTHER SOURCES; AN INDEX TO NAMES AND SUBJECTS. Boston: G.K. Hall, 1977.

> A superior index, covering mostly western states with over 90,000 entries of primarily personal names. Some eastern and Canadian newspapers are included.

AMERICAN NEWSPAPERS, 1821-1936: A UNION LIST OF FILES AVAILABLE IN THE UNITED STATES AND CANADA. Edited by Winifred Gregory under the auspices of the Bibliographical Society of America. New York: H.W. Wilson Co., 1937.

> Identifies black newspapers and lists libraries with newspaper holdings. Because of its early date of publication, some newspapers listed may no longer be available, while holdings of others will have increased. Arranged alphabetically by place of publication (state, subdivided by city).

Brown, Warren Henry. CHECKLIST OF NEGRO NEWSPAPERS IN THE UNITED STATES, 1827-1946. Jefferson City, Mo.: Lincoln University, 1946.

> Contains not only a list of black newspapers, but also a directory of where copies of them can be located. No indexes of names or genealogical information has yet been compiled. Copies of the papers are often not kept in the state or city of their origin, making Brown's CHECKLIST an essential guide.

Bryl, Susan, and Welsch, Erwin K., comps. BLACK PERIODICALS AND NEWSPAPERS: A UNION LIST OF HOLDINGS IN LIBRARIES OF THE UNIVERSITY OF WISCONSIN AND THE LIBRARY OF THE STATE HISTORICAL SOCIETY OF WISCONSIN. Madison: Memorial Library, University of Wisconsin-Madison, 1975.

> This list is very useful for identifying the titles and cities of publications of black newspapers. However, it is not entirely accurate and is arranged alphabetically by title rather than locality.

California. State University, Fullerton. Library. UNION LIST OF NEWS-
PAPERS ON MICROFORMS IN THE CALIFORNIA STATE UNIVERSITY AND
COLLEGES LIBRARIES. 2d ed. Fullerton: California State University, 1975.

Includes many black newspapers.

Jacobs, Donald M., ed., assisted by Paley, Heath; Parker, Susan; and Silver-
man, Dana. ANTEBELLUM BLACK NEWSPAPERS: INDICES TO NEW YORK
"FREEDOM'S JOURNAL" (1827-29), "THE RIGHTS OF ALL" (1829), "THE
WEEKLY ADVOCATE" (1837), AND "THE COLORED AMERICAN" (1837-41).
Westport, Conn.: Greenwood Press, 1976.

Extensive index with citations by subject and name.

LaBrie, Henry G. THE BLACK NEWSPAPER IN AMERICA: A GUIDE. 3d ed.
Kennebunkport, Maine: Mercer House Press, 1973.

A directory.

Mills, Hazel E., and Kloostra, Georgia M., comps. NEWSPAPERS ON
MICROFILM IN THE LIBRARIES OF THE STATE OF WISCONSIN: A UNION
LIST. Olympia: Washington State Library, 1974.

Includes some black newspapers.

Pride, Armistead Scott. NEGRO NEWSPAPERS ON MICROFILM: A SELECTED
LIST. Washington, D.C.: Library of Congress, Photoduplication Service, 1953.

An old but still useful list.

U.S. Library of Congress. Catalog Publication Division. NEWSPAPERS IN
MICROFILMS: UNITED STATES, 1948-1972. Washington, D.C.: Library of
Congress, 1973.

This is the most up-to-date extensive union list available for
newspapers. It includes the approximately 200-title collection,
"Negro Newspapers on Microfilm," which was collected by the
Committee on Negro Studies of the American Council of Learned
Societies. Entries are arranged alphabetically by place of publication (state, subdivided by city), with a title index. Many
libraries will circulate their newspapers on microfilm through
interlibrary loan.

RESEARCH LIBRARIES

Any public library should be able to help you get started on your research.
Most city and state libraries, as well as historical societies, have large genealogical collections. However, there are a few libraries which will be of specific help in black genealogical research:

1. The New York Public Library at 42d Street, and especially its collection
    at the Schomburg Center for Research in Black Culture at 135th and
    Lenox, houses one of the largest collections of genealogical resources in
    the Northeast. The Schomburg Center contains extensive material on
    black life both here and in Africa and has microfilm copies of all the
    Federal Census Population Schedules for the United States from 1790 to
    1880 (see chapter 4, pp. 24-26, for a complete explanation).

2. The Genealogical Department of the Church of Jesus Christ of Latter-day
    Saints has an extensive system of branch libraries throughout the United
    States (see Appendix B for a list of current branch addresses). Any of
    the branches can assist researchers in ordering microfilm copies of the
    voluminous resources owned by the Genealogical Department in Salt Lake
    City. There is a small charge (about $.75) to use each film for a two-
    week period. The Microfilm Card Catalog of the Genealogical Depart-
    ment in Salt Lake City indicates a number of vital records which are
    available through its branch library program. Such records for blacks
    are available for Georgia, Mississippi, and Tennessee. Vital records
    for blacks in Louisiana, Kentucky, North Carolina, and other states may
    be available, but are not separated by race. Since the Genealogical
    Department is constantly updating its vast holdings, it would be wise to
    check the Microfilm Card Catalog in your local Genealogical Department
    branch library for current holdings. Your local public library will not
    have this information.

3. The Southern Historical Collection at the University of North Carolina in
    Chapel Hill has a large manuscript collection (see Black Genealogical
    Records, above, this chapter) of life in the South. Its value for black
    genealogical research is comparatively unknown, but it contains a wealth
    of material such as personal letters, records, diaries, and journals. Its
    published guide lists several hundred entries dealing with slavery in many
    states, including Alabama, Arkansas, California, Connecticut, Florida,
    Georgia, Kentucky, Louisiana, Maryland, Mississippi, New Jersey, New
    York, North Carolina, South Carolina, Tennessee, Texas, Virginia, and
    the West Indies. These resources are not repeated in the survey of states
    below.

4. In addition, there are also available microfilm collections of city direc-
    tories for fifty selected cities for the years 1861-1901 in some larger re-
    search libraries. Of course, nearly all public libraries have extensive
    holdings of the directories for their own areas.

Chapter 3

ORAL HISTORY

Once you have a general awareness of genealogical techniques learned from the suggested guide books, the next step is to conduct interviews with the older members of your family. The process of collecting data concerning genealogy and history through informal but informative conversation is known as oral history. "Informal but informative" means that the conversation is kept flowing while predetermined questions are asked.

The first step is to look over the information you already know, and then determine what you need to find out and which people in your family are likely to know the answers. Write the questions down for easy recall during your conversation. In addition to the names, dates, and places of births, marriages, and deaths, you will want to understand something of the social, economic, and psychological circumstances surrounding each generation. An older person may not initially remember the vital statistics but will probably recall them easily when discussing various experiences. Do not pass up the opportunity to ask about religious, educational, and political practices in the family, as well as local customs. An important part of oral history is understanding how attitudes and experiences have changed or been carried on through the generations. You should also have a basic geographic understanding of the area you are researching and be sure to get the names of counties or cities, not just states. For this, it is a good idea to carry a county or township map with you for easy reference. If you are not able to talk with a particular person, most of these suggestions can be adapted to letter writing.

Since many of the people you will want to interview will be elderly, you should be respectful and considerate. If you appear and dress the way they would like you to, you are likely to make them most comfortable. In addition to holding the interview in a place comfortable to them, their age and health should be considered. Under most circumstances sixty to ninety minutes should be the limit for each interview.

The list of questions should seldom be asked in a sterile form. After asking a question, listen to the response and take notes on points for follow-up. Time allowance should be made for a response, and while they are answering you will be able to restructure one of your questions or ask a probing one suggested below. It should be remembered that in this case, conversation means that you will do most of the listening, not talking.

When a good rapport has been established, they will probably want to share photographs, letters, and family papers with you, and you will want to share what progress you have made in putting the family tree together. Often a family member will not want to let you know, for various reasons, some of the family's past. If this is the case, patience and acceptance of the right to privacy will go a long way. Once they know you will not use the information against them in any way, they will usually be helpful. Asking family members to get involved in the research problems with you will help increase their confidence in the project and make them feel more comfortable about sharing information.

There are a few specific guidelines to follow during the interview:

1. Keep notes while interviewing, even if you use a recorder. The purpose is to keep track of the chronology of events and record information in order to reword questions.

2. Try not to ask a double question or one which you answer yourself. The way you ask questions can influence the answers you receive. Short, clear questions prevent confusion and are easy to answer.

3. Guard against your own feelings by avoiding negative physical mannerisms, and not interrupting their response (except for focusing).

4. Show concern and interest. Try to conceal boredom. Keeping eye contact with the person will help.

Finally, the following questions or responses will help probe the psychological and social factors surrounding particular experiences. They can easily be introduced into the conversation once it is flowing. "Tell me more." "I'm not sure I understand." "Why?" "What led up to that?" "What happened next?" and "How did it turn out?"

The following guide is excellent for oral history interviewing and is applicable to family research:

Baum, Willa K. ORAL HISTORY FOR THE LOCAL HISTORICAL SOCIETY. Stockton: Conference of California Historical Societies, 1969.

Chapter 4

NATIONAL ARCHIVES AND FEDERAL RECORDS

With a preliminary chart of a few generations of your family completed, the next step is to locate the oldest generation in the Federal Population Census. If you have the resources to travel, the National Archives or the Federal Records Center in your area (see appendix C) is the place to start. They have, undoubtedly, the largest government collection of primary source materials for genealogy. If you write the Publications Division you can obtain various guides to the collection. Fortunately, many records within the National Archives have been inventoried and materials relevant to blacks have been identified and extracted.

The two broad areas of records discussed here are Federal Census Schedules and Freedmen's Bureau records. Those records concerning military service which are also located at the National Archives are discussed in the next chapter--"War Records."

FEDERAL CENSUS SCHEDULES

Beginning in 1790 and every ten years afterwards, a federal census was taken. As the years passed and history changed, the records for each census varied. Even though the census taking continues today, the records are not available to the general public for seventy years. This means that, presently, the 1790-1900 census records are open for public use. (The 1900 census still has some restrictions on it.) What follows is a description of the valuable information related to blacks which can be obtained from these records.

Population Schedules

1790--First Census of the United States. Arranged by state and then by county. Lists free blacks who were heads of households by name; other members are numbered, not named; slaves are listed by number within the slave owner's household. Other free blacks living with white families are not named, only numbered.

24

1800--Second Census of the United States. Same as 1790 census.

1810--Third Census of the United States. Same as 1790 census.

1820--Fourth Census of the United States. Arranged by state and then by county. Lists free blacks who were heads of households by name. Other blacks in the household, slaves living with owners, and free blacks living in white households are not named but are numbered within age groupings (under 14, 14-26, 26-45, and 45 and over). The number of persons engaged in agriculture, commerce, and manufacturing is recorded.

1830--Fifth Census of the United States. Same as 1820 census except that the age groupings are under 10, 10-25, 25-36, 36-55, 55-100, and 100 and over. The number of persons engaged in agriculture, commerce, or manufacturing is not included.

1840--Sixth Census of the United States. Same as 1830 census.

1850--Seventh Census of the United States. Arranged by state and then divided into free schedules and slave schedules, both organized by county. Free schedules list names of all members of a household and indicate age; sex; color (black, mulatto, or white--in some cases "Indian"); place of birth; and profession, trade, or occupation for males over fifteen. Other information includes whether married within the year, attending school, unable to read or write, whether pauper or convict. Slave schedules list number of slaves by age and sex under each owner's name; occasionally the slaves are named.

1860--Eighth Census of the United States. Same as 1850 census except that females over fifteen have their profession, trade, or occupation listed, and slaves over age 100 are named, and place of birth is stated.

1870--Ninth Census of the United States. Arranged by state and then by county. This is the first federal census which includes names of all people counted. The same information is noted as for the 1860 and 1850 censuses, but there is no slave schedule since the Emancipation Proclamation had been issued between 1860 and 1870. Chinese ("Y") and Indian ("I") are also included in the "color" designations.

1880--Tenth Census of the United States. Arranged by state and then by county. Includes the same information as the 1870 census with the addition of the relationship to head of household (especially important regarding blacks because of extended family relationships), and birthplace for each person as well as their mother's and father's. The 1880 census has a Soundex for all families with children under ten years of age. This system of indexing by sounds of the last name means that you only need to know the person's name and state of residence in order to locate them on the census for this year, if they lived in a household with children under ten.

1890--Eleventh Census of the United States. As much as 99 percent of the 1890 census was destroyed by a fire in the Commerce Building in 1921. However, a Special Census for 1890 remains. See the discussion below for further information.

1900--Twelfth Census of the United States. Same information as the 1880 census with the addition of a number of socioeconomic facts on each family.

There is a Soundex for the 1900 census which includes all people, not just those who lived in a household with children under ten.

If you have trouble locating census records in your area, the Special List no. 24, FEDERAL POPULATION AND MORTALITY CENSUS SCHEDULES 1790-1890 IN THE NATIONAL ARCHIVES AND THE STATES: OUTLINE OF A LECTURE ON THEIR AVAILABILITY, CONTENT AND USE, published by the National Archives and Records Service, General Services Administration in 1971 and re-printed in 1974 has information on availability of the population censuses out-side the National Archives. Many microfilms of population schedules are owned by public libraries and historical societies. In addition, the National Archives has begun depositing copies in the Federal Records Centers throughout the United States. Consult appendix C for a list of these centers.

Many libraries have the many published indexes to all of the census records. However, their use for black genealogical research is limited. In only a few instances are the "color" designations included in the index, making it difficult to use them for black family information.

Mortality Schedules

Another group of census records taken by the federal government are the mor-tality schedules for 1850, 1860, 1870, 1880 and, for five states, in 1885. Information in these schedules includes name, age, sex, color, birthplace, occupation, and marital status. There is an indication as to whether a black person was slave or free, the month of death and cause, and, by 1880, the birthplace of mother and father and name of attending physician. This group of records is, consequently, a nationwide list of blacks who died from June 1849 to May 1850; June 1859 to May 1860; June 1869 to May 1870; June 1879 to May 1880; and for Colorado, Florida, Nebraska, New Mexico, and the Dakotas, June 1884 to May 1885.

The schedules may not be complete regarding the deaths of slaves; and, al-though indexes to the mortality schedules have been published, they generally omit blacks. Consequently, the originals must be consulted until a complete index is available. The location of the mortality schedules for the various states is noted in the survey of states which follows. See illustration following of mortality schedules.

Special Census Records

In 1890 a special census was taken to record "Persons who served in the Army, Navy and Marine Corps of the United States during the War of the Rebellion (who are survivors) and widows of such persons." The information engendered from these records includes the name of the veteran, post office address, rank, company, regiment or vessel, dates of enlistment and discharge, disability, length of service and, if applicable, the widow's name. These records are housed at the National Archives.

Agricultural information was recorded briefly in 1820, but a more complete list of free black farmers is included in a special census for 1850 and 1880, as well as 1885 for Colorado, Florida, Nebraska, New Mexico, and the Dakotas. The information includes the farmer's name and a description of the land, animals, and equipment.

FREEDMEN'S BUREAU

The records of the Bureau of Refugees, Freedmen, and Abandoned Lands, popularly referred to as the Freedmen's Bureau, are quite valuable. The bureau existed during Reconstruction and kept such important records as marriages, contracts, school reports, and registers of those who deposited money in its Savings and Trust Company. The following groups of records are located at the National Archives and have recently been microfilmed for easier use.

Record Group 101, "Records of the Office of the Comptroller of the Currency"

A "Register of Signatures of Depositions in Branches of Freedmen's Savings and Trust Company from 1865-1874" (M816, 27 rolls) in found in this group of records. Information for each deposition includes account number, name of depositor, date, place of birth, place raised, residence, age, complexion, name of employer or occupation, spouse, children, father, mother, brothers, sisters, signatures, and, for some, name of former owner and plantation. The records are not indexed by name of depositor, but rather by account number. They are, however, broken down by state and by the city where the branch was located. The survey of states which follows indicates those city branches whose depositions are located in this records group.

Record Group 105, "Records of the Bureau of Refugees, Freedmen, and Abandoned Lands"

Another group of Freedmen's Bureau records are found here. There are volumes of letters sent and received, dealing with the operations of the bureau, which are alphabetically arranged by date. The Education Division in this group filed records including monthly reports of pupils' progress, lists of teachers and secretaries, and the sponsoring organizations. The school reports are organized by state.

In addition, there are reports of the Assistant Commissioner and/or Superintendent of Education and the Field Offices for the various states. A brief outline of what is available for each state is included under the Federal Records section for each state in the survey of states which follows. The National Archives publication BLACK STUDIES (Washington, D.C., 1973) gives a complete description of each reel of microfilm.

Example of Mortality Schedules.

MORTALITY SCHEDULES, GEORGIA.
Persons Who Died During the Year Ending 1 June, 1850

Name	Age	Sex	Color	Slave	Md. or Wid.	Place of birth	Mo. Died	Occupation	Cause of Death	Days Ill
APPLING CO.										
Child, name unknown	6/12	M				Georgia	Dec.		Direhea	7
Elizabeth Roberson	53	F				S.C.	Jan.		Phthisic	1/12
John Graham	45	M			M	N.C.	Jan.	Tavernkeeper	Drinking	30
Eda Mobley	60	F	B	S	M	N.A.	Dec.		Old age	40
Mary Mobley	2	F	B	S		Ga.	Feb.		Dysent'ry	6
Christian Mozo	80	F			W	Ga.	Aug.		Dropsey	90
Nancy Dyal	19	F			M	Ga.	July		Childbed	2
Duncan McDuffie	61	M			M	N.C.	Mar.	Farmer	Fever	4
Sebron Sellers	8 m.	M				Ga.	Aug.		Unknown	2
Nancy C. Meadows	30	F			M	Ga.	July		Eating ulcer	2
March Carter	40	M	B	S		Ga.	May		Ovenstain	15
Moses C. A. Taylor	7	M				Ga.	April		Pithitis	6
Child, name unknown	1/12	M				Ga.	Feb.		Cutaneous	30
Thomas Wilson	66	M			M	N.C.	Dec.	Farmer	Suicide	1/12
Jane Ogden	5	F				Ga.	Oct.		Bill. fever	20
Henry Jackson	14	M				Ga.	June		Fever	21
Jane Moody	5	F				Ga.	Oct.		Croup	7
Child, name unknown	6/12	F				Ga.	Jan.		Direhea	5
Rash, Tillman	36	M	B	S	M	Ga.	June		Childbed	180
Jim Carter	2	M	B	S		Ga.	Mar.		unknown	96
Roxy L. Morgan	10	F				Ga.	May		Croup	35
Eliza Reddish	18	F	B	S		Ga.	Sept.		Childbed	4
Delila Middleston	17	F			M	Ga.	Aug.		B. fever	6
Liddia Carter	80	F			M	Ga.	May		Cancer	180
Chrisopher Chauncey	1	M				Ga.	Dec.		Unknown	24
--esinia Arnott	8	F				Ga.	Sept.		Fever	16
Cato Morgan	11	M	B	S		Ga.	June		Worms	2

Chapter 5

WAR RECORDS

Service records for blacks in the various wars of the United States are available and, in some cases, well indexed for general use. This chapter describes the records of the Revolution, War of 1812, Civil War, and other military pursuits.

REVOLUTION, 1776

The number of blacks and their contributions to the Revolution were quite significant. For background reading in trying to trace black ancestors who fought in this war, the following books and articles are suggested:

Foner, Philip Sheldon. BLACKS IN THE AMERICAN REVOLUTION. Contributions in American History, no. 55. Westport, Conn.: Greenwood Press, 1976.

Jackson, Luther P[orter]. "Virginia Negro Soldiers and Seamen in the American Revolution." JOURNAL OF NEGRO HISTORY 27 (1942): 247-87.

> Lists (pp. 257-62) black servicemen who fought for Virginia. Also has scattered names throughout the article.

Moore, George Henry. HISTORICAL NOTES ON THE EMPLOYMENT OF NEGROES IN THE AMERICAN ARMY OF THE REVOLUTION. 1862. Reprint. New York: W. Abbott, 1907.

> Occupational involvement of blacks in the war.

Nell, William Cooper. THE COLORED PATRIOTS OF THE AMERICAN REVOLUTION. 1855. Reprint. New York: Arno Press, 1968.

> This book discusses many blacks involved in the Revolution. A discussion of slave Jonathan Hill, who died in New York and was born in Stonington, Connecticut, led two researchers to the Stonington vital statistics and a well-documented genealogy of Hill's family.

Quarles, Benjamin. THE NEGRO IN THE AMERICAN REVOLUTION. Chapel Hill: University of North Carolina Press, 1961.

> A superior bibliography of articles about blacks who served in the war is on pages 201-23. A must for researchers.

Several states have their own records of blacks in the revolutionary war, but the best and most complete records are at the National Archives and Records Service in Washington, D.C. Special List no. 36, LIST OF BLACK SERVICE-MEN COMPILED FROM THE WAR DEPARTMENT COLLECTION OF REVOLU-TIONARY WAR RECORDS, has been compiled by Debra L. Newman and is available by writing to the National Archives and Records Service, General Services Administration in Washington. It lists the names and home states of those servicemen who could be identified as black from the various records of the War Department.

In addition, there is an index to the pension records of revolutionary war soldiers published by the Genealogical Publishing Company and previously mentioned in chapter 2, p. 18. The volumes are generally available at major libraries and historical societies. Though these records in most cases do not give the names of parents, many times the wives' names are mentioned. It was not uncommon for wives to continue to receive pensions after the death of their husbands. Unfortunately, the indexes do not indicate whether the serviceman was black.

"The Index to Revolutionary War Pension Applications" was published by the NATIONAL GENEALOGICAL SOCIETY QUARTERLY in volumes 35 through 40 and is available in most large libraries. This index includes not only those whose pension applications were accepted, but those whose applications were rejected. The rejected applications often provide more genealogical data.

If you are interested not only in the names of the men but also in their activities during the war, Record Group 93, "War Department Collections of Revolutionary War Records," at the National Archives contains the resources for the complete records of black servicemen. Special List no. 36, mentioned above, can help save much time in locating the records of a particular black serviceman. The entire series of all applications and records, comprising over 5,000 rolls of microfilm, is now available in several major libraries and through the Genealogical Department and its branches throughout the country (see appendix B for list of current branches).

The following is a list of the contents of the 2,670-microfilm-reel index of Record Group 15:

U.S. National Archives and Records Service. REVOLUTIONARY WAR PEN-SION AND BOUNTY-LAND-WARRANT APPLICATION FILES. National Archives Microfilm Publications, Pamphlet Describing M804. Washington, D.C.: General Services Administration, 1974.

WAR OF 1812

Much work is left to be done in identifying all those blacks who served in other wars and conflicts involving the United States. Although not specifically about War of 1812 veterans, Robert Ewell Greene's BLACK DEFENDERS OF AMERICA, 1775-1973 (Chicago: Johnson Publishing Co., 1974) is good for background reading. It has biography and service records for some War of 1812 veterans as well as those who served in the wars from the Revolution through Vietnam. The information gathered from National Archives pension records includes first and last names with short biographies.

CIVIL WAR

Thousands of blacks fought in the Civil War on both the Union and Confederate sides. Most of the records of their services are located at the National Archives, but others can be found at state libraries. Record Group 94, "Records of the Adjutant General's Office, 1780's-1917," at the National Archives contains an index to Compiled Service Records of Volunteer Union Soldiers who served with U.S. Colored Troops. It is an alphabetical card index giving the name of a soldier, his rank, and service unit. The card file will then refer you to the complete service record of the soldier. A second part of this record group is the Compiled Records Showing Service of Military Units in Volunteer Union Organizations. Once the unit has been determined from the card index, this part of the records relates the activities and commanders of each unit.

There are some books on the Civil War which describe the personal experiences and regimental histories found within such records. For example, THE SABLE ARM: NEGRO TROOPS IN THE UNION ARMY, 1861-1865 by Dudley Taylor Cornish (New York: Longmans, Green and Co., 1956) has an excellent bibliography of primary and secondary resources to help in locating black ancestors in the Civil War. There are also published accounts of regimental activities, including:

Chenery, William H. THE FOURTEENTH REGIMENT RHODE ISLAND HEAVY ARTILLERY (COLORED,) IN THE WAR TO PRESERVE THE UNION, 1861-1865. Providence, R.I.: Snow and Franham, 1898. Available on microfilm from Bell and Howell, Wooster, Ohio.

Dornbusch, Charles Emil, comp. REGIMENTAL PUBLICATIONS AND PERSONAL NARRATIVES: SOUTHERN, BORDER, AND WESTERN STATES AND TERRITORIES; FEDERAL TROOPS, UNION AND CONFEDERATE BIOGRAPHIES. Vol. 2, MILITARY BIBLIOGRAPHY OF THE CIVIL WAR. New York: New York Public Library, 1967.

Pages 147-54 contain references for "Colored Troops."

Dyer, Frederick Henry. A COMPENDIUM OF THE WAR OF THE REBELLION, COMPILED AND ARRANGED FROM THE OFFICIAL RECORDS OF THE FEDERAL AND CONFEDERATE ARMIES, REPORTS OF THE ADJUTANT GENERALS OF THE SEVERAL STATES, THE ARMY REGISTERS, AND OTHER RELIABLE DOCUMENTS AND SOURCES. Des Moines: Dyer Publishing Co., 1908.

> Contains the best brief histories of all the black units in the Union Army.

Emilio, Luis Fenollosa. A BRAVE BLACK REGIMENT: HISTORY OF THE FIFTY-FOURTH REGIMENT OF MASSACHUSETTS VOLUNTEER INFANTRY, 1863-1865. 1894. Reprint. New York: Arno, 1969.

> The appendix contains a roster of the men who served in this regiment.

Mickley, Jeremiah Marion. THE FORTY-THIRD REGIMENT UNITED STATES COLORED TROOPS. Gettysburg: J.E. Wible, 1866. Available on microfilm from Bell and Howell, Wooster, Ohio.

As with the pension records for the Revolution, the pension records for the Civil War are valuable sources of genealogical information. If you are able to determine that your ancestor received a pension (or, in the event of death, that his widow, mother, or children received a pension), then it is relatively easy to locate the pensioner's records in the National Archives. First, a nationwide alphabetical list of all pension records is available at the archives. Once located on this list, you can request photocopies of the genealogical material in the soldier's pension file by submitting the request on GSA Form 6751 available by writing the National Archives. The form, when filled out as much as possible, is then sent back to the Military Service Records (NNCC), National Archives Building (GSA), Washington, D.C. 20408. For a small fee (presently $3.00) the photocopies will be sent to you.

"A typical pension file contains the application of the claimant, documents submitted as evidence of identity and service, and records of action taken on the claim. The claimant may have been a veteran or his widow, minor children, or other dependent. Since a claimant could have applied for a pension under several different acts, a pension file may contain more than one application. Documents submitted in support of some pension claims include affidavits attesting to service, pages from family bibles, and copies of records of birth, marriage, and death" (MILITARY SERVICE RECORDS IN THE NATIONAL ARCHIVES OF THE UNITED STATES. General Information Leaflet no. 7. Washington, D.C.: National Archives and Records Service, 1974, p. 9).

Another valuable source in locating black ancestors in the Civil War is William Frayne Amann's PERSONNEL OF THE CIVIL WAR, vol. 2 (New York: T. Yoseloff Co., 1961), which gives a breakdown by states of the "Colored Outfits." In trying to locate a black Civil War veteran, one researcher had only a picture of his grandfather with some indication from the family that he had enlisted at Baltimore. The veteran's regiment was located using Amann's list.

The 1890 Special Census, previously discussed in chapter 4, pp. 26-27, included black Union veterans and their widows. These records have not been indexed.

OTHER MILITARY RECORDS

There were several units of blacks who served in the infantry and cavalry on military posts in the West, in the Indian wars, in the Southwest, and in Cuba during the Spanish-American War. Records of these units are not indexed but are available at the National Archives and described in the publication BLACK STUDIES listed in chapter 2, p. 17.

Chapter 6
MIGRATORY PATTERNS

Until the late eighteenth century the black population remained relatively stable, not moving out of the geographic area in which they found themselves upon arrival in the colonies. At the start of the nineteenth century, and especially by 1830, thousands of blacks began moving toward the cities or the western frontier. They, like the thousands of whites they migrated with, moved to other areas for a myriad of military, economic, and social reasons growing out of industrialization and western expansion.

In addition to this general migratory pattern in which blacks and whites moved, there were two important migratory patterns in which blacks alone were involved: (1) the domestic slave trade, and (2) the escape of slaves with and without the Underground Railroad.

The domestic slave trade resulted in the displacement of many blacks. Consequently, it is significant to understand the areas and routes of trade in order to explore successfully black genealogical roots.

The areas for slave sales and distribution, such as Charleston and Columbia, South Carolina, were busy and prosperous places. In fact, over 40,000 slaves were imported from Africa to Charleston in anticipation of prohibition of foreign slave trade, which began in 1808. By the end of the 1850s, Columbia and Charleston were larger markets in the domestic slave trade than Richmond, Virginia. The southern counties in Virginia and Maryland supplied the largest number of slaves to the Deep South. Baltimore was the center for slave sales and Alexandria the port of debarkation for slaves and free blacks to be transported by boat to New Orleans (see chapter 13, "Virginia and West Virginia").

Two methods frequently used for transporting slaves to distant markets were by ship--either along the Atlantic coast or down the Ohio and Mississippi rivers and their tributaries--or overland by march and, later, railroad. The largest coast cargoes of slaves were shipped from Alexandria, Norfolk, and Richmond, Virginia; Baltimore, Maryland; or Charleston, South Carolina, to ports of Natchez, Mobile, and New Orleans, where they were sold inland. The Mississippi River was a great inland channel of slave trade, with numerous blacks being sold along the way.

The relationship between migratory patterns and the domestic slave trade needs to become a major focus of black genealogy in the future. Some of the sources described in the various state chapters, along with the resources listed below, can be utilized as the basis for such research. In addition, there are massive amounts of slave sale advertisements found in early newspapers and early residential directories which can be a rich source of slave traders. For example, the largest slave traders in Memphis, Tennessee, were Bolton and Dickens. The New York Historical Society has Bolton and Dickens's list of over 1,500 slaves and their purchasers. Alphabetizing and tracing the names in this list would be an excellent contribution to black family ancestry. The same process could be applied to the Chicago Historical Society's microfilmed records of Hector Davis and Company. Hundreds of other lists could be reclaimed and published for similar purposes. For those interested in beginning the reclaiming process from materials dealing with the domestic slave trade, the following book is an important resource:

Bancroft, Frederic. SLAVE TRADING IN THE OLD SOUTH. New York: Frederick Ungar Press, 1959.

> Extensive discussion of slave advertisements. Good beginning for locating advertisements for possible publication.

The second black genealogical migration pattern was established by the escape of slaves and the Underground Railroad. Slaves escaped from nearly every geographical area and then traveled north and west. Slaves were known to have traveled from as far as Greenwich, Connecticut, to northern Ohio by freight car and to have stowed away on barges up the Ohio River from Virginia and Kentucky. Blacks also traveled by the Underground Railroad from Columbia, South Carolina, and Wilmington, Delaware, to New Haven, New Bedford, Boston, Portland, and Canada. Another route on the Railroad existed from North Carolina, through Tennessee, Kentucky, and Indiana, to Michigan. The following background reading will be necessary for understanding the scope of migratory patterns created by escaped slaves and the Underground Railroad:

Campbell, Stanley W. THE SLAVE CATCHERS: ENFORCEMENT OF THE FUGITIVE SLAVE LAW, 1850-1860. Chapel Hill: University of North Carolina Press, 1970.

> Contains names of some slaves along with an excellent bibliography on this aspect of slavery.

The following books relate migration trails, train lines, and stations of the Underground Railroad, as well as the people involved:

McDougall, Marion Gleason. FUGITIVE SLAVES, 1619-1805. Prepared under the direction of Albert Bushnell Hart. 1891. Reprint. Freeport, N.Y.: Books for Libraries Press, 1971.

Siebert, Wilbur Henry. THE UNDERGROUND RAILROAD FROM SLAVERY TO FREEDOM. 1898. Reprint. New York: Arno Press, 1968; Russell and Russell, 1967; Gloucester, Mass.: Peter Smith, 1968.

_____. "The Underground Railroad in Massachusetts." In AMERICAN ANTI-QUARIAN SOCIETY, WORCESTER, MASS. PROCEEDINGS, vol. 45, pp. 25-100. Worcester, Mass., 1935.

_____. "The Underground Railroad in Ohio." In OHIO ARCHAEOLOGICAL AND HISTORICAL QUARTERLY, vol. 4, pp. 44-63. Columbus, 1895.

_____. VERMONT'S ANTI-SLAVERY AND UNDERGROUND RAILROAD RECORD, WITH A MAP AND ILLUSTRATIONS. Columbus, Ohio: Spahr and Glenn Co., 1937.

Strother, Horatio T. THE UNDERGROUND RAILROAD IN CONNECTICUT. Middletown, Conn.: Wesleyan University Press, 1962.

Chapter 7
SLAVERY

Throughout the Western world and Africa, there are thousands of records dealing with slavery. In many cases they were dutifully kept because of their importance to the growth of capitalism. When Africans were seized from their homeland and brought to the Americas, the slave ship captain recorded it in his manifest. Such records still exist in vast quantities in the United States and several European and Caribbean countries. That was only the beginning of slave records. Once off the ship, if able to survive the journey, the slaves' lives were recorded in many ways--sometimes in separate records, but more often as part of the normal course of events in the slave owner's business affairs. There has, however, been no concerted effort to find or publish all these records for black genealogical research.

Once you have traced your ancestors through oral history, census, and vital statistics records back to slavery, you will need to be familiar with the techniques of establishing family relationships through slave records. It is sometimes tedious work which will probably take you longer than you would like. If slave records were published and as easily accessible as other genealogical information, it would be much easier.

The following sections provide a description, with some illustrations, of various types of records which are known to be available for some states. This chapter is concluded with the genealogy of the Hallam-Ross family, an example of how the records can be used to document black family ancestry.

SLAVE TRADING RECORDS

Valuable information on migration trails can be found in these records. Examples of the small number of these can be found in chapter 6, "Migratory Patterns." In addition naval shipping lists (which include slave arrivals) for east Florida, Georgia, Maryland, Massachusetts, New Hampshire, New Jersey, New York, South Carolina, and Virginia are on microfilm (1) at Columbia University in New York City, (2) at the National Archives, and (3) through the branch libraries of the Genealogical Department (see appendix B for a current list of branches).

BILLS OF SLAVE SALES

In most cases these records, as well as those for indentured servants, are found as part of land deeds, since slaves were considered property. The name of the slave, the value, and some description of age, plus the buyer's name, the seller's name, their counties of residence, and the date of the sale are usually included. Occasionally, such deeds are separate from land deeds or are in miscellaneous records at historical societies, libraries, and archives. They can be used in conjunction with other records to construct a genealogy. William Latham's deed (illustration following) is an example of such land deeds.

SLAVE ADVERTISEMENTS

Advertisements were carried in local papers naming runaways, and slaves for sale or hire. Little has been done to collect the genealogical information from these advertisements. Even when the genealogical data has been extracted and it included blacks, most often only those with last names are listed in the index, making it very difficult to use unless you know the slave owner's name.

BIRTH, BAPTISM, MARRIAGE, AND DEATH RECORDS

Vast numbers of such records exist in historical societies, archives, state libraries, and in the possession of private individuals. During the colonial period such records were often part of white church records, family papers, and wills. This was true for the North as well as the South. Local customs determine whether the records were kept separately or not.

CENSUS AND TAX RECORDS

In addition to the Federal Census Schedules already discussed, tax and census records were necessary to keep for business and governmental purposes since slaves were considered property. There are census records for slaves as early as 1619 when twenty blacks arrived in Jamestown, Virginia. By 1623 another census was taken which included the names of many of the blacks. But most often tax and census records contained numbers only and did not include names.

Slaves were assessed periodically and valuations were placed on them when estates were broken up. Often it is possible to approximate the ages and relationships of slaves by their value and order on such lists.

DEED, WILLIAM LATHAM, GROTON, NEW LONDON, CONNECTICUT, APRIL 18, 1725

COURT RECORDS

Local customs and laws will determine how accessible the records of slaves in court records are. They are, however, among the most voluminous of existing records dealing with slavery. In Georgia, for example, separate tribunals were set up to try slaves, although little has been done to index the wealth of information in these records, found at the Georgia State Archives. In addition, slave owners bringing slaves into this state had to register the names of their slaves in court. Other states handled court records and slavery in different ways.

PLANTATION RECORDS AND DIARIES

Plantation owners kept meticulous records of their slaves. They included birth, marriage, and death information in their recording, along with supplies distributed, health and illnesses of slaves, productivity, beatings (or "corrections"), and personal anecdotes. By carefully documenting a plantation record, genealogies can be constructed. Herbert George Gutman's THE BLACK FAMILY IN SLAVERY AND FREEDOM, 1750-1925 (New York: Pantheon Books, 1976) is an excellent example of the history that can be documented from plantation records.

Diaries are similar to plantation records, but are usually more anecdotal. Chapter 1 of this book has already pointed out how JOSHUA HEMPSTEAD'S DIARY (pp. 7-8) was essential in documenting the life of his slave Adam Jackson. Other diaries need to be scanned for their relevance to black genealogical research. There are several annotated bibliographies of diaries available at most libraries. Among the most recent is William Matthews's AMERICAN DIARIES IN MANUSCRIPT, 1580-1945: A DESCRIPTIVE BIBLIOGRAPHY (Athens: University of Georgia Press, 1974). Matthews's annotations indicate which diaries may have some value for black genealogical research. Consequently, those diaries have been included in the survey of states which follows. There are probably thousands of diaries in other places, however, which contain black genealogical information. One researcher, while looking for material on her ancestors in Alabama, located a diary of the slave-owning family and found her ancestor referred to by initials within the recorded daily life of the family.

MEDICAL RECORDS

Most slaves received some kind of care from doctors and hospitals. Miscellaneous medical records, which may be part of plantation records, and doctors' journals found at various state libraries and archives could be appropriate sources. All owners or employers were required to make health reports to the federal government during the pre-Civil War period in order to keep track of various epidemics. Among these records are the Mortality Schedules for 1850, 1860, 1870, 1880, and 1885, discussed in chapter 4, p. 26.

. Four sugarboxes 9/o Slait 2/o - . . . . £0 - 11 - 0
. large Cupboard 18/o tennant Saw 8/o five augres 7/o - . . 1 - 13 - 0
. Chest with Carpenters tools 30/o whipsaw 15/o - . - 2 - 5 - 0
. Crosscutsaw 4/o two handsaws 4/o addos & axe 2/o — 0 - 10 - 0
. two Iron squares 3/o two Beetles & two wedges 6/o — 0 - 9 - 0,
. Set old Cartboxes 2/o two draw shaves 1/6 Grindstone 12/o 0 - 15 - 6
. old prowirns 7/o dutch plow 14/o Cart & wheels 100/o 0 - 6 - 1 - 0
. Clove Spin 1/6 two ox yokes & ring & Staple 9/o — 0 - 10 - 6
. Set of Horstackling 9/o two pitchforks 3/o three rakes 1/o 0 - 13 - 0
one sledge 6/o two draft Chains 12/o log dog 6/o — 1 - 4 - 0
two old hoes 2/o pair old wheels 20/o two old axes 2/o 1 - 4 - 0
Iron bar 8/o spaid 3/o two hammers 3/o - — . . . 0 - 14 - 0
meataxi 1/o one Mare 300/o . - — . — — —15 - 1 - 0
Negro Boy Primas 300/o Brunitte Negro girl 120/o —21 - 0 - 0
Negro boy Brister 180/o - — — . — . — 9 - 0 - 0
three loads & half english hay 14 0/o — . . 7 - 0 - 0
Five bushels Rye 30/o ten bushels Potatoes 15/o - — 2 - 5 - 0
bushel & half Turnips 3/o two bushel Barley 12/o — —0 - 15 - 0
twenty lb flax in the bundle 8/o half bushel Pease 2/6 - 0 - 10 - 6
Farm & Buildings - . . . - — — 450 - 0 - 0
twenty bushels endiancorn 9/o - — . . — 4 - 10 - 0
                                                      526 11 - 6

INVENTORY, JOSEPH STARR,
NEW LONDON, CONNECTICUT, NOVEMBER 20, 1725

WILLS, INTESTATE RECORDS, AND INVENTORIES

Essential to all genealogical documentation is the information obtained from these records. Their importance cannot be overstated. Whether someone died having left a will or not, if they owned property, courts were required to appoint administrators to divide the property and care for the dependents. When a will was left, the administrator was the executor appointed by the deceased. If there was no will (an intestate estate), administrators were appointed from the community.

The job of the administrator or executor was to itemize and value all the property, which included slaves, and distribute it among the heirs. Illustration on previous page, Joseph Starr's Inventory, is an example of such an itemized inventory. Such itemizations and valuations, along with the final disposition of the property, are very important in constructing genealogies. The following will and genealogy will help to illustrate how a will can be used to construct genealogies:

Will of Elliott Futrell written September 20, 1836,
in Northampton County, North Carolina*

In the name of God Amen. I Elliott Futrell of Northampton County, State of North Carolina being sick but of sound mind and memory do make and ordain this my last will and testament in manner as follows. Item 1st. I give and bequeath unto my nephew Sander D. Futrell my plantation whereon I now live, also Negro woman Bridget and Negro girl named Elizabeth to him and his heirs forever.
Secondly, I give and bequeath unto my niece Penelope Futrell daughter of Noah Futrell Negro girl named Notice to her and her heirs forever.
3rd. I give and bequeath unto my niece Mary Futrell Negro woman Nancy and her child to her and her heirs forever.
4th. I give and bequeath unto my niece Irene Futrell and daughter of Noah Futrell Negro woman Lavina and her child Isabel to her and her heirs forever.
5th. I give and bequeath unto my nephew Noah Futrell son of Noah Futrell Negro boy named Moses to him and his heirs forever.
6th. I give and bequeath unto my niece Matilda Futrell daughter of Noah Futrell Negro girl Nancey to her and her heirs forever.
7th. I give and bequeath unto my brother Littleburg Futrell my track adjoining Willie Fennell and others, to him and his heirs.
Item 8th. I give and bequeath unto my niece Mitchel Futrell

---

*From JOURNAL OF NEGRO HISTORY 16 (July 1931): 332-33.

daughter of Noah Futrell Negro girl named Amy to her and her heirs forever.

Item 9. I give and bequeath unto my brother Hosea Futrell Negro woman America and her three children named Henry, William, Daisy to him and his heirs forever.

It is my will and desire that all of my property not herein given away be disposed of by my executor and so much thereof as may be necessary for the payment of my just debts to be equally divided between my brother Hosea Futrell and Sander D. Futrell, my nephew.

I nominate and appoint my friend Bryan Randolph my lawful executor in witness thereof.

I have hereunto set my hand and seal this 20th day of September in the year of our Lord 1836 in the presence of Jordan Bell and Jacob Outland.

(signed) Elliott Futrell

From Elliott Futrell's will, it can be determined that he had three brothers and no (?) children. The children of his brothers, and the slaves who were distributed by the will, are shown in the following chart. Abbreviations used are (g) girl, (w) woman, and (b) boy.

BROTHER	CHILDREN	BEQUEST
Noah Futrell	i. Penelope	Notice (g)
	ii. Irene	Lavinia (w)
		i. Isabel (g)
	iii. Noah	Moses (b)
	iv. Matilda	Nancey (g)
	v. Mitchel	Amy (g)
	vi. (?) Mary	Nancy (w)
		i. child (unnamed)
Hosea Futrell		America (w)
		i. Henry (b)
		ii. William (b)
		iii. Daisy (g)
	i. Sander D.	Bridget (w)
		Elizabeth (g)
		plantation
Littleburg Futrell		land

In order to follow the lives of these slaves further, one would have to check the marriage records of any sisters of Futrell, researching wills and bills of sale of the sisters and their husbands. The same records must be examined for the Futrell males Sander, Noah, and Hosea.

MANUMISSIONS

Before the Emancipation Proclamation, some slaves did gain their freedom for various reasons. This process was called manumitting, and a freedom certificate was granted to the slave upon manumission. Freed slaves were required to carry their certificates of freedom at all times. In states where manumissions are found they are usually in separate court records. In the North, however, you will sometimes find manumissions filed with land records or recorded in the will of the slave owners. The following is an example of the information in a New York State manumission record, located at the New York Historical Society:

> Ball, James (master)
> Laws, Leroy (Mulatto slave)
> Age 17
> Comments: Leroy is 5'2". He was born free in Lancaster County, Virginia
> (statement dated August 8, 1788)

SECONDARY SOURCES

Once you have located an ancestor living in a particular area or with a particular slave owner, you will want to research <u>every</u> aspect of that area or family you can find. The sources listed in Chapter 2 will be a start, but only a start. No guide book or bibliography can tell you everything you need to know. The records listed in the survey of states which follows are only those which specifically identify blacks and not the immense volume of genealogically valuable material available in every state archive, historical society, and library. In addition, there are probably thousands of primary and secondary sources which exist but have not yet been identified or recorded.

HALLAM-ROSS FAMILY

The following genealogy is an example of the type and scope of information which can be found in documenting black family ancestry. While two family members, Elizabeth L.H. Jordan Miller and Robert Freeman Jordan, provided much of the information, it was verified by vital statistics in Stonington and Groton, Connecticut. In addition, the slave information was provided by James Rose and Mrs. Barbara Brown from their unpublished manuscript TAPESTRY: A LIVING HISTORY OF BLACK AND WHITE IN SOUTHEASTERN CONNECTICUT.

Inventory of Deacon William Morgan of Stonington, June 21, 1778: mulatto boy Jack Ł20; services of Negro man named Pero, time of 4 years, 5 mo., Ł20. (Stonington Probate Dist./Town of Stonington, 1778, File #2269, located at Connecticut State Library.)

Will of Captain Peleg Brown of Stonington dated March 14, 1796: to daughter Mary, Negro girl Cate.

Inventory, August 6, 1796: Negro woman, Phyllis, aged ca. 56; Negro boy Pero, aged 17, slave for life; Negro girl, Lucy, aged about 15, slave for life; Negro girl Cate, aged 7, free at age 25. Distribution--August 30, 1797: Cate went to daughter, Mercy, who married Nathaniel Palmer, Jr.; old Phyllis and girl, Lucy, remained with the widow, Nancy Brown, Phyllis to be supported by the widow for life. (Stonington Probate Dist./Town of Stonington, 1796, File #562, located at Connecticut State Library.)

Children of Pero and Phyllis Hallam:

    I.   Lucy born ca. 1781; evidently unmarried; probably died July 26, 1821.
   II.   Pero m. (1) Pamela ?; (2) Mercy Miner, January 31, 1822.
  III.   Pardon born ca. 1787 son of Pero and Phyllis (Morgan) Hallam.
  IV.   Nancy born 1788; married Gerant Ross died March 2, 1876.
   V.   Catherine born April 22, 1790 Stonington, Connecticut.
  VI.   Fanny born ca. 1791; married Peter Dorrell; died May 14, 1872.
 VII.   Margaret born ca. 1800; died unmarried September 23, 1852. (Perhaps the daughter of Pero Jr. On her stone in Hillard Cemetery in Stonington, her parents are given as Pero and Pamelia Hallam. Fanny (Hallam) Dorrell is buried with her.)
VIII.   Adam married June.
  IX.   Simeon.

Children of Nancy Hallam and Gerant Ross:

   i. Frank Benjamin Ross   m. Maria E. Gates (black Indian)
      b. ca. 1801, Stonington   b. ?, Block Island
      m. 12-15-1833
      d. 11-23-1892, Stonington   d. 8-8-1822, Stonington

  ii. Milly Ross   m. Peter Sands (from Black Island)
      b. ?   b. ?
      m. ?
      d. ?   d. ?

 iii. Alexander Ross   m. Lorana Gates
      b. ca. 1815   b. ?
      m. 12-15-1833
      d. ?   d. ?

  iv. Alfred D. Ross   m. Sarah J. Gates (Lorana's sister)
      b. 6-18-1816, Stonington   b. 8-15-1821
      m. ?
      d. 5-23-1892   d. 2-20-1887, Stonington

   v. Horace Ross   m. Betsey
      b. ca. 1820   m. Emily
      d. ?   m. Elizabeth Niles

vi.	Caroline Ross	m.	Henry Cowen Scott
	b. 2-14-1823, Stonington	m.	John Eastern
	d. ?		
vii.	Stiles Ross	m.	Flora Ann Hallam
	b. 1827	b. ?	
	m. ?		
	d. 12-30-1886	d.	9-27-1900
viii.	Enoch Ross	m.	Ann
	b. ca. 1827	b. ?	
	m. ?		
	d. 8-18-1883	d. ?	
ix.	Eliza Ross	m.	George Freeman
	b. ca. 1829, Stonington	b. ca. 1824	
	m. 1-27-1850, Stonington		
	d. 12-30-1904	d.	3-21-1896
x.	Angeline Ross	m.	Stephen Carter
	b. ?, Stonington	b. ?	
	m. ?		
	d. ?	d. ?	
xi.	Lavina Ross		
xii.	Amelia Ross		

Additional generations are listed in James M. Rose and Barbara Brown's unpublished manuscript TAPESTRY.

Part II

SURVEY OF THE UNITED STATES,
THE WEST INDIES, AND CANADA

Part II

SURVEY OF THE UNITED STATES,
THE WEST INDIES, AND CANADA

What is attempted here is a brief survey of the types of records known to be available for black genealogical research. This survey tries not to duplicate other genealogical surveys. For that reason, many other guides and sources should be consulted in the process of research. One guide in particular is the DIRECTORY OF AFRO-AMERICAN RESOURCES, edited by Walter Schatz for the Race Relations Information Center (New York: R.R. Bowker Co., 1970).

This part of BLACK GENESIS is divided into four geographic areas, keeping in mind the history of slavery and the addition of states to the Union. The first area--the South--surveys the extensive records of slave ship port states and then moves inland to those states active in the domestic slave trade whose records are not as easily available. Next are the northern states, again with port states first, where separate records dealing with blacks were rarely kept and little has been done to find and index records of blacks found within the abundant New England resources. The third area is the Midwest, whose giant waterways served as conduits for blacks on the early frontier. Finally, the western states, the West Indies, and Canada are surveyed. The Western states came later into the Union and their black citizens were more likely ex-slaves than slaves.

The discussion for each geographic area is divided by states. For every state there is a general description and an annotated bibliography of appropriate background reading. Each survey is concluded with an outline of federal, state and county or town records and miscellaneous material, including cemetery records, church records, unpublished diaries, military records, newspapers, personal papers, and slavery records related to black genealogical research. The general nature of all these records has been previously discussed in the introductory chapters.

A large part of the diaries, journals, and papers listed in the survey can be found in the NATIONAL UNION CATALOG OF MANUSCRIPT COLLECTIONS cited in chapter 2, p. 15. The manuscript numbers (e.g., MS 64 389) have been included to assist the researcher. In addition, the majority of the newspaper holdings listed in the following survey were taken from NEWSPAPERS IN MICROFILM: UNITED STATES, 1948-1972 also cited in chapter 2, p. 20. In most cases titles with only one to three issues available in a library have been excluded from the survey here as well as most titles published in the twentieth century. When a final date of publication is not listed, it should be assumed that it was still published up to 1972, the publication date of the union list.

If the user wants to have any of the records listed microfilmed for personal use (such as a diary or state record), many state archives, in addition to the National Archives, have the facilities to make such copies at a moderate cost. If the records are unobtainable through the Genealogical Department or interlibrary loan at the local library, microfilming and xeroxing are less expensive than traveling.

Chapter 8
GEORGIA (South)

Georgia is the birthplace of many black families, some of whose ancestors came from Virginia. The port of Savannah was a nucleus area for black families. There are many publications, too numerous to mention here, dealing with the history of slavery in Georgia. Some books, however, are of particular genealogical value in the study of blacks and are excellent primary sources. In addition, records found at the Georgia Department of Archives and History in Atlanta are listed below. These records, which are microfilmed, represent only the obvious records which deal with blacks in Georgia. The bulk are still under other titles and need to be sought out. The following is a list of published sources which will be of value for Georgia research:

Flanders, Ralph Betts. THE FREE NEGRO IN ANTE-BELLUM GEORGIA. Wooster, Ohio: Bell and Howell Black Culture Collection, #279-9.

> An excellent and interesting resource which is available on microfilm from the publishers and may be found at some state libraries.

Georgia. Department of Archives and History. SOME EARLY TAX DIGESTS OF GEORGIA. Collected and edited by Ruth Blair. 1926. Reprint. Easley, S.C.: Southern Historical Press, 1971.

> This very valuable record contains names of whites who owned slaves, in addition to a record of free blacks in Chatham County, Georgia.

Grant, Hugh Fraser. PLANTER MANAGEMENT AND CAPITALISM IN ANTE-BELLUM GEORGIA: THE JOURNAL OF HUGH FRASER GRANT, RICEGROWER. Edited by Albert Virgil House. Columbia University Studies in the History of American Agriculture, no. 13. New York: Columbia University Press, 1954.

> This journal contains many names, and birth and death records of slaves on the Elizafield Plantation in Glynn County, Georgia. Many other plantation records can be as helpful as this one in tracing ancestors.

Jones, Ruby Mae. THE NEGRO IN COLONIAL GEORGIA, 1735-1805. Wooster, Ohio: Bell and Howell Black Culture Collection, #564-2, 1938.

> All materials in this series are available on microfilm from Bell and Howell and may be found at some state libraries.

Perdue, Robert E. THE NEGRO IN SAVANNAH, 1865-1900. New York: Exposition Press, 1973.

> Gives a good general history of blacks in Savannah and lists a number of names of free blacks. Also contains a good account of migrations into and out of the city. Good bibliography, pages 142-53.

Phillips, Ulrich Bonnell, ed. PLANTATION AND FRONTIER, 1649-1863. 2 vols. 1910. Reprint. Selected Essays in History, Economics, and Social Science, no. 99. New York: B. Franklin, 1969.

> Contains a record of names of blacks on the Gourie and East Heritage estates, which were operated as one plantation on Argyle Island on the Savannah River in Georgia (I, 134). This work also has an official register of free persons "of color" in Richmond County, Georgia, in 1819 (II, 143). (See chapter 21, "Connecticut," p. 154, for notes on Phillips's personal papers which may contain more material than was published in these volumes.)

Reed, Ruth. THE NEGRO WOMEN OF GAINESVILLE, GEORGIA. University of Georgia, Phelps-Stokes Fellowship Studies, no. 6. Athens, Ga.: 1921.

> Available on microfilm from Bell and Howell, Wooster, Ohio.

Scott, Olivia Barbara. A CLASSIFIED SOCIOLOGICAL SOURCE BIBLIOGRAPHY OF PERIODICAL AND MANUSCRIPT MATERIALS ON THE NEGRO IN ATLANTA, GEORGIA. Wooster, Ohio: Bell and Howell Black Culture Collection, #571-1, 1948.

> Available on microfilm from Bell and Howell and at local, state, and college libraries in Georgia.

Sweat, Edward Forrest. "The Free Negro in Ante-Bellum Georgia." Ph.D. dissertation, Indiana University, 1957. Available from University Microfilms, Ann Arbor, Mich., order no. 22709.

Trevor Arnett Library. GUIDE TO MANUSCRIPTS AND ARCHIVES IN THE NEGRO COLLECTION OF TREVOR ARNETT LIBRARY, ATLANTA UNIVERSITY. Atlanta: 1971.

FEDERAL RECORDS

Mortality Schedules

   1850, 1860, 1870, 1880 (DNA, DNDAR)

Population Schedules

   1800-20 (G-Ar); 1820-1900 (DNA); 1830, 1850, 1880 (GU)

Special Census   - none

Record Group 101 (DNA)

   For a description of these records see chapter 4, p. 27.   Georgia
   branches with deposits recorded: Atlanta, Augusta, Savannah.

Record Group 105 (DNA)

   For a description of these records see chapter 4, p. 27.   Georgia
   records contain school reports, letters sent and received (alphabetical).

Record Group 36, "Records of the Bureau of Customs" (DNA)

   Contains slave manifests for Savannah before 1808.

U.S. Adjutant General Records (G-Ar)

   The Negro in the Military Service of the U.S. 1639-1886.

      Seven volumes of materials, including employment,
      civil status, battles, and treatment and exchange of
      prisoners.

U.S. Bureau of the Census (G-Ar, DNA)

   Schedule of Slave Owners, 1850 and 1860.

      Includes all Georgia counties.   Ten reels of microfilm.

U.S. Department of Interior (G-Ar)

   African Slave Trade and Negro Colonization Records 1854-72.

Owsley Charts (T)

   These charts contain land and slave information compiled from all
   counties from Federal Census of Georgia 1840-60.

STATE, COUNTY, AND TOWN RECORDS

The list of records which follows indicates what is available on microfilm from the Georgia Department of Archives and History in Atlanta. These records are similar in nature to records available in most southern states and should be used not only as a guide for Georgia, but an indication of what ought to be found in other southern states as well. This list of materials relating to black genealogical research is by no means definitive. It represents only those records on microfilm which specifically state that they concern blacks (e.g., the marriage records listed are only the black marriages). Counties not mentioned on the list may have kept similar records, but interspersed them with white ones. An actual check of other films will be necessary to determine the existence of other county records relating to blacks.

Appling County

　　Free Persons of Color, 1843-56

Baker County

　　Marriages, 1905-25; 1925-43

Baldwin County

　　Free Persons of Color, 1832-64

　　Trials of Slaves, Inferior Court Minutes:　1812-38; 1812-26

Berrien County

　　Marriages, 1905-27; 1927-49

Bibb County

　　Marriages, 1828-39; 1865-71; 1869-74; 1874-82; 1882-88; 1888-97; 1892-95; 1895-99; 1899-1911; 1902-8; 1906-10; 1913-19; 1917-19; 1919-21 and 1934; 1921-25 and 1929; 1936; 1963; 1964

　　Index to Marriages, 1823-1963

Brooks County

　　Marriages, 1894-1904; 1904-13; 1911-25; 1924-37; 1937-49; 1949-66

Bryan County

　　Marriages, 1870-97

Bulloch County

    Marriages, 1912-25; 1925-39; 1939-66; 1952-69

Burke County

    Slave List, 1798 (Second District C)

Butts County

    Marriages, 1882-1903; 1903-29; 1929-48

Camden County

    Affidavits of Persons Bringing Slaves into Georgia, 1818-47

    Affidavits of Persons Bringing Slaves into Georgia, 1818-47 (Superior Court)

    Free Persons of Color, 1819-43

    Marriages, 1931-49; 1949-52

Campbell County

    Marriages, 1898-1928

Carroll County

    Marriages, 1892-1906

Chatham County

    Free Persons of Color, 1780-1865; 1837-49; 1861-64; 1826-35 (some also at GHS)

    List of Negroes Freed (Superior Court) (Compiled by General Robert J. Travis)

Chatooga County

    Free Persons of Color, 1847-62

    Marriages 1909-16; 1916-43; 1943-56

Clay County

    Indentures for Free Persons of Color, 1866-67

    Marriages, 1906-18; 1922-33

Clinch County

    Marriages, 1922-65

Colquitt County
>Marriages, 1942–46; 1946–50; 1950–62; 1962–67

Columbia County
>Affidavits of Persons Bringing Slaves into Georgia, 1818–35
>Free Persons of Color, 1819–36
>Marriages, 1914–43; 1943–52

Coweta County
>Index to Marriages, 1827–1966

Crawford County
>Marriages, 1909–43

Decatur County
>Voters Registration (Superior Court), 1902

DeKalb County
>Marriages, 1893–1908

Dodge County
>Marriages, 1893–1940; 1905–19; 1919–37; 1937–52; 1952–66
>Index to Marriages, 1871–1958

Dooly County
>Marriages, 1852–75; 1868–90; 1885–91; 1890–99; 1899–1908

Douglas County
>Marriages, 1894–1941

Elbert County
>Affidavits of Persons Bringing Slaves into Georgia, Volume A, 1822–47
>Free Persons of Color, 1819–59
>Marriages, 1882–91; 1889–99; 1898–1909
>Slave Trials, 1837–49

Emanuel County
>   Free Persons of Color, 1855
>   Marriages, 1905-17; 1917-33; 1933-47; 1948-61; 1952-61

Fayette County
>   Superintendent of Schools
>   School Census, 1928; 1933; 1938

Forsyth County
>   Marriages, 1895-1900

Franklin County
>   Importation of Slaves, 1818-31
>   Marriages, 1893-1938

Fulton County
>   Marriages, 1866-78; 1878-84; 1884-89; 1889-93; 1893-96; 1896-1900; 1900-1902

Glascock County
>   Marriages, 1871-1920; 1921-45; 1945-66

Glynn County
>   Marriages, 1898-1905; 1905-18

Gordon County
>   Marriages, 1908-65

Greene County
>   Marriages, 1866-75; 1875-77; 1878-83

Hall County
>   Marriages, 1866-1900; 1900-1920; 1920-53

Hancock County
>   Free Persons of Color, 1855-62
>   Slave Trials, 1834-50 (Inferior Court)

Harris County
>   Marriages, 1859-72; 1870-83; 1890-1923

Hart County
>   Marriages, 1867-99; 1899-1923

Henry County
>   Marriages, 1851-85; 1881-92; 1885-1916; 1916-33
>   Index to Marriages, 1821-1939

Houston County
>   Licenses to Sell Spiritous Liquor to Free Persons of Color, 1834-62

Irwin County
>   Marriages, 1854-74; 1904-17; 1917-54

Jackson County
>   Affidavits of Persons Bringing Slaves into Georgia, 1818-30
>   Marriages, 1895-1911

Jefferson County
>   Free Persons of Color, 1818; 1820-22; 1840-59
>   Marriages, 1866-90; 1899-1917; 1896-1917; 1918-30; 1929-58;
>   1942-56

Johnson County
>   Marriages, 1907-28; 1928-52; 1952-66

Jones County
>   Index to Slave Deeds (Superior Court)
>   Grantor and Grantee, 1791-1864

Laurens County
>   Marriages, 1897-1907; 1907-15; 1915-33; 1921-29

Lee County
>   Marriages, 1867-1905

Liberty County

> Bonds of Apprenticeship, 1866-73
>
> Free Persons of Color, 1852-64
>
> Marriages, 1819-96; 1897-1909; 1909-37; 1936-56; 1867-72

Lincoln County

> Docket of Slaves Indicted for Capital Crimes, 1814-38 (Inferior Court)
>
> Free Persons of Color, 1819-63
>
> Marriages, 1866-75; 1875-84; 1884-96; 1896-1925; 1925-68
>
> Index to Marriages, 1866-1939

Lowndes County

> Marriages, 1904-10; 1909-16; 1916-21; 1921-29; 1925-34

Lumpkin County

> Free Persons of Color, 1848-64

McDuffie County

> Voters Register (Ordinary), 1886-94

Marion County

> Voters List, 1898, 1900, 1903, 1906 (Superior Court)

Meriwether County

> Superintendent of Schools
>
> School Census, 1898, 1903, 1913

Miller County

> Marriages, 1939-53; 1965-66

Mitchell County

> Marriages, 1909-17; 1915-24; 1924-35; 1935-43; 1943-52

Montgomery County

> Marriages, 1893-1946

Morgan County

    Marriages, 1866-91; 1891-1904

    Slave Register (Ordinary), 1818-24

    Tax Digests, 1890-1910; 1895

Oconee County

    Marriages, 1932-66

Oglethorpe County

    Marriages, 1873-94; 1897-1908

    Marriage Licenses Issued to Freedmen, 1865-73

Polk County

    Marriages, 1917-19 and 1928; 1916-47; 1947-65

Pulaski County

    Free Persons of Color, 1840-65

    Marriages, 1894-1910; 1910-19

    Slave Records (Ordinary), dates not stated

Putnam County

    Trials of Slaves, 1813-43

Richmond County

    Slave Requisition, 1818-20; 1822-30; 1835-37 (Superior Court)

Rockdale County

    Marriages, 1891-1902

Screven County

    Docket for Trials of Slaves and Free Persons of Color, 1844-48 (Inferior Court)

Spalding County

    Marriages, 1893-98; 1898-1903; 1903-10; 1910-17; 1917-23; 1923-34; 1933-42; 1942-51; 1951-52

Sumter County

    Marriages, 1888-97

    Voters Register, 1909; 1911-13

Taliaferro County

    Free Persons of Color, 1796-1865, Book A

    Free Persons of Color, 1829-64, Books A and B

    Marriages, 1866-1929; 1875-1905

    Trials of Free Persons of Color, Book A, 1857-58

Tattnall County

    Marriages, 1866-72; 1910-50

Terrell County

    Marriages, 1869-88; 1888-1906

    Voters Registration, 1895-1909

Thomas County

    Free Persons of Color, 1858-62

    Marriages, 1868-74

Troup County

    Marriages, 1892-1908

Upson County

    Marriages, 1866-76; 1893-1908

Walton County

    Marriages, 1896-1908; 1905-19

Warren County

    Free Persons of Color, 1844-63

    Marriages, 1888-1902

    Slave Owner's List, 1798 (Superior Court)

Wayne County

    Marriages, 1907-55

Webster County

    Marriages, 1914-60

MISCELLANEOUS RECORDS

Cemetery Records (G-Ar)

Baldwin County

    Central State Hospital Cemetery Records, 1880-1951

        Negro: male and female, name, date of burial, grave number, section number, and remarks.

Chatham County

    Laurel Grove Cemetery Records

        Records include deaths, burials, and title to lots, 1852-1942; not indexed.

Sumter County

    Oak Grove Cemetery Records, 1903-59; indexed.

Thomas County

    Old Negro Cemetery

        Transcribed records, histories, loose notes related to the cemetery.

Church Records (G-Ar)

Baptist

    First Baptist Church for the Colored, Macon, Bibb County

    Jordan Grove Baptist Church, Lee County, Palmyra District

    Sandy Creek Baptist Church, Morgan County

        Minutes and membership rolls, 1808-66; 1905-50.

    Bethlehem Baptist Church, Appalachee, Morgan County

        Minutes, 1859-96.

Episcopal

St. Anthanasius Episcopal Church, Brunswick, Camden County

Records include the monthly publication WORTH and a short sketch of church, 1915-24; the will of Mary Rhinelander King of New York, with bequest to the church is also included.

St. Bartholomew's Episcopal Church, Chatham County

There are records of baptisms, marriages, burials, and memberships, 1877-1925.

Methodist

Bethel Methodist Church, Screven County

Records contain appointments and list of members, 1836-78.

Presbyterian

Hebron Presbyterian Church, Banks County

Church records, 1847-84.

Independent Presbyterian Church, Chatham County

Minutes of First African Sabbath School, 1826-39; colored Sunday School, 1844; colored marriages and members, 1829-87.

New Hope Presbyterian Church, Madison County

Minutes, 1838-61; church history, 1788-1838; baptisms, marriages, and members, 1849-59.

City Records (G-Ar)

Atlanta

Tax Digest; includes Negro property for all of Fulton County, 1890.

Milledgeville

Census, 1911; contains name, age, color, residence, and remarks.

Treasurer: Tax Digests, 1859-67; 1869 lists black taxpayers.

Savannah

Free Persons of Color Register, 1817-29; 1860-63 (also at GHi).

Georgia

Diaries

Allen, Eliza Harriet (Arnold), 1831; 1837; 1841 (RHi)
Records visits on brother's Savannah plantation.

Barrow, Clara Elizabeth, 1869; 1875 (GU)
Records Oglethorpe County, Milledgeville, and Americus daily life.

Barrow, Col. David Crenshaw, 1847-49; 1851-52; 1856-58; 1863; 1876; 1879 (GU)
An Oglethorpe County plantation diary. MS 64-219

Couper, James Hamilton, 1839-54 (NcU)
A Hopeton Plantation journal, Glynn County.

Dickey, William J., 1858-59; 1879-80; 1884-89 (GU)
Thomas County plantation diary.

Lumpkin, Wilson, 1838-63 (GHi)
Births and deaths of slaves are listed.

Parker, William Foster, 1859-60 (GHi)
A Savannah slave dealer's journal.

Ravenel, Miss, 1865 (GHi)
Describes plantation conditions.

Ravenel, Henry, Jr., 1806-22 (GHi)
This diary lists blacks inherited and their descendants (1780-1820).

Ravenel, Dr. Henry, 1830-32 (GHi)
Records slave births, 1809-29.

Ravenel, Thomas Porcher, 1845-1903 (GHi)
Describes plantation life.

Richardson, Gilbert M., 1860-61 (GHi)

A Lumpkin plantation diary.

Spratlin, James A., 1866 (GHi)

An Oglethorpe County overseer's record.

Military Records (G-Ar)

Confederate record: An official request for use of the slave of J.J. Jones of Burke County from CS Engineering Department, Office Enrollment of Slave, Savannah, December 9, 1836.

Forms: "Military Impressment of Negroes for the Defense of Georgia." Two forms filed by estate of S.A. Jones for use of slaves, August 5, 1862.

Record Group 109, "War Department Collection of Confederate Records" (DNA)

Medical Department, Ordinance: Macon records of slaves hired, letters to owners and returns for work done by black laborers, carpenters, and bricklayers.

Newspapers

LOYAL GEORGIA (Augusta). January 13, 1866, to 1868. Weekly.

Holdings: 1866-68; CSdS, CSS, WHi.

SAVANNAH TRIBUNE. 1875 to September 24, 1960. Weekly.

Holdings: December 4, 1875; 1889; December 1891 to 1943; ATT, DHU, DLC, GAU, MH, MoJcL, NN, OC1, OKentU, TNF, ViHal, WHi.

December 4, 1875, to December 25, 1924; Cty, CU.

October 23, 1886, to December 15, 1888; GSSC, CU.

SAVANNAH WEEKLY ECHO. 1879-84. Weekly.

Holdings: 1883-84; CSdS, CSS, CU, DLC, FTaSU, KHi, LU-NO, MdBMC, MiKW, TNF, WHi.

Personal Papers

Allen, Eliza A., 1841-63 (G-Ar)

Personal correspondence and business papers, Burke County plantation.

Georgia

Anderson, Edward Clifford. Papers, 1813-82 (NcU)

> Includes miscellaneous plantation and slave records of Savannah. MS 64-389

Berrien, John McPherson, 1781-1856 (G-Ar)

> Conditions of slaves.

Cameron Family Papers, 1739-1929 (NcU)

> Contains some slave registers for a planter of Orange County and Raleigh. MS 64-445

Cooper, Mrs. Mark, 1790 (G-Ar)

> Includes deed for slave Reuben Payne to Thomas Cooper.

Cooper, Mark Anthony, 1794-1875 (G-Ar)

> Includes deeds, warrants, grants, and slave deeds.

Cowan, Mrs. F.B., 1837 (G-Ar)

> Includes receipts of slave, December 1, 1837, Franklin County.

Greene, Richard Appling. (G-Ar)

> Lists of slaves owned in Macon County.

Jones, John J., 1835-65 (G-Ar)

> Includes records relating to slavery.

Jones, William B., M.D. (G-Ar)

> Includes bills of slave sales.

King, Parrington. (G-Ar)

> Includes deeds, receipts, and bills of sale of slaves, from Darien and Rosewell, Georgia.

Moye Collection. (G-Ar)

> Includes an 1844 bill of sale for a slave, signed by Joseph and E.O. Forbes and Isaac Tull.

Nephew, James. (G-Ar)

> Includes deeds for land and slaves, McIntosh County.

Orr, James M. (G-Ar)

Includes bills of sale for slaves, Gwinnett County.

Turner, Daniel. (G-Ar)

Includes economic, social, and political conditions related to slavery. Turner was a physician at St. Mary's, 1805-08.

Yancey, B.C. Account Book for Coosa River Plantation, 1853-66 (G-Ar)

These records are from Cherokee County, Alabama, and Blue Spring Plantation in Dougherty County, Georgia. Includes birth and deaths of slaves, and accounts of freedmen working, 1865-66.

Slavery Records

In addition to those records of slaves already listed under Diaries, the Georgia Historical Society in Savannah has the following:

Bills of Sale, miscellaneous.

Plantation Records for Argyle, 1828-31; papers of Beverly Berwick, 1874-76; papers from the Telfair Family Plantation, 1794-1864.

Slave Ship Manifests.

Chapter 9

LOUISIANA (South)

New Orleans was a main conduit for slave sales to Louisiana, Alabama, Mississippi, and other southern states. New Orleans, being a nucleus area of many black families, is therefore a primary area for the study of black genealogy. The records of blacks in New Orleans and Louisiana are massive and can be found in both obvious and obscure places. There are several published sources available which are of considerable interest:

Barrow, Bennet Hilliard. PLANTATION LIFE IN THE FLORIDA PARISHES OF LOUISIANA, 1836-1846, AS REFLECTED IN THE DIARY OF BENNET H. BARROW. By Edwin Adams Davis. Columbia University Studies in the History of American Agriculture, no. 9. 1943. Reprint. New York: AMS Press, 1967.

　　Bennet Barrow's diary contains an excellent example of the types
　　of plantation records that were kept by slave owners.

Everett, Donald E. "Free Persons of Color in New Orleans, 1803-1865." Ph.D. dissertation, Tulane University, 1953.

　　An excellent book for background reading. It can be obtained
　　from the Howard Tilton Memorial Library of Tulane University.

Hebert, Donald J. SOUTHWEST LOUISIANA RECORDS; CHURCH AND CIVIL RECORDS OF SETTLERS. Vol. 2: 1811-1830. Eunice, La.: Published by the author, 1974. Available through the Genealogical Society in Salt Lake City, Utah, and the following libraries: GU, LU, ICU, NcD, NN, TxU, WHi.

　　A superior survey is on the preliminary pages (xii-xix) of this
　　volume. It covers the laws involving blacks and is very extensive
　　in surveying the vast number of records on blacks (some in French)
　　in southwest Louisiana churches. A very important contribution to
　　black genealogy.

Hiss, Roscoe R. DESCRIPTIVE CATALOGUE OF THE DOCUMENTS RELATING TO THE HISTORY OF THE UNITED STATES IN THE PAPELES PROCEDENTES DE CUBA DEPOSITED IN THE ARCHIVO GENERAL DE INDIAS AT SEVILLE.

Washington, D.C.: Carnegie Institute, 1932.

Especially valuable for genealogical research in Louisiana. Examples of records follow. ("Legajo" numbers are category and finding references.)

Legajo 191. Census of New Orleans, 1778.

Legajo 192. Census of Baton Rouge, 1782, 1786; census of the district of Nueva Feliciana, 1798; census of Negroes in the district of Cannes Brulles, 1799; census of the district of La Meteaire.

Legajo 122-1. List of families, including slaves, arriving at Tinzas, 1788 and June 1, 1792.

Legajo 189-1. Census of the left bank of the Mississippi from Bayou de Placaminas to Ile au Marais, May 10, 1772; census of Rapide, February 1, 1773; census of Negro and Indian slaves at Natchitoches, February 25, 1774; census of Negroes and Mulattoes at Natchitoches, January 17, 1774.

Legajo 189-2. Census of slaves at Cabahannocer, 1775; list of slaves and masters at Pointe Coupee, 1776.

Legajo 206. Lists of free "Mulattoes and Negroes" found in Florida in 1772.

Legajo 211. Census of slaves at Allemands, 1795; at Atakapas, 1795; at Natchitoches, 1795; census of slaves at the Quartier de la Metarie of New Orleans in 1796.

Legajo 212. Census of Negroes at Chapitoulas; lists of inhabitants of Mobile possessing slaves; census of third ward of New Orleans, of slaves of the second ward; of slaves' masters who contributed to indemnity for slaves lost at Pointe Coupee (all for the year 1795).

Legajo 582. List of licenses granted for purchases of vessels and cargoes of Negroes for 1802.

Leland, W.G. GUIDE TO MATERIALS FOR AMERICAN HISTORY IN THE LIBRARIES AND ARCHIVES OF PARIS. Washington, D.C.: Carnegie Institute, 1932-43.

Especially valuable for research in Louisiana. It contains a guide to records of the French period of Louisiana history and includes some of the following records:

Census of Louisiana--transmitted by Perrier and Salmon in January 1732. (CF. Arch Colonies, G1, carton 464 F.166 in MSS. FR. NOUVELLES ACQUISITIONS.)

Census returns of New Orleans and Louisiana for 1722, 1724, 1732.

Subjects, emigration, indentured servants, women, volunteers, Negroes found in BIBLIOTHEQUE NATIONALE.

Numerous extracts relating to vessels engaging in the slave trade found in the BIBLIOTHEQUE NATIONALE.

General census of the French West Indies including 36,655 people for the year 1687.

Maduell, Charles R. THE CENSUS TABLES FOR THE FRENCH COLONY OF LOUISIANA FROM 1699 THROUGH 1732. Baltimore: Genealogical Publishing Co., 1972.

Lists some blacks named in the census.

_____. MARRIAGE CONTRACTS, WILLS AND TESTAMENTS OF THE SPANISH COLONIAL PERIOD IN NEW ORLEANS, 1770-1804. New Orleans: Published by the author, 1969.

Lists some black marriages.

McConnell, Roland Calhoun. NEGRO TROOPS OF ANTEBELLUM LOUISIANA: A HISTORY OF THE BATTALION OF FREE MEN OF COLOR. Louisiana State University Studies, Social Science Series, no. 13. Baton Rouge: Louisiana State University Press, 1968.

Excellent background reading for tracing black veterans before the Civil War. Especially good for the War of 1812.

McGowan, Emma. "Free People of Color in New Orleans." Master's thesis, Tulane University, 1939.

An excellent discussion. Available in the Howard Tilton Memorial Library at Tulane.

Menn, Joseph Karl. THE LARGE SLAVEHOLDERS OF LOUISIANA, 1860. New Orleans: Pelican Publishing Co., 1964.

Lists white slaveholders from the 1860 census.

Porteous, Laura L. "Index to the Spanish Judicial Records of Louisiana." LOUISIANA HISTORICAL QUARTERLY 6 (1926): 145-63.

Contains some slave sale transactions.

Sterkx, H.E. THE FREE NEGRO IN ANTE-BELLUM LOUISIANA. Rutherford, N.J.: Fairleigh Dickinson University Press, 1972.

Gives names of free blacks. Good background and excellent bibliography, pages 316-37.

Taylor, Joe Gray. NEGRO SLAVERY IN LOUISIANA. Baton Rouge: Louisiana Historical Association, 1963.

> Lists some black genealogical sources found at the Louisiana State Archives. Good bibliography.

FEDERAL RECORDS

Mortality Schedules

> 1850-80 (DNA, DNDAR)

Population Schedules

> 1810-80 (DNA, LU-Ar); 1900 (DNA): and many libraries throughout the state have schedules of a few years.

Special Census 1890 (DNA, LU-Ar)

Record Group 101 (DNA)

> For a description of these records see chapter 4, p. 27. Louisiana branches with deposits recorded: New Orleans, Shreveport.

Record Group 105 (DNA)

> For a description of these records see chapter 4, p. 27. Louisiana records contain school reports.

Record Group 36, "Records of the Bureau of Customs" (DNA)

> Contains slave manifests for New Orleans 1819-56.

Record Group 56, "General Records of the Department of the Treasury" (DNA)

> Third Special Agency: Supervisory Special Agent's dealings with freedmen before the Freedmen's Bureau was established 1863-65.

STATE, PARISH, AND COUNTY RECORDS

The greatest source of black genealogical materials for Louisiana is at the Louisiana State Archives located at the Louisiana State University in Baton Rouge. No published survey exists of the records found in this collection. The archives has a large number of family papers of slaveholders; church records (which list slave and free black members); business records of merchants dealing with freedmen and black farmers; slave inventories arranged in family groups or listing mothers with names and dates of birth of their children. For the Civil War period there is a large number of papers of free black families, predominantly planters from the Francophone area. The best plantation records found in this collection have been microfilmed and can be purchased from Greenwood Press, New Haven, Connecticut. A survey and cataloging of all Louisiana State Archives records is an essential research project. A few of the diaries found at the archives are listed below.

Another important group of parish records is located at the New Orleans Public Library. The state of Louisiana ordered that all free blacks who arrived in Louisiana would have to enroll their names with the parish judge. The registers for 1840-57, 1856-59, 1859-61, and 1861-64 are available at the library.

The U.S. Works Project Administration's INVENTORY OF PARISH ARCHIVES OF LOUISIANA (New Orleans: Historical Records Survey, 1940) is an important reference. Their work gives an indication of just where to look for various manumission records. The court and colonial records are still held in the parishes and, in some cases, the colonial records give names of the slave's African tribe.

The court minutes contain records of slave trials and manumissions because the 1825 legislature set up a separate court to try fugitive slaves. The WPA survey on the Federal Archives in Louisiana lists an alphabetical and chronological digest of the ACTS AND DELIBERATIONS OF THE CABILDO, 1769-1803. The ten volumes in this digest are in typescript form at the Louisiana State Archives located on the Baton Rouge campus of the Louisiana State University. They relate to activities involving blacks both in Louisiana and Florida. Included in the survey is a nineteen-volume typescript report of the Archives of the Spanish Government of West Florida which has records on blacks in that area.

MISCELLANEOUS RECORDS

Cemetery Records

Availability not known.

Church Records

St. Louis Cathedral Archives, New Orleans.

> First book of marriages of Negroes and mulattoes in the parish of St. Louis in the city of New Orleans, 1777-1830. Marriage register of Negroes and mulattoes of St. Louis Cathedral from July 1, 1720, to December 4, 1730.

Also see Donald J. Hebert's SOUTHWEST LOUISIANA RECORDS cited in the introductory section of this chapter.

Diaries

Anonymous, 1835-37 (LU-Ar)

Plantation life.

Batchelor, Albert A., 1856-1930 (LU-Ar)

Plantation life.

Bateman, [Mary], 1856 (LU-Ar)

Her plantation life. Original manuscript is at the University of North Carolina.

Capell, Eli J., 1842-50; 1867 (LU-Ar)

Pleasant Hill Plantation diary, Amite County, Mississippi.

DeClouet, Paul L., 1866-70; 1880-88 (LU-Ar)

Plantation operations. MS 75-732

Foster, Robert Watson, 1862-64 (RHi)

Plantation life near Apolousas, Louisiana.

Hickman-Bryan. Papers, 1796-1920 (MoU)

Missouri, Louisiana, and Kentucky families with land and slave records. MS 60-1817

Hilliard, Mrs. Isaac H., 1849-50 (LU-Ar)

Describes plantation life at Vicksburg. Also available at Shreve Memorial Library in Shreveport.

Jenkins, Dr. John Carmichael, 1841-55 (LU-Ar)

Includes purchases and health of slaves. MS 70-220

Liddell, St. John R., 1839-44; 1867-68 (LU-Ar)

Health of slaves.

McCollan, Ellen E., 1842-51 (LU-Ar)

Plantation and family life.

Magruder, Eliza L., 1846-57 (LU-Ar)

> Treatment of slaves.

Marston, Henry W., 1822-32; 1855-84 (LU-Ar)

> Plantation problems.

Mather, Joseph, 1852-59 (LU-Ar)

> Sugar plantation, health of slaves.

Monette, James, 1848-63 (LU-Ar)

> Plantation diary.

Moreland, William F., 1834-50 microfilm (LU-Ar)

> Plantation diary.

Palfrey, William T., 1842-68 (LU-Ar)

> Palfrey Plantation, St. Martin and St. Mary parishes, Louisiana.

Pascal, Paul, 1830 (MH)

> New Orleans slave dealer's letters to B. Raux of Norfolk, Virginia, with bills of sale.

Seale, H.M., 1853-57 (LU-Ar)

> Daily accounts of plantation.

Taylor, William, 1838-42 (LU-Ar)

> Sugar and cotton plantation life.

Newspapers

BLACK REPUBLICAN (New Orleans). April 15, 1865, to ? Weekly.

> Holdings: April 15, 22, 29, May 13, 20, 1865; CSdS, CSS, CU, DLC, FTaSU, KHI, LU-NO, MBAt, MdBMC, MiKW, TNF, WHi.

NEW ORLEANS DAILY CREOLE. June 16, 1856, to ? Daily.

> Holdings: July 1856 to January 1857; CSdS, CSS, CtY, DLC, InNd, LN, LU-NO, MdBJ, MnU, MoSW, NcU, TxFS, WHi.

SEMI-WEEKLY LOUISIANIAN (New Orleans). December 18, 1870, to April 21, 1872. Semiweekly.

> Title varies as LOUISIANIAN. Continued by WEEKLY LOUISI-ANIAN (next entry).

> Holdings: 1870-72; CSS, CtY, CU, DLC, InNd, LN, LU, LU-NO, MB, MdBJ, MnU, MoSW, NcU, NjP, TNF, TxFS, WHi.

WEEKLY LOUISIANIAN (New Orleans). April 27, 1872, to June 17, 1882. Weekly.

> Continues SEMI-WEEKLY LOUISIANIAN (see above).

> Holdings: 1872-74; CSdS, CSS, Cty, DLC, InND, LN, LU, LU-NO, MB, MdBJ, MnU, MoSw, NcU, NjP, TNF, WHi.

WEEKLY PELICAN (New Orleans). December 4, 1886, to 1889. Weekly.

> Holdings: December 1886 to November 1889; CSdS, CtY, DLC, InNd, LN, LU, LU-NO, MB, MdBJ, MnU, MoSW, NcU, TNF, WHi.

Personal Papers and Slavery Records

Bolton and Dickens Company Slave Trade Records (NHi)

> A record of slave purchases and sales to the Memphis and New Orleans areas. Contains about 1,500 names of slaves. A copy is also located at the Ethnic Genealogy Center at Queens College.

Chelette, Atala. Family Papers, 1819-1919 (LU-Ar)

> Includes personal and business papers of Joseph Perot, free Negro, land and slave owner, and other papers of the family of free Negroes, of Natchitoches Parish, 1840-99. MS 71-241

Descriptions of Slaves Being Transported (NHi)

> Manifests of "Negroes, Mulattoes, and Persons of Color" taken on board various vessels, particularly from Alexandria, Virginia. The manifests give slave's name, age, sex, height, color, and the owner or shipper's name and place of residence. Many of the records indicate that the slaves were going to New Orleans.

McCollam, Andrew. Papers, 1795-1935 (NcU)

> Planter of Donaldsonville. Papers include records of slaves. MS 64-1054

Martin, Charles. Civil War Papers, 1864–65 (DHU)

> Includes poll tax records of "colored people" in Louisiana. MS 62–4285

Murrell Family Papers, 1704–1886 (ViU)

> Correspondence includes sales of slaves of "Tally Ho" near New Orleans. MS 71–1960

New Orleans. Mayor. Papers, 1811–43 (NN-Sc)

> Papers, bonds, and reports of the mayor on the employment of slaves.

New Orleans Slave Trade. 118 items (NNC)

> Miscellaneous sources and letters dealing with the slave trade to New Orleans, and police reports on blacks sentenced to gangs, 1780–1833.

Norton Family Papers, 1760–1926 (NcU)

> Includes slave records (1820–32) for families in Virginia, Mississippi, and New Orleans. MS 64–594

Chapter 10

MARYLAND (South)

Maryland is a key state for the study of the black family, and, fortunately, the records for Maryland are excellent. The following records published in various books are of particular importance for black genealogical research in Maryland.

Brumbaugh, Galus Marcus. MARYLAND RECORDS. 2 vols. 1924. Reprint. Baltimore: Genealogical Publishing Co., 1975.

> These volumes contain records on Maryland parishes with actual photos of some records. There are hundreds of names of blacks listed in the records, in most cases giving only the first name, although surnames are sometimes recorded. The names of blacks are grouped with the white families they were living with, making the records even more valuable.

Hartdagen, Gerald E. "The Vestry as a Unit of Local Government in Colonial Maryland." MARYLAND HISTORICAL MAGAZINE 64 (1972): 363-88.

> Pages 363-64 illustrate the practice of bringing slaves before the vestry to have their ages adjudged and certified. The example given in the article includes the names, estimated ages, and names of owners for several slaves.

Koger, Azzie Briscoe. HISTORY OF THE NEGRO BAPTISTS OF MARYLAND. Baltimore: Clarke Press, 1942.

_____. THE MARYLAND NEGRO; 501 FACTS, FIGURES, AND FANCIES ABOUT THE MARYLAND NEGRO. Baltimore: The author, 1953.

_____. THE MARYLAND NEGRO IN OUR WARS. Baltimore: Clarke Press, 1942.

> Available at Duke University, Durham, North Carolina.

_____. THE NEGRO LAWYER IN MARYLAND. Baltimore: Clarke Press, 1948.

> All four of Koger's works are short, but contain good background material and some bibliographic resources. They are difficult to locate but at least one copy of each is at the Library of Congress.

Magruder, J.M. INDEX OF MARYLAND COLONIAL WILLS, 1634-1777, IN THE HALL OF RECORDS, ANNAPOLIS, MARYLAND. 1933. Reprint, 3 vols. in 1. Baltimore: Genealogical Publishing Co., 1967.

> Contains wills of whites and slave owners.

Maryland Historical Society. THE MANUSCRIPT COLLECTIONS OF THE MARYLAND HISTORICAL SOCIETY. Compiled by Arvil J. Pedley. Baltimore: 1968.

> This is an excellent guide to family papers containing a wealth of slave records. A survey of records here involving blacks would be an essential contribution to black genealogy.

Stein, Charles Francis. A HISTORY OF CALVERT COUNTY, MARYLAND. Baltimore: Published in cooperation with the Calvert County Historical Society, 1960.

> The appendix of this county history has an excellent census for the county for 1782, including blacks and slaves. Many other county histories have good census or tax records which include blacks. They should not be overlooked as sources of black family information.

Wright, James Martin. THE FREE NEGRO IN MARYLAND, 1634-1860. 1921. Reprint. Studies in History, Economics and Public Law, no. 222. New York: Octagon Books, 1971.

> Thorough background book on free blacks in Maryland.

FEDERAL RECORDS

Mortality Schedules

> 1850-80 (MdPM)

Population Schedules

> 1790-1900 (DNA); 1800-1890 (MdPM). Also available for some years in a few other libraries in the state.

Special Census 1890 (DNA, MdAA, MdPM, MdHi)

Record Group 101 (DNA).

> For a description of these records see chapter 4, p. 27. Maryland branches with deposits recorded: Baltimore.

Record Group 94, "Records of the Adjutant General's Office, 1780's-1917" (DNA)

> Slave Claims Commission's register of claims for 1864-67.

STATE AND COUNTY RECORDS

The following is a list of records found at the Hall of Records in Annapolis and in county courthouses. It is an updated synopsis of the Works Progress Administration's survey of Maryland. All the records listed were scanned and found to contain black genealogical material. Land records, in many instances, include records of manumissions, bills of sale, and other black records. Wills and inventories contain names of blacks who were left to white family members. In many cases, blacks mentioned in the will were not listed in the inventories, especially if the will freed the slave or if the slave was in a favored position. Naturalization records contain names of blacks who were considered aliens. Indentures contain records of blacks who were indentured to the service of a family voluntarily or by force. Guardian Bonds include records of blacks who were placed under the guardianship of whites, in some cases as a legal guise for slavery. Orphan Court records contain names of blacks who came before that court for manumission, indentures, or to be made wards. (HR indicates those records at the Hall of Records, CH indicates those records found in the various court houses.)

Allegheny County

> Inventories, 1791-1899. HR
>
> Land Records, 1791-1949 (microfilmed). HR
>
> Naturalization Dockets, 1945. CH
>
> Naturalization Petitions, 1906. CH
>
> Orphans Court Wills, 1790-1955 (indexed). HR

Anne Arandel County

> Assessment Books of Negro Slaves for the City of Annapolis. CH
>
> Bills of Sale, 1829-62. HR
>
> Certificates of Freedom, 1810-64 (indexed). HR
>
> Certificates to Free Negroes, 1805-64; 1807-20. HR (in Orders and Petitions)
>
> Guardian Bonds, 1780-1820 (microfilmed). HR (in Administration

Books section)

Indentures, 1796-1919. HR (in Orders and Petitions)

Inventories, 1777-1962 (microfilmed). HR

Land Records, 1653-1853 (microfilmed). HR

Land Records Index, 1653-1853 (microfilmed). HR

Manumission Records, 1797-1866 (indexed). HR

Naturalization Record of Declaration and Naturalization. CH

Receipts and Releases, 1826-42. HR

Slave Statistics, 1867 (indexed). HR

Wills, 1777-1961 (microfilmed and indexed). HR

Baltimore City

Certificates of Freedom, 1805-64. CH

Chattel Records, 1750-1814. HR

Guardian Accounts, 1786-1851. HR

Indentures, 1794-1916. HR

Inventories, 1666-1852 (microfilmed). HR

Land Records, 1661-1949 (microfilmed). HR

Land Records Index, 1659-1849. HR

Naturalization Docket and Naturalization Record of Minors. CH

Wills, 1852-1950 (microfilmed). HR

Baltimore County

Assessments, 1805, 1813, 1818, 1823-24, 1833, 1841. HR

Chattel Records, 1851 (microfilmed). HR

Chattel Records Index. CH

Indentures, 1851-1913. CH

Inventories, 1851. CH

Land Records, 1851-1949 (microfilmed). HR

Land Records Index (microfilmed). HR

Orphans Court Proceedings, 1851-1954 (microfilmed). HR

Wills, 1851 (microfilmed). HR

Calvert County

Inventories, 1882-- .

Land Records, 1840-1952 (microfilmed). HR

Wills, 1882-- .

Caroline County

Administration Bonds, 1679-1851 (microfilmed; also containing certificates of freedom). HR

Certificates of Freedom, 1806-57 (microfilmed). HR. See also Administration Bonds.

Indentures, 1785-1970. HR

Inventories of Caroline and Dorchester, 1680-1850 (microfilmed). HR

Land Records, 1774-1950 (microfilmed and indexed). HR

List of Orphans Placed under Guardians or as Apprentices, 1760-77. HR

Naturalization Records, 1905. CH

Wills, 1688-1853 (microfilmed and indexed). HR (includes Dorchester County)

Wills Index of Dorchester County (microfilmed). HR

Carroll County

Certificates of Freedom, 1838-64 (indexed by name of slave). CH

Chattel Records, 1837 (includes manumissions). CH

Court Proceedings, 1824-1904 (includes naturalizations). CH

Guardian Accounts, 1837-52 (microfilmed). HR

Inventories, 1837-52 (microfilmed). CH

Land Records, 1837 (microfilmed). HR

Land Records Index. HR (in Liber index)

Manumissions. See Chattel Records.

Naturalization Records. See Court Proceedings.

Returns of Luther Walsh Commissioner of Slave Statistics, 1864. Basement Room of CH

Wills, 1837-1910 (microfilmed). HR

Cecil County

Assessment of Slaves, 1852-64. CH

Guardian Bonds, 1778-97. HR

Indentures, 1794-1894 (in Guardian Bonds). CH

Inventories, 1675-1850 (microfilmed). HR

Land Records, 1674-1949 (microfilmed). HR

Land Records Index (Liber index). HR

Naturalization Records, 1860-1903. CH

Orphans Court Proceedings, 1798-1955 (microfilmed). HR

Wills, 1675-1961 (microfilmed). HR

Wills Index (microfilmed). HR

Charles County

Apprentices (Indentures), 1915-27. CH

Guardian Accounts, 1788-1823 (microfilmed). HR

Guardian Bonds, 1778-1825. HR

Inventories, 1673-1951 (microfilmed). HR

Land and Court Records (includes probate and vital records), 1658-1949 (microfilmed). HR

Land Court and Records Index (Liber index microfilmed). HR

Manumission Records, 1826-60. CH

Naturalization Records, 1911-29. CH

Orphans Court Proceedings, 1791-1951 (microfilmed). HR

Wills, 1665-1958 (microfilmed). HR

Wills Index, 1665-1948 (microfilmed). HR

Dorchester County

Inventories, 1857. CH

Land Records, 1669-1875 (microfilmed). HR

Land Records Index, 1669-1875 (microfilmed). HR

Naturalization Certificates, 1898-1926. CH

Orphans Court Proceedings, 1845-1952 (microfilmed). HR

Slave Statistics (Robert Bell's Book), 1867. CH

Wills. Most Dorchester County wills were destroyed by fire.

Wills Index. HR

Frederick County

Certificates to Free Negroes, 1815-63. HR

Certificates of Free Negroes Record, 1865. HR

Guardian Bonds, 1778-1853 (microfilmed). HR

Guardian Bonds Index. CH

Indentures, 1794-1815 (microfilmed). HR

Inventories, 1749-1851 (microfilmed). HR

Land Records, 1748-1949 (microfilmed). HR

Land Records Index (microfilmed). HR

Naturalization Records, 1799-1906. CH

Orphans Court Proceedings, 1853 (microfilmed). HR

Orphans Court Proceedings Index (microfilmed). HR

Wills, 1748-1948 (microfilmed and indexed). HR

Garrett County

Indentures (includes date of contract, names of parents, name of master, race, and sex). CH

Land and Mortgage Records, 1873-present. CH

Harford County

Certificates of Freedom, 1774-1842. HR

Free Negroes List, 1832. HR

Guardian Accounts, 1801-73 (microfilmed). HR

Inventories, 1777-1852 (microfilmed). HR

Land Records, 1773-1949 (microfilmed). HR

Land Records Index, 1773-1946. HR

Orphans Court Proceedings, 1800-1953 (microfilmed). HR

Wills, 1774-1950 (microfilmed). HR

Howard County

Chattel Records, 1840 (Clerk of Circuit Court, 19 vols.). CH

Chattel Records Index. HR

Civil Commissions Trustees and Officers Bonds, 1840--Twelve volumes under Liber of Successive Clerks Commissioners and Negroes. One volume--1840-63, contains "Record of Free Negroes." CH

Guardian Bonds, 1840-1942 (microfilmed). HR

Inventories, 1840-54 (microfilmed). HR

Land Records, 1839-1949 (microfilmed). HR

Manumissions, 1943-63 (Justice of the Peace; records include one volume of Records of Release of Slaves). CH

Naturalization Records, 1847-1902. CH

Slave Statistics, 1868. CH

Wills Index (microfilmed). HR

Kent County

Bonds: Bills of Sale, 1751-1851. HR

Bonds: Indentures. HR

Bonds Index, 1750-1845. HR

Certificates of Freedom, 1849-61. HR

Guardian Bonds, 1778-1860 (microfilmed). HR

Inventories, 1709-1850 (microfilmed). HR

Land Records, 1648-1949 (microfilmed). HR

Land Records Index (microfilmed). HR

Naturalization Records, 1822-1908. HR

Orphans Court Proceedings, 1803-1952 (microfilmed). HR

Slave Records, 1864. HR

Wills, 1674-1950 (microfilmed). HR

Montgomery County

Assessment Books, 1798 (records of slaves). CH

Certificates of Freedom, 1806-63. CH

Deeds. See Guardian Bonds.

Guardian Bonds, 1777-1858 (from Record Books; contain deeds, mortgages, and indentures of orphaned Negroes). CH

Indentures. See Guardian Bonds.

Inventories. CH

Land Records, 1777-1949 (microfilmed). HR

Mortgages. See Guardian Bonds.

Naturalization Certificates, 1905. CH

Naturalization Records, 1906. CH

Orphans Court Minutes and Proceedings, 1779-1954 (microfilmed). HR

Record Books, 1777-1858 (microfilmed). HR

Slave Statistics, 1864. CH

Wills Index, 1777-1942. HR

Wills in Record Books. HR

Prince George's County

    Certificates of Freedom, 1820-52. HR

    Guardian Bonds. See Orphans Court Proceedings.

    Indentures. See Orphans Court Proceedings.

    Inventories, 1697-1795 (microfilmed). HR

    Inventories Index, 1697-1948 (microfilmed). HR

    Land Records, 1696-1949 (microfilmed). HR

    Land Records Index. HR

    Manumission Records, 1806-29. HR

    Naturalization Certificates, 1904-26. HR

    Orphans Court Proceedings, 1802-1954 (contains guardian bonds and indentures). HR

    Slave Statistics, 1867-69. HR

    Wills, 1698-1955 (microfilmed). HR and CH

    Wills Index, 1698-1948 (microfilmed). HR

Queen Anne's County

    Administration Accounts, 1790-1952 (microfilmed). HR

    Assessment of Negroes, 1813, 1817, 1826, 1832, 1840, 1852. HR

    Certificates of Freedom, 1807-63. HR

    Indentures, 1771-1880. CH; 1815-61. HR

    Inventories, 1791-1950 (microfilmed). HR

    Land Records, 1707-1949 (microfilmed and indexed). HR

    Manumission Records, 1828-64. HR

    Orphans Court Proceedings, 1799-1954 (microfilmed). HR

    Wills, 1706-91 and 1791-50 (microfilmed). HR

St. Mary's County

    Assessment Books, 1793-1826 (microfilmed). HR

    Guardian Bonds, 1779-1862 (microfilmed). HR

    Inventories, 1795-1953 (microfilmed). HR

    Land Records, 1781-1851. HR

    Land Records Index, 1781-1851 (microfilmed). HR

    Naturalization Certificates, 1908-17. CH

Orphans Court Proceedings, 1777-1949 (microfilmed). HR

Wills, 1658-1950 (microfilmed). HR

Somerset County

Certificates of Freedom, 1821-64. HR

Indentures, 1864-1909. HR

Inventories, 1726-1850 (microfilmed). HR

Land Records, 1665-1850 (microfilmed). HR

Land Records Index (microfilmed). HR

Orphans Court Proceedings, 1778-1938. HR

Wills, 1664-1950 (microfilmed). HR

Talbot County

Administration Bonds, 1664-1852. HR

Census of Free Negroes, 1832. HR

Certificates of Freedom, 1807-60. HR

Land Records, 1662-1949 (microfilmed and indexed). HR

Negro Docket (record of Negroes seized in the county), 1855-67. HR

Orphans Court Proceedings, 1787-1946 (microfilmed). HR

Wills, 1668-1955 (microfilmed). CH and HR

Washington County

Assessments of Land (valuation of slaves), 1803. CH

Certificates of Freedom, 1827-63. CH

Certificates of Freedom, Juvenile Court, 1836-57. CH

Guardian Bonds, 1780. HR

Indentures, 1794-1917. HR

Inventories, 1777-1850 (microfilmed). HR

Judgment Records, 1798 (24 vols.; contains records of litigations between masters and slaves). CH

Land Records, 1777-1949 (microfilmed and indexed). HR

Manumission Records, 1827-63. HR

Naturalization Records, 1798-1906. CH

Orphans Court Proceedings, 1806-1954 (microfilmed). HR

Wills, 1749-1955 (microfilmed). HR

Wicomco County

Indentures, 1868-1900. CH

Land Records, 1867. CH

Naturalization Certificates. CH

Orphans Court Minutes, 1867-1944 (microfilmed). HR

MISCELLANEOUS RECORDS

Cemetery Records, Church Records, Diaries, Military Records

Availability not known.

Newspapers

AFRO-AMERICAN (Baltimore). August 1892-present. Weekly.

Holdings: 1892-present; Publisher, WaU.

1892-98 (incomplete); CSS, WHi.

1892-1969; WaOE.

1894-present; CFIS.

Personal Papers and Slavery Records

Gittings Family Papers, 1815-96 (MdHi)

Includes a list of slaves belonging to David S. Gittings (1822-59). MS 71-266

Maryland State Colonization Society Papers, 1827-71 (MdHi)

Manumission books; registers of births, deaths, and marriages of names of blacks who went to Liberia from Maryland.

Peabody, George Foster, 1830-57 (MSaE)

Extensive slave trading records for Massachusetts, Washington, D.C., and Maryland.

Richardson, Levin. Papers, 1831-61 (MdHi)

James L. Dorcey of Church Creek, Dorchester County, describes his slaves. MS 67-1661

Chapter 11

NORTH CAROLINA (South)

There are several sources that should be consulted in searching for black ancestors in North Carolina. The first is the Duke University Library. An out-of-print, 362-page guide to the collection entitled A GUIDE TO THE MANUSCRIPT COLLECTIONS IN THE DUKE UNIVERSITY LIBRARY, prepared by Nannie M. Tilley and Noma Lee Goodman (Durham: Duke University Press, 1947), gives a good indication of the massive amount of records available. The private family papers are of particular value because they include bills of sale, names of free blacks, and many records of genealogical value. Some of the diaries in this collection are listed below.

The second important genealogical resource is the Southern Historical Collection of the University of North Carolina Library in Chapel Hill. The index in THE SOUTHERN HISTORICAL COLLECTION: A GUIDE TO MANUSCRIPTS, by Susan Sokol Blosser and Clyde Norman Wilson, Jr., reveals that records on slavery, blacks, and plantations are extensive (see chapter 2, p. 16, Research Libraries, for a description).

In addition, there are various publications that will be valuable in the research process:

Blount, John Gray. THE JOHN GRAY BLOUNT PAPERS. Edited by Alice Barnell Keith. Raleigh: North Carolina State Department of Archives and History, 1952.

Includes Blount's will and the names of his slaves in the appendix.

Franklin, John Hope. THE FREE NEGRO IN NORTH CAROLINA, 1790-1860. 1942. Reprint. New York: W.W. Norton, 1971; Russell and Russell, 1969.

This book, in addition to being an excellent bibliographic source, contains a list of free blacks having property valued at more than $2,500, and a list of free black slave owners in 1790 and 1830.

Heyward, Duncan Clinch. SEED FROM MADAGASCAR. 1937. Reprint.

Spartanburg, S.C.: Reprint Co., 1972.

> Anyone who is able to trace their ancestry back to the Heyward
> Plantation will find this an interesting source book.

North Carolina. Secretary of State. ABSTRACTS OF NORTH CAROLINA
WILLS, COMPILED FROM ORIGINAL AND RECORDED WILLS IN THE OFFICE
OF THE SECRETARY OF STATE. By J. Bryan Grimes. 1910. Reprint. Balti-
more: Genealogical Publishing Co., 1975.

> Blacks mentioned in this book have been indexed by the Ethnic
> Genealogy Center. However, in most cases no names of slaves
> were given in the abstracts.

_____. NORTH CAROLINA WILLS AND INVENTORIES, COPIES FROM ORI-
GINAL AND RECORDED WILLS AND INVENTORIES IN THE OFFICE OF THE
SECRETARY OF STATE. By J. Bryan Grimes. 1912. Reprint. Baltimore:
Genealogical Publishing Co., 1967.

> This is of incomparable value and gives an index of some eighteenth-
> century wills. The blacks named in these wills have been indexed
> by the Ethnic Genealogy Center at Queens College, but the index
> has not yet been published.

Olds, Fred A. AN ABSTRACT OF NORTH CAROLINA WILLS, FROM ABOUT
1760 TO ABOUT 1800. 1965. Reprint. Baltimore: Genealogical Publishing
Co., 1972.

> This, while a continuation of Grimes's earlier work (see above,
> under North Carolina. Secretary of State), does not include
> black names. Instead it is a name index of the wills filed, and
> will be helpful if you know the name of the slave's owner.

Wellman, Manly Wade. THE COUNTY OF WARREN, NORTH CAROLINA,
1586-1917. Chapel Hill: University of North Carolina Press, 1959.

> Includes a list of those taxable in the county in 1781, with names
> of each slave owner and number of slaves owned.

FEDERAL RECORDS

Mortality Schedules

> 1850-80 (DNA, Nc-Ar)

Population Schedules

> 1790-1900 (DNA); 1800-1880 (NcAr); schedules for some years
> are available at libraries throughout the state.

Special Census 1890 (DNA, NcU), and several public libraries.

Record Group 105 (DNA)

> For a description of these records see chapter 4, p. 27, North Carolina. Records contain school reports.

STATE AND COUNTY RECORDS

The North Carolina State Department of Archives and History is in the process of microfilming its vast holdings of county records. An index to some of the microfilms already completed and the original records not yet microfilmed can be found in the GUIDE TO RESEARCH MATERIALS IN THE NORTH CAROLINA STATE ARCHIVES (Raleigh: Division of Archives and History, 1974). The following records, which are of obvious value in black genealogical research, have been extracted from the guide. However, there are other records listed in the guide which are probably of value for research. In addition, Beth G. Crabtree's GUIDE TO PRIVATE MANUSCRIPT COLLECTIONS IN THE NORTH CAROLINA STATE ARCHIVES (Raleigh: North Carolina State Department of Archives and History, 1964) has been reprinted by the Genealogical Publishing Company in Baltimore.

Craven County

> Civil Actions Concerning Slaves and Free Persons of Color, 1788, 1806-60, 1885
>
> Criminal Actions Concerning Slaves and Free Persons of Color, 1781-1868
>
> Slaves and Free Negroes, 1775-1861

Duplin County

> Marriages of Freed People, 1860
>
> Marriage Certificates, 1866-1868

Durham County

> Marriage Licenses, Colored, 1898-1968

Edgecombe County

> Slave Papers, 1780-1857

Granville County

> Certificates of Marriage, 1851-68
>
> Marriages of Freed People, 1866-67

Records of Slaves and Free Persons of Color, 1755-1874

Greene County

Marriage Register (Negro), 1875-1958

Guilford County

Marriage Licenses (Colored), 1872-1961

Marriage Register (Colored), 1867-1937

Lincoln County

Record of Freedmen: Marriages, 1866

Mecklenburg County

Marriage Record (Colored), 1850-67

Nash County

Division of Slaves, 1829-64

Marriages of Colored People and Division of Slaves, 1862-66

Slave Records, 1781-1864

New Hanover County

Slave Records, 1795-1864

Northhampton County

Slave Records, 1785-1867

Orange County

Negro Cohabitation, 1866-68

Slave Records, 1783-1865

Pasquotank County

Apprentice Bonds for Negroes, 1842-61

Perquimans County

Slave Records, 1759-1864

Randolph County
    Records of Slaves and Free Persons of Color, 1788–1887

Rockingham County
    Slave Records, 1803–60

Stokes County
    Slave Records, 1806–60

Washington County
    Freedmen's Marriage Records, 1866–72

Wayne County
    Records of Slaves and Free Persons of Color, 1798–1869

Wilson County
    Slave Records, 1855–64

MISCELLANEOUS RECORDS

Cemetery Records

Availability not known.

Church Records

Advent Episcopal Parish Register (white and black), Williamston, N.C.
    Records of 1850–1917. (Nc-Ar, US1GD 44684)

First Christian Church (white and black), Williamston, N.C.
    Records of 1939–62. (Nc-Ar, US1GD 44606)

Diaries

Anonymous, 1814–47 (NcU)
    Plantation diary.

Anonymous, 1822-80 (NcWsM)

St. Philips Negro Mission of the Moravian Church.

Ardrey, William E., 1862-1907 (NcD)

Discusses farming during Reconstruction and use of blacks.

Bateman (Mary), 1856 (NcU, original at LU-Ar)

Plantation life.

Beale, Edward, 1817-18 (NcD)

Includes an account of Beale's personal servant Horace. Records treatment of blacks.

Burgwyn, Capt. William Hyslop Sumner, 1858-64 (NcHiC)

Plantation in Welden, N.C. MS66-1852

Crudup, E.A., 1857-72 (NcD)

Plantation diary.

Erwin, William, 1846-56 (NcU)

Plantation records.

Gwyn, James, 1852-84 (NcU)

Personal and plantation diary. MS 64-512

Harden, Edward, 1834-49 (NcD)

Plantation records. MS 61-2449

Hill, Col. John, 1830 (NcU)

Plantation diary.

Justis, Horace Howard, 1857-59 (NcD)

Notes on slaves by law student and country schoolmaster.

King, Richard Hugg, 1819-23 (Nc-Ar)

Records of slave deaths.

Kollock, 1837-61 (NcU)

Diaries from Coffee Bluff, Rosedew, and Ossabaw Island plantations.

Lawton, Alexander James, 1810-40 (NcU)

Comments on crops, slaves, and wealth. MS 64-544

Lovell, William S. (NcU)

Plantation diary.

Pringle, Elizabeth W., 1868-1915 (NcU)

Woman rice planter's diary.

Shaffer, J.J., 1876-79 (NcU)

Sugar plantation diary.

Simpson, Samuel, 1795 (Nc-Ar)

Plantation affairs.

Skinner, Tristin Lowther, 1820-62 (NcU)

Plantation diary.

Warmoth, Henry Clay, Papers, 1842-1931 (NcU)

Plantation journals including the Magnolia Plantation. Reports conditions of blacks after the Civil War.

Military Records

Availability not known.

Newspapers

GAZETTE (Raleigh). 1883-1900? Biweekly, weekly.

Holdings: January 16, 1893; 1896-1898 (incomplete); January 13, 1900; CSdS, CSS, CU, DLC, FTaSU, KHi, LU-NO, MdBMC, MiKW, TNF, WHi.

Personal Papers

De Rosset Family Papers, 1581-1940 (NcU)

> Some of the papers contain records of births of slaves in Wilmington, North Carolina. MS 64-995

Foy, Robert Lee. Collection, 1762-1875 (NcGrE)

> Includes slave records for Popular Grove Plantation, Scotts Hill, New Hanover County. MS 73-505

Frazor Family Papers, 1784-1884 (TxU)

> Includes slave records. MS 64-747

Galloway, James Clarence. Collection, 1756-1868 (NcGrE)

> Slave sale and rental records included. MS 73-499

Hubard Family Papers, 1741-1907 (NcU)

> Papers of the family in Virginia, Washington, D.C., North Carolina, Tennessee, and Florida, including slave lists. MS 64-1031

Rowell, James. Papers, 1809-1928 (NcGrE)

> Includes his slave records, Brunswich County. MS 73-517

Smith, Ephram H. Collection, 1795-1919 (NcGrE)

> Includes slave records of a family in Chicod, Pitt County. MS 73-519

Smith, Peter Evans. Papers, 1738-1944 (NcU)

> A Halifax County family. The papers include a list of Negroes, 1858-66. MS 64-649

Slavery Records

In addition to those already listed, there was a 1755 Tax List for Beaufort, Cumberland, Currituck, Granville, New Hanover, Orange, and Tyrell counties which contains names of black slaves. It is on microfilm and available at the North Carolina Department of Archives and History and at the Genealogical Department in Utah.

Chapter 12

SOUTH CAROLINA (South)

Several published sources are of particular genealogical importance for South Carolina research.

Bleser, Carol K. Rothrock. THE PROMISED LAND: THE HISTORY OF THE SOUTH CAROLINA LAND COMMISSION, 1869-1890. Tricentennial Studies, no. 1. Columbia: University of South Carolina Press, 1969.

Reports on land given to whites and free blacks.

Moore, Caroline T., and Simmons, Agatha Aimar. ABSTRACTS OF THE WILLS OF THE STATE OF SOUTH CAROLINA, 1670-1740. 2 vols. Charleston, S.C.: C.T. Moore and A.A. Simmons, 1960-64.

Slave names not included.

South Carolina. University. Library. INDEXES TO COUNTY WILLS OF SOUTH CAROLINA. Compiled by Martha L. Houston. 1939. Reprint. Baltimore: Genealogical Publishing Co., 1975.

Few blacks are included, but this is an excellent source for information on slave-owning families.

Tindall, George Brown. SOUTH CAROLINA NEGROES, 1877-1900. 1952. Reprint. Baton Rouge: Louisiana State University, 1966; Columbia: University of South Carolina Press, 1970.

Short history of prominent blacks; with bibliography.

Turnbull, Robert J. A BIBLIOGRAPHY OF SOUTH CAROLINA, 1563-1950. 6 vols. Charlottesville: University of Virginia Press, 1956-60.

Historical bibliography for background work.

Wood, Peter H. BLACK MAJORITY: NEGROES IN COLONIAL SOUTH
CAROLINA FROM 1670 THROUGH THE STONO REBELLION. New York:
Knopf, 1974.

Excellent background history.

FEDERAL RECORDS

Mortality Schedules

1850–80 (DNA, DNDAR, Sc–Ar)

Population Schedules

1790–1880 and 1900 (DNA); 1800–1880 (Sc–Ar); several other
county, college, and historical society libraries have population
schedules for some years.

Special Census 1890 (DNA, Sc–Ar, ScRhW)

Record Group 101 (DNA)

For a description of these records see chapter 4, p. 27. South
Carolina branches with deposits recorded: Beaufort, Charleston.

Record Group 105 (DNA)

For a description of these records see chapter 4, p. 27. South
Carolina records contain school reports, letters sent and received
(alphabetical), and records relating to restoration of property and
issuance of rations.

Record Group 45, "Naval Records Collection of the Office of Naval Records
and Library" (DNA)

Logbooks of an African Squadron including list of slaves employed
at Charleston, South Carolina, 1862–64.

Record Group 56, "General Records of the Department of the Treasury" (DNA)

Fifth Special Agency: "Port Royal Correspondence" records of the
Sea Islands, South Carolina, with reports of the earliest care and
education of freedmen.

Record Group 217, "Records of the United States General Accounting Office"
(DNA)

South Carolina Direct Tax Commission certificates for land sold
to black heads of family 1863–65; state and county records.

STATE AND COUNTY RECORDS

One of the most important contributions to the study of genealogy in South Carolina has been the microfilming of county records by the South Carolina Department of Archives and History. These records are extensive and a list of them can be obtained by writing the Publication Division, South Carolina Department of Archives and History, 1430 Senate Street, P.O. Box 11699 Capitol Station, Columbia, South Carolina 29211. The list of microfilm rolls does not indicate those records which specifically relate to blacks. However, the following list of records, extracted from the Works Progress Administration's survey of records, is a good example of the types of records that have black genealogical information in this state. It has been noted that some records listed here are not found on the South Carolina Department of Archives list of their central records. Each county's records need to be completely surveyed in order to compare them with the state list. There was no WPA records survey of Charleston, an important city for black genealogical records. This survey also needs to be undertaken.

Allendale County

   Old Records Negro Census, 1833

Anderson County

   Judge of Probate Office Slave Records, 1812–60

   Record of Magistrates and Freeholders, 1842–46, 1789–1811, 1814–18, 1861–68

Dillion County

   Official Roster of South Carolina Soldiers in World War I, Vol. 2.

Jasper County

   Pension Records, years not stated.

Oconee County

   Judge of Probate, Pension Applications of Negroes Who Served the Confederacy, 1919–32

   Clerk of Court, Military Records Official Roster of South Carolina Soldiers in World War II, Vol. 2, Colored

Parish Records

   St. Helene's Parish, 1800–1821 (ScHi)

      Plantation records.

St. John's Parish, 1760–1853, Berkeley County (ScHi)

Property owners lists and records of dealings with
runaway or owned slaves. MS 65–851

St. Stephen's Parish, 1833–40

Same as above.

Pickens County

Board of Education Census, years not stated

Court of Magistrates and Freeholders (all black cases were held
under jurisdiction of this court)

Negro Convictions, 1828–65
Trials of Vagrants, 1829–56
Guardians for Free Person of Color, 1844–63
Index, Circuit Court of Common Pleas (appearance and file books)

Richland County

Board of Education, Annual Report, Register of Negro Pupils,
1914–28

Census Reports, 1917–20

Pension Records, Confederate (Negro)

Saluda County

Pension Record of Confederate Veterans and Negroes, Vol. 1

South Carolina State Records

Comptroller General Free Negro Roll Books, 1821–46 (ScAr)

Names and addresses of free blacks in Charleston.

Low Country Land Records, 1696–1854 (ScHi)

Wills, deeds, indentures, and bills of sale involving slaves.
MS 63–312

Secretary of the Province and Secretary of State, 1671–1903
(ScAr)

Extensive collection of bills of sale, manumissions, guardianship papers, certificates of freedom, and free birth records.

MISCELLANEOUS RECORDS

In addition to the microfilm collection at the South Carolina Department of
Archives and History, there are excellent collections of personal papers and
slavery records housed there, at the South Carolina Historical Society, and at
the University of South Carolina. A few of their materials are listed below.

Cemetery Records

Availability not known.

Church Records

South Carolina Episcopal Church Records, 1694-1962 (ScHi)
   Church registers with some references to blacks.

Diaries

Grimball, John Berkely, 1832-84 (ScCC, NcU)
   Plantation records. MS 61-2642

McIver, Sarah Witherspoon Ervin, 1854-89 (ScU)
   Family and plantation life.

Mulberry Plantation Journal, 1853-89 (ScU)

Trapier, Paul (ScHi)
   Autobiography of an Episcopal minister's work with blacks during
   Confederacy and postbellum period.

Webb, Daniel Cannon, 1817-50 (ScHi)
   Plantation journal and personal diary. MS 63-313

Military Records

In addition to Record Group 45 and those listed under state and county records,
above.

Confederate States of America, 1861-65 (ScU)
   Work and payroll records of blacks.

Newspapers

Brown, John H. RESEARCH MATERIAL IN SOUTH CAROLINA: A GUIDE.
Columbia: University of South Carolina Press, 1967.

Includes a description of the university's manuscript and newspaper files.

SOUTH CAROLINA LEADER (Charleston).   October 7, 1865, to 1867?   Weekly.

Holdings: 1865 to May 12, 1866 (incomplete); CSdS, CSS, CU, DLC, IHi, KHi, LU-NO, MBAt, MdBMC, MiKW, TNF, WHi.

Personal Papers

Allston-Pringle-Hill Collection, 1812-1920 (ScHi) MS 63-273; Robert Francis Withers Allston Papers, 1757-1929 (ScHi) MS63-272

Extensive materials on rice plantation, including diaries, overseer's reports, and plantation receipts.   The family includes a governor of South Carolina and his daughter, Elizabeth Waites Allston, who wrote extensively on her daily life and "lowcountry" blacks.

Bacot, Peter Samuel.   Papers, 1757-1946 (ScU)

Includes lists of Negroes of a Darlington County planter.   MS 70-1863

Bacot-Huger Collection, 1754-1927 (ScHi)

Cooper River Plantation materials, family genealogy, and materials on refugees at Society Hill, South Carolina, 1862-65.   MS 63-291

Bratton Family Papers, 1779, 1859-1953 (ScU)

Land and slave holdings are included.   The family is from York County.   MS 72-1261

Broughton Family Papers, 1703-1854 (ScHi)

Relates to Mulberry Plantation on Cooper River and St. George Plantation at Dorchester County.   MS 65-845

Chestnut-Miller-Manning Papers, 1744-1900 (ScHi)

Indenture, leases, etc.   MS 63-279

Cheves Family Papers, 1777-1938 (ScHi)

Advice on plantation managements, plat records, and indentures.   MS 63-280

Cox Family Papers, 1787-1875 (ScU)

Records of slave sales are among the papers of this Marlboro District, Columbia, and Charleston family. MS 72-1263

Cross, Paul. Papers, 1768-1803 (ScU)

Slave traders bills and receipts. MS 66-525

Jefferies Family Papers, 1771-1936 (ScU)

Contracts made with freedmen are included in the papers of this Union District and Cherokee County family. MS 69-1133

Laurens, Henry. Papers, 1747-96 (ScHi)

Some materials related to slaves. MS 63-293

Law, Thomas Cassels. Papers, 1770-1899 (ScU)

Contains some slave records of Law, a resident of Darlington District. MS 66-565

Manigault Family Papers, 1685-1873 (ScHi)

This collection includes Silk Hope Plantation records and memorandum book, 1861-73. MS 63-297

Middleton, Nathaniel Russell. Papers, 1761-1919 (NcU)

Includes plantation account book and slave list (1785-1812) of Thomas Middleton of Charleston. MS 64-1076

Perrin Family Papers, 1790-1918 (NcU)

Includes slave records, chiefly 1830-62, relating to the Thomas County plantations of James M. and Lewis W. Perrin of Abbeville District. MS 72-1096

Porcher-Ford Family Papers, 1797-1925 (ScU)

Almanacs with notes on slave births and deaths. MS 66-920

Ravenel Family Papers, 1790-1918 (NcU)

Includes slave lists of the Ravenel and related families in Charleston and Berkeley counties. MS 72-1100

Richardson-Nelson Families Papers, 1765-1935 (ScU)

Some papers concerning slaveholding for firms in Charleston and Sumter. MS 69-1137

Sams Family Papers, 1826-1934 (ScU)

>Births of family and black members of plantation, 1837-70.
>MS 66-605

Smith, Daniel Elliot Huger, 1846-1932 (ScHi)

>A Charleston historian's notebook with will abstracts, records of
>Charleston houses, and records of a low-country plantation. MS
>63-304

Stapleton, John. Papers, 1790-1839 (ScU)

>A London lawyer's papers with plantation journals and lists of
>blacks, chiefly from the Bull family estate of St. Helena Island,
>Beauford. MS 67-956

Weston Family Papers, 1786-1869 (ScHi)

>Peedee River, Georgetown District, family with lists of blacks
>and estate settlements for the Plowden Weston Plantation. MS
>63-317

Slavery Records

Ball, John, Sr., 1802-13 (ScHi)

>Account books.

Brinckerhoff, Isaac W., 1862-63 (NjR)

>"Port Royal Gazette" experiences of Freedmen's Bureau superinten-
>dent on a plantation at Beaufort.

Coker [W.C.] and Co., Society Hill, S.C. Records, 1842-1932 (ScU)

>Papers of a planter and merchant's company. Papers include
>William Coker's plantation book, 1868-69. MS 66-1360

Council Journals, Saluda County, 1671-80, 1692, 1721-76 (Sc-Ar)

>These journals contain information on runaway slaves going to
>St. Augustine, records of the Stono slave revolt, and information
>on the 1749 slave revolt alarm.

Hinson, Joseph Benjamin, 1801-22 (ScHi)

>Account books of Hinson, from Stiles Point, James Island.

Lee, Huston. Papers, 1858-65 (ScHi)

Records slave auctions.

Oakes, Ziba B., 1854-48 (MB)

Papers of a Charleston broker dealing in slaves. MS 69-6

Plantation Papers, 1748-1914 (ScHi)

Includes tax returns, lists of blacks, indentures for cotton and rice plantations on the Ashley, Cooper, Cumbabee, and Peedee rivers, and for plantations in Georgetown County, St. John's Parish, Berkeley County, St. Mark's Parish, and Orangeburg County. MS 63-313

Smyth, Thomas, 1850-99 (ScHi)

Account books. MS 63-308

Chapter 13

VIRGINIA AND WEST VIRGINIA (South)

Virginia is a key state for researching black family ancestors. Fortunately, the records for research in Virginia are massive. County records, census records, vital statistics from 1853, and other sources have been centralized and can be found at the Virginia State Library in Richmond. It is important to remember that all of West Virginia was included in the state of Virginia until 1860. Consequently, West Virginia's records are also covered in this chapter.

There are several good primary source materials which are of particular value to black genealogy. They go back to the seventeenth century when blacks were first brought into the colony. At that time they were given headrights (fifty acres of land), which in almost all cases were held by the slave's owner. In that way, the slave owners increased their wealth and land at the same time. Headrights were given to free blacks like Anthony Johnson and Benjamin Doyle (Doll), who were two of the original blacks to arrive in the colony. The headright records can be found in the Land Patent Records housed at the land office in Richmond, the state library in Richmond and on microfilm at the Genealogical Department in Utah. Two examples listing blacks' headrights are Jennings Cropper Wise's YE KINGDOM OF ACCAWMACKE: OR, THE EASTERN SHORE OF VIRGINIA IN THE SEVENTEENTH CENTURY (Baltimore: Regional Publishing Co., 1967) and Nell Marion Nugent's CAVALIERS AND PIONEERS, ABSTRACTS OF VIRGINIA LAND PATENTS, AND GRANTS, 1623-1666. Vol. 1. (1934. Reprint. Baltimore: Genealogical Publishing Co., 1969).

Another primary source is the Tithable (taxable) Records. In 1657-58, a law was passed in Virginia requiring that all white males imported into Virginia under articles of indenture, however young, be subject to the county levies. In addition, all imported black slaves above sixteen years of age, whether male or female, were to be held equally liable and their names entered in parish registers and tithable books. A further act was passed that required the owners of young slaves to bring them into court within three months after their arrival in the colony. On the whole, however, white women were not included in the Tithable Records.

In many cases the tithable entry may read, "John Smith (20)." This would only indicate the number of slaves owned. The names of blacks were, however, often recorded in the Tithable Records. For an excellent guide to these Virginia records, Earl Gregg Swem's VIRGINIA HISTORICAL INDEX (2 vols. in 4. 1934-36. Reprint. Gloucester, Mass.: Peter Smith, 1965) should be consulted. In addition, THE HISTORY OF PITTSYLVANIA COUNTY, VIRGINIA by Maud Carter Clement (Lynchburg, Va.: J.P. Bell, 1929) has a list of tithables for that county in 1767.

The third primary source for blacks in Virginia is the Tax Property Records, which can be found at the state library in Richmond. These records do indicate whether the property owner was black.

Other primary source materials include Legislative Petitions of Free Negroes of Virginia, 1776-1860, located at the state library; court records for all counties; and parish records, which contain hundreds of slave birth, death, burial, and christening records. Two examples of these fine, priceless records have been copied and published by the National Society of the Colonial Dames of America: (1) THE PARISH REGISTER OF CHRIST CHURCH, MIDDLESEX COUNTY, VA., 1653-1812 (Baltimore: Genealogical Publishing Co., 1964) and (2) THE PARISH REGISTER OF SAINT PETER'S, NEW KENT COUNTY, VA., 1680-1787 (Baltimore: Genealogical Publishing Co., 1966). The Ethnic Genealogy Center at Queens College has indexed all blacks listed in these records and arranged them alphabetically by owner. While the index is not presently published, information from it can be obtained by writing the center.

The following books are suggested for background reading:

Boddie, John B. COLONIAL SURRY. 1948. Reprint. Baltimore: Genealogical Publishing Co., 1974.

> This book contains a census of Sussex County in 1782 and the tithable census record.

Bradshaw, Herbert Clarence. HISTORY OF PRINCE EDWARD COUNTY, VIRGINIA. Richmond, Va.: Dietz Press, 1955.

> Excellent example of a county history and a good background source for searching for ancestors in this county.

Carter, Landon. THE DIARY OF COLONEL LANDON CARTER OF SABINE HALL, 1752-1778. Edited by Jack P. Greene. Virginia Historical Society, Documents, vols. 4-5. Charlottesville: University Press of Virginia, 1965.

> This is an excellent example of the valuable black genealogical source material found in diaries. All the names of the Carter slaves are listed under "Slave." There are probably many black families from Virginia with the name Carter whose ancestral search will lead them to one of the Carter plantations. Further sources

of Carter slaves include Louis Morton's ROBERT CARTER OF NO-
MINI HALL (Williamsburg: University Press of Virginia, 1941)
which is excellent reading for records of the Carter slaves. Robert
Carter's will, which contains many black names, can be found in
the Baltimore City Court House. His papers are at Duke University, the Virginia Historical Society, and the Library of Congress.
A good survey of the Landon Carter Papers can be found in Walter Ray Wineman's THE LANDON CARTER PAPERS IN THE UNI-
VERSITY OF VIRGINIA LIBRARY (Charlottesville: University Press
of Virginia, 1962).

Dorman, John Frederick, comp. CULPEPER COUNTY VIRGINIA WILL BOOK
A, 1749-1770. Washington, D.C.: The author, 1956.

These wills contain many names of blacks, as do those wills in the
compilations by Dorman listed below.

_____. ESSEX COUNTY, VIRGINIA, WILLS, BONDS, INVENTORIES, ETC.,
1722-1730. Washington, D.C.: The author, 1961.

_____. ORANGE COUNTY, VIRGINIA, WILL BOOK I, 1735-1743. Wash-
ington, D.C.: The author, 1958.

_____. ORANGE COUNTY, VIRGINIA, WILL BOOK II, 1744-1788. Wash-
ington, D.C.: The author, 1961.

_____. PRINCE WILLIAM COUNTY, VIRGINIA, WILL BOOK C, 1734-1744.
Washington, D.C.: The author, 1956.

Fitzhugh, William. WILLIAM FITZHUGH AND HIS CHESAPEAKE WORLD,
1676-1701. Edited by Richard Beale Davis. Chapel Hill: University of North
Carolina Press, 1963.

Contains the will of William Fitzhugh and the names of his slaves.

Guild, June Purcell. BLACK LAWS OF VIRGINIA. 1936. Reprint. New
York: Negro University Press, 1969.

This book contains abstracts from all the laws that pertain to
blacks in Virginia. It is an excellent book for manumissions
and is indicative of the types of records that exist.

Harrison, Fairfax. LANDMARKS OF OLD PRINCE WILLIAM. 1924. Reprint.
Berryville, Va.: Chesapeake Book Co., 1964.

This is an excellent summary of Prince William County records.

Jackson, Luther Porter. FREE NEGRO LABOR AND PROPERTY HOLDING IN VIRGINIA, 1830-1860. 1942. Reprint. New York: Atheneum, 1969; Russell and Russell, 1971.

> Includes a list of free black property owners.

_____. NEGRO OFFICE-HOLDERS IN VIRGINIA, 1865-1895. Norfolk: Guide Quality Press, 1945.

> This book contains an excellent biographical account of blacks who held office during this period. It gives their names and the city and county they were representing.

James, Edward W. "Slave Owners of Spotsylvania County, 1783." VIRGINIA MAGAZINE OF HISTORY AND BIOGRAPHY 10 (1902): 229-35.

Jefferson, Isaac. MEMOIRS OF A MONTICELLO SLAVE, AS DICTATED TO CHARLES CAMPBELL IN THE 1840'S BY ISAAC, ONE OF THOMAS JEFFERSON'S SLAVES. Charlottesville: University Press of Virginia, 1951.

> Has a fair genealogy of the Hemings family, who are reputed to be mulatto decendents of a union between Thomas Jefferson and Sally Hemings.

Jefferson, Thomas. THOMAS JEFFERSON'S FARM BOOK. Edited by Edwin Morris Betts. Princeton, N.J.: Princeton University Press, 1953.

> This includes extensive records of births, deaths, and other records of Thomas Jefferson's slaves. A truly outstanding example of the types of records plantation owners kept on their slaves.

Jester, Annie Lash, ed. ADVENTURERS OF PURSE AND PERSON, VIRGINIA, 1607-1625. Princeton, N.J.: The editor, 1956.

> This includes a census of blacks in 1623.

Mason, Polly Cary. RECORDS OF COLONIAL GLOUCESTER COUNTY, VIRGINIA. 2 vols. in 1. 1946-48. Reprint. Berryville, Va.: Chesapeake Book Co., 1965.

> This book contains various land abstracts, with some names of blacks and a tax list for 1782 listing whites and their number of slaves.

Pendleton, William Cecil. HISTORY OF TAZWELL COUNTY AND SOUTHWEST VIRGINIA, 1748-1920. Richmond: W.C. Hill Publishing Co., 1920.

> A fine example of the usefulness of county histories.

Russell, John. "The Free Negroes in Virginia." JOHNS HOPKINS UNIVERSITY STUDIES 8 (1913): 9-194.

Good study of a historically interesting group of people.

Sams, Conway Whittle. THE CONQUEST OF VIRGINIA: THE THIRD ATTEMPT, 1610-1624. 1916. Reprint. Spartanburg, S.C.: Reprint Co., 1973.

This account has an inaccurate point of view on blacks but has a chapter on those blacks brought to Virginia and gives some leads as to their African ancestry.

"Slave Owners, Westmoreland County, Virginia, 1782." VIRGINIA MAGAZINE OF HISTORY AND BIOGRAPHY 10 (1902): 229-35.

Snavely, Tipton Ray. THE TAXATION OF NEGROES IN VIRGINIA. Publications of the University of Virginia, Phelps-Stokes Fellowship Papers. Charlottesville, Va.: Michie Co., 1916.

Swem, Earl Gregg. VIRGINIA HISTORICAL INDEX. 2 vols. in 4. 1934-36. Reprint. Gloucester, Mass.: Peter Smith, 1965.

This index is available in most genealogical libraries and indexes the CALENDAR OF VIRGINIA STATE PAPERS, HENNING'S STATUTES AT LARGE, LOWER NORFOLK COUNTY VIRGINIA ANTIQUARY, TYLER'S QUARTERLY HISTORICAL AND GENEALOGICAL MAGAZINE, VIRGINIA HISTORICAL REGISTER, the VIRGINIA MAGAZINE OF HISTORY AND BIOGRAPHY, and the WILLIAM AND MARY QUARTERLY, Series 1 and 2.

Torrence, Clayton. VIRGINIA WILLS AND ADMINISTRATIONS, 1632-1800. 1930. Reprint. Baltimore: Genealogical Publishing Co., 1972.

Supplements Dorman's work on Virginia County wills, cited above.

VIRGINIA COUNTY RECORDS. Edited by William A. Crozier. 11 vols. 1905-13. Reprint. Baltimore: Genealogical Publishing Co., 1971-73.

This contains good census records and other county records of the Shenandoah Valley.

Virginia Gazette. VIRGINIA GAZETTE INDEX, 1736-1780. By Lester J. Cappon and Stella F. Duff. Williamsburg: Institute of Early American History and Culture, 1950.

An excellent guide to black source material, such as advertisements of sales, and ship arrivals. The listing of "Slave" in the index gives an idea of the value of this index.

Virginia. General Assembly. Joint Committee on the State Library. COLONIAL RECORDS OF VIRGINIA. 1874. Reprint. Baltimore: Genealogical Publishing Co., 1973.

These records contain a census of February 16, 1623, with a list of blacks living and dead at the time.

West Virginia. University. West Virginia Collection. GUIDE TO MANU-SCRIPTS AND ARCHIVES IN THE WEST VIRGINIA COLLECTION. Compiled by James W. Hess. Morgantown: West Virginia University Library, 1974.

The guide includes short descriptions of many of the materials.

William and Mary College. Earl Gregg Swem Library. A GUIDE TO HISTORICAL MATERIALS IN THE SWEM LIBRARY: A SELECTED BIBLIOGRAPHY OF REFERENCE WORKS WITH EMPHASIS ON VIRGINIA HISTORY. Library contributions, no. 5. Williamsburg, Va.: 1968.

Excellent guide to an important Virginia library.

FEDERAL RECORDS

Mortality Schedules

Virginia: 1860-70; 1860 (DNA, NcD); 1870 (US1GD)

West Virginia: 1860-80 (Wv-Ar)

Population Schedules

Virginia: 1810-80 and 1900 (DNA); 1810-80 (Vi, ViU)

West Virginia: 1870-80 and 1900 (DNA); 1870-80 (Wv-Ar)

Some population schedules are at several other libraries in both states.

Special Census 1890, Virginia (DNA, ViU, and several other public libraries)

Special Census 1890, West Virginia (DNA, Wv-Ar, and several other public libraries)

Record Group 101 (DNA)

For a description of these records see chapter 4, p. 27. Virginia branches with deposits recorded: Lynchburg, Norfolk, Richmond.

Record Group 105 (DNA)

For a description of these records see chapter 4, p. 27. Records contain school reports for Virginia.

Record Group 109, "War Department Collection of Confederate Records" (DNA)

Bureau of Conscription, Virginia, 1864-65.

This service list contains details of free blacks at Camp Lee, naming free blacks enrolled and assigned, giving age and birthplace. There is also a register of slaves who impressed the enrolling officers.

Medical Department

These records contain the Farmville, Virginia, General Hospital lists of free blacks and slaves employed. Registers of slaves hired and of patients are also included for the Richmond, Virginia, Chimborazo General Hospital and the General Hospital.

Record Group 94, "Records of the Adjutant General's Office, 1780's-1917" (DNA)

Slave Claims Commission register of claims for West Virginia, 1864-67, is included here.

MISCELLANEOUS RECORDS FOR VIRGINIA

Cemetery Records

Availability not known, but there are numerous black cemeteries throughout the state.

Church Records

See Parish Records, above, this chapter.

Diaries

Carter, Robert Wormley, 1776 (ViW)

"Sabine Hall" personal and business affairs (see Carter, Landon. THE DIARY OF COLONEL LANDON CARTER OF SABINE HALL, discussed earlier in this chapter). MS 66-272

Gray, M.R., 1822-31 (ViU)

Includes his slave sales.

Jaeger, 1885-94 (NcD)

> Jaeger was the founder of the Rustburg, Virginia, orphanage for black children.

Taylor, Francis, 1786-92; 1794-99 (Vi)

> Midland Plantation births, deaths, and marriages in Orange County, Virginia.

Military Records

See Record Group 109 listed, above, this chapter, under Federal Records.

Newspapers

PEOPLE'S ADVOCATE (Alexandria). 1876-? Weekly.

> Moved to Washington, D.C. some time before April 19, 1879.

> Holdings: April 22, September 9, 1876; CSdS, CtY, CU, DLC, InNd, MB, MdBJ, MnU, NcD, NcU, NcU, NjP, TNF,

RICHMOND PLANET. December 1883-1945? Weekly.

> Holdings: February 21, 1885, to July 12, 1890 (incomplete); 1895-1898; July 1899, to September 1900; CSdS, CtY, CU, DLC, FTaSU, ICU, InNd, MB, MdBJ, MnU, NcD, NcU, NjP, TNF, WHi.

> 1890-94; 1899-1945; McP, Vi.

> 1890-94; 1899 to May 1938 (incomplete); ViU, ViW.

VIRGINIA GAZETTE (Williamsburg). 1736-80. Weekly.

> Holdings: 1736-80; A-Ar, ArU, AU, CFIS, CLS, CoU, CSdS, CSmH, CSt, CU, DeU, DLC, FTaSU, GEU, GStG, IaHi, IaU, IHi, InNd, KyHi, KU, LU-No, MB, MBAt, MdAA, MdBJ, MeU, MiD, MiDW, MiMtpT, MiU, MnU, MoS, MoSHi, MoSW, MoU, MsHaU, MsSM, MU, MWA, NbOU, NcD, NcU, NdU, NhD, NHi, NIC, NjP, NjR, NmU, NN, NvU, OC, OC1, OKnetU, OkS, OrU, OU, PHi, PPiD, PPiU, ScU, TU, TxF, TxU, ViU, ViW, WaBeW, WaU, WHi, Wv-Ar.

> Includes extracts related to runaway slaves and slave sales.

VIRGINIA STAR (Richmond). April 1877-1888? Weekly.

> Holdings: September 8, 1877; May 11, 1878, to September 27, 1879

(incomplete); April 30, 1881, to December 23, 1882 (incomplete); CSdS, CSS, CU, DLC, FTaSU, KHi, LU-NO, MdBMC, MiKW, TNF, WHi.

Personal Papers

Brock, Robert Alonzo. Collection of Virginiana, 1582-1914 (CSmH)

Extensive county records, family papers, and slave merchants' records, manumissions, etc. MS 61-1834

Carter, Robert [Wormley]. Papers, 1775-95 (ICH)

Includes manumissions, baptism, and emancipations of Northumberland County, Virginia.

Glasgow Family Papers, 1795-1889 (TxU)

Virginia planter's family letters and bills of sale for slaves and land. MS 64-751

Madden Family Papers, 1760-1874 (ViU)

Correspondence and other papers of a free black family of Spotsylvania and Culpeper counties. MS 69-1289

May, Samuel, 1825-1912 (MsHS)

Correspondence with Caroline F. Putnam about Holley School for blacks at Lottsburgh, Virginia.

Murphy, Thomas G. Papers, 1861-1904 (De-Ar)

Murphy was chaplain and missionary to freedmen at Amelia Courthouse, Virginia. MS 61-1619

Parkhill, John. Papers, 1813-91 (NcU)

Includes correspondence with a former slave, 1866-75. MS 64-602

Virginia. University of. COLLECTION IN THE MANUSCRIPT DIVISION . . . CONTAINING REFERENCES TO SLAVERY FOR THE PERIOD FROM 1820-1865. 1967.

Excellent guide to manuscripts; not surveyed for genealogical materials.

Slavery Records

Bill of Sale, 1787 (NN)

>Collection contains bonds for delivery after the 1783 sale of Savage Nathan Lyttleton, a Virginia planter. Also included is his account book concerning blacks, 1768-85.

Cabell Family Papers, 1719-1839 (ViW)

>Includes a list of Dr. William Cabell's slaves of Amherst, Albemarle, and Nelson counties, Virginia. MS 67-735

Cummins Family Papers, 1815-80 (ViU)

>Includes slave lists for the Cummins family of Fauquier County, Virginia. MS 69-1254

Davis Preston and Company, Lynchburg and Bedford, Virginia. (FTaSU) MS 69-204

>This company bought and hired out slaves to farmers for commodities (cotton, tobacco, wheat, etc.). Also available at NHi.

Description of Slaves Being Transported. Manifests of Negroes, Mulattoes and Persons of Color taken on Board Various Vessels, 1835-55 (NHi)

>Most vessels went from Alexandria, Virginia, to New Orleans. Document gives slave's name, age, sex, height, color, and owner or shipper's name and place of residence.

Gilliam Family Papers, 1794-1920 (ViU)

>Includes indentures and slave records (1830-60) of this family from Dinwiddie County, Virginia. MS 69-1269

Marshall Family Papers, 1742-1951 (ViHi)

>Includes papers of the Digges family of Fauquier County, Virginia. Includes births and deaths (1758-1859) of their slaves. MS 72-816

Massie, William. Papers (Vi)

>Includes a Slave Book, 1836-1913?: "A register of Negroes ages, made out February 1836" including name, date of birth, and in some cases, death, age, how obtained, and value. Additional papers are available at ViW (MS 67-749); NcD (MS 61-3159); and TxU (MS 70-890).

Picot Family Papers, 1753-1907 (ViHi)

> Lists of blacks, 1863-67, at "Ampthill," Chesterfield County, Virginia, owned by Elizabeth Skyren Temple. MS 64-1242

Records of the Society for the Prevention of the Absconding and Abduction of Slaves, Richmond, Virginia (NHi)

Sheperd Family Papers, 1732-1907 (ViHi)

> Among the papers are lists of slaves of the Princess Ann County and Norfolk family. MS 69-552

Vice Consulate of France, 1833, Norfolk, Virginia (NHi)

> Official papers of Martin Oster, 1811-15; has indentures, birth certificates, and enfranchisements of West Indian slaves.

Washington, George, 1796-99 (NN)

> Correspondence regarding his slaves.

Winn Family Papers, 1780-1925 (NcD)

> Includes records of births and deaths of slaves, Fluvanna County, Virginia. MS 63-145

MISCELLANEOUS RECORDS FOR WEST VIRGINIA

Cemetery Records

Lambert, Frederick B. Collection, 1809-1959 (WvU)

> Materials include cemetery records and obituaries from Guyandotte Valley and area. MS 66-692

Church Records

Availability not known.

Diaries

McCalla, John Moore, Jr., 1860 (NcD)

> Journal of "Star of the Union" voyage to Liberia, chartered by the American Colonization Society. MS 63-207

Military Records

Availability not known.

Newspapers

PIONEER PRESS (Martinsburg, W. Va.) 1882-1918? Weekly.

Holdings: September 1886 to November 1888; Wv-Ar, WvU.

September 6, 1890; January 16, 1892; August 28, 1915; CSdS, CSS, CU, DLC, LU-NO, MdBMC, MiKW, TNF, WHi.

Personal Papers and Slavery Records

Campbell Family Papers, 1795-1901 (WvU)

Microfilm of plantation and store operations near Arden in Berkeley County, West Virginia. MS 66-634

Fox, William. Papers, 1762-1895 (WvU)

Accounts and items related to slaves in Romney and in Hampshire County, West Virginia. MS 60-2389

Goff, David. Papers, 1826-1904 (WvU)

Berkeley County letters and slave sales. MS 60-1463

Lewis Family Papers, 1825-1936 (WvU)

Kanawha County slave sales. MS 60-320

Morgan County Archives, 1772-1923 (WvU)

The Free Negro Register and numerous county records are held in these archives. MS 66-984

Chapter 14

ALABAMA (South)

Most records on black families in Alabama are buried in other state records and need to be extracted. Examples of other states' records (see chapter 8: "Georgia," for example) show clearly the types of records which should be available in Alabama but have not yet been clearly identified.

There are several publications which should be helpful in doing family research in Alabama:

Alabama. Department of Archives and History. ALABAMA CENSUS RETURNS, 1820, AND AN ABSTRACT OF FEDERAL CENSUS OF ALABAMA, 1830. Edited by Marie Bankhead Owen. 1967. Reprint. Baltimore: Genealogical Publishing Co., 1971.

> Contains census of population before the first available federal census for Alabama (1830).

Alabama Genealogical Society. "Genealogical Materials to be Found in Alabama County Court Houses." ALABAMA GENEALOGICAL SOCIETY MAGAZINE 1 (April 1967): 29-34; (July 1967): 21-25; (October 1967): 27-36; 2 (January 1968): 20-27; (April 1968): 56-61.

> Contains a helpful guide to county records.

Daughters of the American Revolution, Alabama. INDEX TO ALABAMA WILLS, 1808-1870. Baltimore: Genealogical Publishing Co., 1955.

> An important index to slaveholders' wills.

Davis, Charles S. THE COTTON KINGDOM IN ALABAMA. Perspectives in American History, no. 3. 1939. Reprint. Philadelphia: Porcupine Press, 1974.

> Excellent guide to Alabama records.

Fuller, Willie J. BLACKS IN ALABAMA, 1528-1865. Council of Planning

Librarians, Exchange Bibliography no. 1033. Monticello, Ill.: Council of Planning Librarians, 1976.

> Short, but important bibliography for background work.

Menn, Joseph Karl. "The Large Slaveholders of the Deep South, 1860." Ph.D. dissertation, University of Texas, 1964. Available from University Microfilms, Ann Arbor, Mich., order no. 65-4333.

> Contains a list of slaveholders in Alabama, Mississippi, and Georgia based on the 1860 federal census.

Sellers, James Benson. SLAVERY IN ALABAMA. University: University of Alabama Press, 1950.

> A fine description of the laws, customs, and effects of slavery in Alabama.

FEDERAL RECORDS

Mortality Schedules
> 1850-80 (A-Ar)

Population Schedules
> 1820-80 and 1900 (DNA); 1830-80 (A-Ar, and Mobile and Birmingham public libraries)
>
> 1860 Slave Schedules (A-Ar)

Special Census   - None

Record Group 101 (DNA)
> For a description of these records see chapter 4, p. 27, Freedmen's Bureau. Alabama branches with deposits recorded: Huntsville, Mobile.

Record Group 105 (DNA)
> For a description of these records see chapter 4, p. 27, Freedmen's Bureau. Alabama records contain Education Division reports, letters sent and received, narratives of conditions, and rosters of personnel.

Record Group 56, "General Records of the Department of the Treasury" (DNA)
> Third Special Agency: Supervisory Special Agent's dealings with freedmen before the Freedmen's Bureau was established.

Record Group 109, "War Department Collection of Confederate Records" (DNA)

Medical Department.

Mobile, Alabama, register of patients and federal troops at Engineer Hospital 1-64 to 1-65.

Territorial Commands and Armies.

District of Gulf records, rolls of civilians, blacks, including slaves hired at Mobile.

STATE RECORDS

The Works Progress Administration survey uncovered the following records, although the survey did not indicate whether these records might be available in other counties.

Marengo County

Probate Office

Reports of slave sales at auction, appraisement and division of slaves, 1820-45.

Sale of Slaves, 1820-45

Four file drawers of records are available.

The Alabama State Department of Archives and History in Montgomery has not been surveyed for black family primary source material, but this would be an excellent project. They do have a number of family papers (listed below) as outlined in DIRECTORY OF AFRO-AMERICAN RESOURCES described in chapter 2, pp. 16-17.

The Tuskegee Institute Library and Museum, as well as the University of Alabama Library, have extensive collections on black resources, but their relevance for genealogical research has not been determined. DIRECTORY OF AFRO-AMERICAN RESOURCES gives an indication of what is available.

Finally, the following was located at the Tennessee State Library and Archives:

Owsley Charts, 1840-60

Charts on land and slaveholdings for all counties in Alabama; taken from the federal census returns.

MISCELLANEOUS RECORDS

Cemetery Records and Church Records

Availability not known.

Diaries

Chadwick, Mary Ione (Cook), 1862-65 (NcD)
>   Notes on local slaves in Huntsville, Alabama.

Reed, Seth, 1863 (MiU)
>   Notes on slaves from a member of the U.S. Commission with the Army of Cumberland in Alabama and Tennessee. MS 65-506

Military Records

See Record Groups discussion above, this chapter, under Federal Records. Further availability not known.

Newspapers

HUNTSVILLE GAZETTE. November 22, 1879, to October 29, 1894. Weekly.
>   Holdings: 1881-94 (incomplete); AU, CSdS, CtY, DLC, ICU, InNd, MB MdBJ, MnU, MoSW, NcU, TNF, WHi.

Personal Papers and Slavery Records

Buckner, Mary Elizabeth (Stay). Papers, 1818-1923 (T)
>   Includes slave lists of the Buckner family in Montgomery. MS 65-876

Coffee, John. Family Papers, 1796-1887 (A-Ar)
>   Includes information on the family slaves. MS 60-1164

Criglar, William Louis. Papers, 1848-85 (NcU)
>   Includes descriptive list (1862) of slaves belonging to Criglar, Batch-elder & Company. MS 62-4455

Donnell, James Webb Smith. Papers, 1820-1932 (T)

>Contracts with freedmen to work his farm in Limestone County are included. MS 73-867

France, Charles B. Papers, 1857-90 (MoHi)

>Banker of St. Joseph, Missouri. Some items are related to freed slaves in the Mobile, Alabama, area. MS 64-270

Hill and Howth Plantation Records (A-Ar)

>"Rules and Regulations for the Management of . . . " by William P. Gould.

Lewis, Ivey Foreman. Business Records, 1857-1916 (NcU)

>Includes births and deaths of slaves on a plantation in Hale and Marengo counties.

Pickens, Isreal. Family Papers, 1805-84 (A-Ar)

>Includes information on the family slaves. MS 60-1166

Torbet, James, and Tait, Charles. Family Papers, 1768-1874 (A-Ar)

>Includes information on the family slaves. MS 60-1444

Chapter 15
ARKANSAS (South)

The first black slaves arrived in Arkansas with German settlers from Old Biloxi, Mississippi. They had originally come from Guinea during the 1720s. However, the number was evidently small because by 1769 there were only sixteen blacks in Arkansas; and in 1810 only 287 slaves and five free blacks were listed as residents in the state. Conceivably many of them were descendants of the original sixteen.

During the period 1820–30, the slave population increased markedly, with a corresponding increase in the white population. The slaves came from Alabama, Tennessee, Mississippi, and other states east of the Mississippi River. Most were settled along the river where, by the 1850 census, the number of slaves was greater than the white population of the state.

Taylor, Orville Walters. NEGRO SLAVERY IN ARKANSAS. Durham, N.C.: Duke University Press, 1958.

> Provides an excellent discussion of the above details, along with much information regarding the laws of slavery in Arkansas.

FEDERAL RECORDS

Mortality Schedules
    1850–80 (Ar–Hi)

Population Schedules
    1830–80 and 1900 (DNA); 1830–80 (Ar–Hi)

Special Census –   none

Record Group 101 (DNA)

For a description of these records see chapter 4, p. 27, Freedmen's Bureau. Arkansas branch with deposits recorded: Little Rock.

Record Group 105 (DNA)

For a description of these records see chapter 4, p. 27, Freedmen's Bureau. Arkansas records contain school reports.

Record Group 36, "Records of the Bureau of Customs" (DNA)

Time book for mechanics and slaves employed at Fort Morgan, Arkansas, 1861-62.

Record Group 56, "General Records of the Department of the Treasury" (DNA)

Third Special Agency: Supervisory Special Agent's dealings with freedmen, 1863-65, before the Freedmen's Bureau was established.

STATE RECORDS

The Arkansas History Commission at the State Archives in Little Rock is an excellent place for state records. However, it is not known if they have specific records related to blacks. They do have a collection of miscellaneous Arkansas black newspapers in addition to the ones listed below.

MISCELLANEOUS RECORDS

Cemetery Records, Church Records, Diaries, Military Records

Availability not known.

Newspapers

ARKANSAS MANSION (Little Rock). 1884-87? Weekly?

Holdings: June 1883 to April 1884; CSS, CtY, CU, DLC, InNd, KHi, MB, MdBJ, MnU, NcU, NjP, TNF, WHi.

Personal Papers and Slavery Records

Brown, John, 1821-1865 (U)

Experience as a lawyer and plantation owner in Arkansas.

Arkansas

Dobbins, Archibald S.   Papers, 1852–69 (TxGR)

> Phillips County planter who escaped to Brazil after the Civil War; letters concern moving his slaves to Mexico and Cuba.   Land deeds and a will are included in these papers.

Gulley, L.C. (Ar-Hi)

> Discusses freedmen with whom he had dealings.

Woodruff, William Edward, 1810–82 (Ar-Hi)

> Slave indentures included.   MS 68–527

Chapter 16
DISTRICT OF COLUMBIA (South)

Although not usually considered part of the South, the District of Columbia was an early home of many Southern ex-slaves. Research in the District of Columbia should not be attempted without referring to the DIRECTORY OF AFRO-AMERICAN RESOURCES described in chapter 2, pp. 16-17, for the District is the home office of a multitude of organizations involved with the lives of black Americans. The archives of these organizations may contain considerable biographical information. Among the important groups whose archives are located here are the American Colonization Society and the African Methodist Episcopal Church. In addition, the Civil Rights Documentation Project, with over 500 extensive taped interviews with those active in the Civil Rights, and the Delta Archives of Delta Sigma Theta may have some genealogical materials. Howard University Library's 100,000 items include over 100 manuscripts which have not been surveyed for genealogical material in the same manner as the collections of Duke University and the University of North Carolina.

One book, in addition to the DIRECTORY OF AFRO-AMERICAN RESOURCES, is essential reading for a genealogical perspective of history in the District of Columbia:

Brown, Letitia Woods. FREE NEGROES IN THE DISTRICT OF COLUMBIA, 1790-1846. The Urban Life in America Series. New York: Oxford University Press, 1972.

The appendix contains a list of early free blacks in the District.

FEDERAL AND DISTRICT RECORDS

Mortality Schedules

    1850-80 (DNA, DNDAR)

Population Schedules

    1800-1880 and 1900 (DNA); 1800-1880 (DNDAR)

District of Columbia

Special Census – none

Record Group 101 (DNA)

> For a description of these records see chapter 4, p. 27, Freedmen's Bureau. City with deposits recorded: Washington, D.C.

Record Group 105 (DNA)

> For a description of these records see chapter 4, p. 27, Freedmen's Bureau. Records contain school reports.

Record Group 21, "Records of District Courts of the United States" (DNA)

> Includes District of Columbia records relating to slaves, 1851-63; fugitive slave cases—alphabetical; records of the Board of Commissioners for the Emancipation of Slaves in the District of Columbia, 1862-63; manumission and emancipation records for the District of Columbia, 1821-62.

Record Group 48, "Records of the Office of the Secretary of the Interior" (DNA)

> Contains the record of appointments, 1849-1908, and list of personnel at the Freedmen's Hospital and at Howard University. Includes all registers of deeds in the District of Columbia. There is much biographical material on prominent blacks.

MISCELLANEOUS RECORDS

Cemetery Records

Sluby, Paul E. COLUMBIAN HARMONY CEMETERY RECORDS, DISTRICT OF COLUMBIA, 1831-1899. Washington, D.C.: Sluby, 197-?

> A very important contribution to black genealogy.

Church Records

See DIRECTORY OF AFRO-AMERICAN RESOURCES described in chapter 2, pp. 16-17, for a list of national churches with headquarters in the District of Columbia.

Diaries

Wiltburger, Christian, Jr., 1821 (DLC)

Describes the NAUTILUS voyage to Liberia with African colonists.

There are probably a good number of other diaries located at the Library of Congress.

Military Records

Record Group 92, "Records of the Office of the Quartermaster General" (DNA)

These records contain lists from the Civil War period of black troops buried and ex-slaves who were contraband.

Record Group 94, "Records of the Adjutant General's Office, 1780's-1917" (DNA)

Bureau of Colored Troops, 1863-89; applications, registers, rosters.

Record Group 109, "War Department Collection of Confederate Records" (DNA)

Compiled Records of Treasury Department

Claims for lost property, including slaves; list of black workers.

Quartermaster General's Rolls and Payrolls

Slave payrolls giving period of service, 1861-65, and owner's name; alphabetical index to payrolls, including slaves with their overseer's names, county, and owner's name.

Record Group 110, "Records of the Provost Marshal General's Bureau" (DNA)

National draft enrollment lists giving residence, age, race, profession, marital status, and place of birth, 1863-65; and emancipation applications, 1862-63.

Record Group 217, "Records of the United States General Accounting Office" (DNA)

Office of Comptrollers and Auditors payments to black troops, 1863-65; Freedmen's Bureau accounts, 1867-82; naval payments to black sailors.

Newspapers

AFRICAN REPOSITORY. March 1825 to January 1892.

Holdings: 1825-92; WHi.

BEE.   June 3, 1882, to July 1884.   Weekly.

Continued by the WASHINGTON BEE (see below).

Holdings: 1882-84; CSdS, CtY, CU, DLC, FTaSU, ICU, InNd, MB, MdBJ, MnU, MoJcL, MoSW, NcU, NhD, TNF, TxFS, ViW, WHi.

COLORED AMERICAN.   1893-1904?   Weekly.

Holdings: August 11, 1894; March 12, 1898, to November 12, 1904 (incomplete); CSS, CtY, CU, DLC, FTaSU, ICU, InNd, MB, MdBJ, MnU, MoSW, NcU, NjP, TNF, WHi.

NEW ERA.   January 13, to September 1, 1870.   Weekly.

Continued by NEW NATIONAL ERA (see below).

Holdings: January to September 1870; CU, DLC, ICU, MnU, NhD, NHi, NRU, WHi.

NEW NATIONAL ERA.   September 8, 1870, to April 10, 1873.   Weekly.

Continues NEW ERA (see preceeding entry); continued by NEW NA-TIONAL ERA AND CITIZEN (next entry).

Holdings: 1870-73; DLC, ICU, MnU, NhD, NHi, .NRU, WHi.

NEW NATIONAL ERA AND CITIZEN.   April 17, 1873, to October 22, 1874. Weekly.

Continues NEW NATIONAL ERA (see above).

Holdings: 1873-74 (incomplete); DLC, ICU, MnU, NhD, NHi, NRU, WHi.

PEOPLE'S ADVOCATE.   1879?-1884?   Weekly.

Holdings: April 19, 1879, to April 12, 1884; CSdS, CtY, CU, DLC, InNd, MB, MdBJ, MnU, NcU, NhD, NjP, TNF, WHi.

WASHINGTON BEE.   August 1884 to January 21, 1922.   Weekly.

Holdings: 1884-1922 (incomplete); CSdS, CtY, CU, DLC, FTaSU, ICU InNd, MB, MdBJ, MnU, MoJcL, MoSW, NcU, NhD, TNF, TxFS, ViW, WHi.

Personal Papers and Slavery Records

The Library of Congress has the Slave Narrative Collection of the Federal Writ-ers Project.   In addition, there are more than 5,000 items in the manuscript collection and many groups of personal papers appropriate to black genealogy. There are also the following materials:

1. Accounts Book Collection
2. African Colonization Society lists of immigrants
3. NAACP and National Urban League papers
4. Slave papers with appraisal, mortgages, birth certificates, and emancipation certificates

The DIRECTORY OF AFRO-AMERICAN RESOURCES described in chapter 2, pp. 16-17, cites some of these holdings. A complete survey of the Library of Congress and the Daughters of American Revolution Library for black genealogical materials has not been undertaken. Two groups of fascinating papers at the Library of Congress are:

Fleetwood, Christian Abraham. Papers, 1797-1945 (DLC)

Diaries, correspondence, legal documents, genealogical records, photos, and scrapbook of a free black soldier and civic leader. MS 60-3194

Roberts, Jonathan. Family Papers, 1734-1944 (DLC)

Includes information on a group of free blacks who left North Carolina and moved to Roberts Settlement, Indiana. A notebook for 1734-1813 with a family genealogy is part of this group of papers.

Finally, the following is available outside the District of Columbia:

Peabody, George Foster, 1830-57 (MSaE)

Extensive slave trading records for Massachusetts; Washington, D.C.; and Maryland.

Chapter 17

FLORIDA (South)

Florida was the new home of many escaped slaves. The Florida Historical Collection at the University of Florida Library in Gainesville has a unique group of materials on blacks in Florida. However, there is no published guide and it has not been surveyed for genealogical material. The following publications will be quite helpful for black genealogical research in Florida:

CATALOG OF THE NEGRO COLLECTION IN THE FLORIDA AGRICULTURE AND MECHANICAL UNIVERSITY LIBRARY AND THE FLORIDA STATE UNIVERSITY LIBRARY. Tallahassee, 1969.

   Lists many primary sources located at both university libraries.

Jones, George Noble. FLORIDA PLANTATION RECORDS FROM THE PAPERS OF GEORGE NOBLE JONES. Edited by Ulrich Bonnell Phillips and James David Glunt. St. Louis: Missouri Historical Society, 1927.

   Excellent background reading and guide to Florida plantations.

Rooks, Milton Perry. THE FREE NEGRO IN FLORIDA, 1565-1863. Wooster, Ohio: Bell and Howell Black Culture Collection, 1946, #564-9.

   Indicates availability of some Florida records related to blacks.
   Good background reading.

Smith, Julia Floyd. SLAVERY AND PLANTATION GROWTH IN ANTEBELLUM FLORIDA, 1821-1860. Gainsville: University of Florida Press, 1973.

   Good background material, including bibliography.

FEDERAL RECORDS

Mortality Schedules
   1885 (DNA)

Population Schedules

> 1830-80 (DNA, FM, FTaSU); 1900; and 1825 Territorial Census (DNA). Schedules for some years are also available at other libraries in the state.

Special Census - none

Record Group 101 (DNA)

> For a description of these records see chapter 4, p. 27, Freedmen's Bureau. Florida branch with deposits recorded: Tallahassee.

Record Group 105 (DNA)

> For a description of these records see chapter 4, p. 27, Freedmen's Bureau. Florida records contain school reports.

Record Group 56, "General Records of the Department of the Treasury" (DNA)

> Third Special Agency: Dealings with freedmen before the Freedmen's Bureau was established, 1863-65.

STATE AND COUNTY RECORDS

Although Florida had special tribunals established to try fugitive slaves, the court records have not been located. This would make an excellent research project. There are a few groups of records on Florida described in the chapter on Louisiana, including the following:

> List of Free Blacks and "Mulattoes," 1772.

> Archives of the Spanish Government in Florida.

The following records are also available for research:

Columbia County

> List of Slave Owners, 1850 (G-Ar)

Owsley Charts (T)

> 1840-60 charts of land, slaves, etc., for all counties from the Federal Census Schedules.

MISCELLANEOUS RECORDS

Cemetery Records, Church Records, Diaries, Military Records, Personal Papers

Availability not known.

Newspapers

FLORIDA EVANGELIST (Jacksonville). 1896-1902. Weekly.

Holdings: January 20, 1900; CSdS, CSS, CU, DLC, FTaSU, KHi, LU-NO, MdBMC, MiKW, TNF, WHi.

FLORIDA SENTINEL (Pensacola). 1887-1913. Weekly.

Holdings: January 26, 1900; CSdS, CSS, CU, DLC, FTaSU, KHi, LU-NO, MdBMC, MiKW, TNF, WHi.

Slavery Records

Jefferson County Plantation Records (FTaSU)

Includes Bunker Hill, Nacossa, Freelawn, and Mt. Vernon plantation records.

Chapter 18

KENTUCKY (South)

Research in Kentucky should begin with the following books:

Ardery, Julia Hope. KENTUCKY COURT AND OTHER RECORDS. Vol. 2, KENTUCKY RECORDS. 1932. Reprint. Baltimore: Genealogical Publishing Co., 1972.

> This reference is good as an example of the types of records which include black names.

Coleman, John Winston. SLAVERY TIMES IN KENTUCKY. 1940. Reprint. New York: Johnson Reprint Corp., 1970.

> Excellent description of slavery in Kentucky; good background reading.

Jillson, Willard Rouse. OLD KENTUCKY ENTRIES AND DEEDS. Filson Club Publications, no. 34. 1926. Reprint. Baltimore: Genealogical Publishing Co., 1972.

> Lists group of early deeds filed in Kentucky State Court of Appeals. Some of the deeds were for slaves.

Johnson, William Decker. BIOGRAPHICAL SKETCHES OF PROMINENT NEGRO MEN AND WOMEN OF KENTUCKY. 1897. Reprint. New York: Books for Libraries, 1973.

> Includes discussion of British and American slaveholders.

King, Junie Estelle Stewart, comp. ABSTRACT OF EARLY KENTUCKY WILLS AND INVENTORIES. 1933. Reprint. Baltimore: Genealogical Publishing Co., 1969.

> Mostly a listing of white wills, but in some cases the names of the slaves contained in them are listed.

McDougle, Ivan E. SLAVERY IN KENTUCKY, 1792–1865. 1918. Reprint. Westport, Conn.: Negro University Press, 1970.

Originally a Ph.D. dissertation; contains good bibliography.

FEDERAL RECORDS

Mortality Schedules

1850–80 (DNA, DNDAR)

Population Schedules

1810–80 (DNA, KyLoF, KyHi, KyBgW) and 1900 (DNA). Also available for some years at other public libraries.

Special Census 1890 (DNA, KyLoF, KyHi)

Record Group 101 (DNA)

For a description of these records see chapter 4, p. 27, Freedmen's Bureau. Kentucky branches with deposits recorded: Lexington, Louisville.

Record Group 105 (DNA)

For a description of these records see chapter 4, p. 27, Freedmen's Bureau. Kentucky records contain school reports.

Record Group 109, "War Department Collection of Confederate Records" (DNA)

Regiments, battalions, and companies of Kentucky troops including a list of black cooks.

Record Group 94, "Records of the Adjutant General's Office, 1780's–1917" (DNA)

Slave Claims Commissions register of claims for Kentucky, 1864–67.

STATE AND COUNTY RECORDS

The Kentucky Historical Society in Frankfort has extensive county records for every county, including wills, marriages, births, and deaths for 1852–61 and 1874–78; pensions; cemetery records; and tax records; in addition to an excellent collection of Kentucky state and county histories. The following are available in other parts of the state:

Breckenridge County Courthouse

Eighty volumes of deeds, including slave deeds and affidavits of slave ownership filed when entering the state.

Jessamine County Courthouse

Deed books with slave sale records, dates not noted.

Meade County Courthouse

Life estate records with affidavits of slave ownership.

MISCELLANEOUS RECORDS

Cemetery Records

The Kentucky Historical Society in Frankfort has cemetery records for every county.

Church Records

Beech Creek Baptist Church, Shelby County, 1825–40 (KyLoF)

List of black members.

Buffalo Lick Baptist Church, 1805–38 (KyLoF)

List of black members.

Christenburg Baptist Church, 1810–75 (KyLoF)

Church records including black members.

Newburg Christian Church, Newburg, Kentucky (KyLoF)

Church records; list of black members.

Diaries

Hord, William, 1798–1823 (KyLoF)

Account book with list of black births and the names of their children.

Miller, Howard, 1857–67; 1878–88 (KyLoF)

    Civil War diary of events involving freeing of the slaves.

Taylor, Francis, 1786–92; 1794–99 (KyLoF)

    Midland Plantation business and military pursuits in Orange County, Virginia, and Kentucky.

Military Records

Other than the pension records at the Kentucky Historical society, the availability is not known.

Newspapers

The Filson Club in Louisville, Kentucky, has an excellent collection of newspapers which have not been indexed for black genealogical material.

LEXINGTON STANDARD. 1892–1912? Weekly.

    Holdings: March 1900 to February 7, 1903; KyLxT

    January 27, 1900; CSdS, CSS, CU, DLC FTaSU, KHi, LU-NO, MdBMC, MiKW, TNF, WHi.

Personal Papers and Slavery Records

Bills of Sale, Kentucky Papers, 1787–1883 (NHi)

    Records for Fayette and Lincoln counties. MS 66–1792

Hickman-Bryan. Papers, 1796–1920 (MoU)

    Missouri, Louisiana, and Kentucky families with land and slave records. MS 60–1817

Kentucky Colonization Society Reports and AFRICAN REPOSITORY, 1830–74 (KyBgW)

    Includes diaries and letters from Liberia. Library also has an excellent research collection which needs to be surveyed for black genealogical material.

Strange, Agatha Jane (Rochester). Papers, 1852–89 (KyBgW)

    Includes slave records of families in Bowling Green. MS 70–2088

At the Filson Club in Louisville is a superior collection of family papers and manuscripts including bills of sale, records of fugitive slaves, inventories of estates, manumissions, and letters referring to specific slaves. The DIRECTORY OF AFRO-AMERICAN RESOURCES (pp. 16-17) cites some of these, but an excellent research project would be to develop an index to the black genealogical information found in this fine collection.

Another large group of slavery materials can be found at the Kentucky Historical Society in Frankfort. They, also, have not been indexed specifically for black genealogical material, although the society has a card index file of much of its holdings. Material here includes slave compensation papers, emancipation deeds, bills of sale for slaves, evaluation papers for slaves, and an extensive collection of Kentucky family Bibles.

Chapter 19
MISSISSIPPI (South)

The following books are excellent sources of black family names and guides to Mississippi black genealogical materials:

King, June Estelle Stewart, comp. MISSISSIPPI COURT RECORDS, 1799-1835. 1936. Reprint. Baltimore: Genealogical Publishing Co., 1969.

Indicates court records, some of which include blacks.

McBee, May Wilson, comp. MISSISSIPPI COUNTY COURT RECORDS. 1958. Reprint. Baltimore: Genealogical Publishing Co., 1967.

Contains court records and wills, with names of slaves included.

Sydnor, Charles Sackett. SLAVERY IN MISSISSIPPI. 1933. Reprint. Baton Rouge: Louisiana State University Press, 1966; Gloucester, Mass.: Peter Smith, 1965.

Excellent background reading.

Wharton, Vernon Lane. THE NEGRO IN MISSISSIPPI, 1865-1890. 1947. Reprint. New York: Harper and Row, 1965.

Good background; records on blacks and slaves are indicated.

Williams, E. Russ, comp. ORPHANS COURT RECORDS (ABSTRACTS OF WILLS AND ESTATES), 1812-1859, MARION COUNTY, MISSISSIPPI, PRESERVED IN THE OFFICE OF CLERK OF CHANCERY. Bogolusa, La.: The compiler, 1962.

Orphans Court Records are valuable black genealogical sources. This is a fine example of the material which should be available in such court records for every county and state.

FEDERAL RECORDS

Mortality Schedules

1850-80 (Ms-Ar)

Population Schedules

1830-80 (DNA, Ms-Ar, MsSM, MsU); and 1900 (DNA). Libraries in Aberdeen, Booneville, Cleveland, Greenwood, Hattiesburg, Kosciusko, Louisville, and Meridan also have 1830-80 population schedules on microfilm.

Territorial Census for 1805, 1810 and 1816 (Ms-Ar).

Special Census 1890 (DNA, Ms-Ar, MsHaU)

Record Group 101 (DNA)

For a description of these records see chapter 4, p. 27, Mississippi branches with deposits recorded: Columbus, Natchez, Vicksburg.

Record Group 105 (DNA)

For a description of these records see chapter 4, p. 27, Mississippi records contain school reports; letters sent and received; station books and rosters; labor contracts between planters and freedmen; and register of indentures and marriages, August 1865 to May 1866. The indenture records include name and age of orphan, date of indenture, terms of agreement, and name and residence of employer. Marriage records include names, residence, color and age of couple, date of marriage, color of parents, and names of ministers and witnesses. Both are arranged chronologically.

Record Group 56, "General Records of the Department of the Treasury" (DNA)

Third Special Agency: Dealings with freedmen before the establishment of the Freedmen's Bureau, 1863-65.

STATE AND COUNTY RECORDS

The records in Mississippi are probably similar to those of Georgia. An indication of this is found in the GUIDE TO VITAL STATISTICS RECORDS IN MISSISSIPPI (Jackson: Mississippi Historical Records Survey, 1942).

The Mississippi Department of Archives and History at Jackson, Mississippi, should be the first stop for beginning research in this state. Although most black genealogical records have yet to be uncovered, there are indications of valuable records at the archives. There are tax lists for the nineteenth century which include the valuation of slaves and records of slave sales. For example, Adams County records contain such sale records for 1827-59. The source material at the archives is vast and only waits for someone to organize and publish it.

The records which follow are found in the JOURNAL OF MISSISSIPPI HISTORY and are especially valuable sources of black names. The census data does not have any names of free blacks, but does have names of whites who owned slaves.

Capers, Charlotte, ed. "Census of Franklin County Mississippi Territory, 1810." JOURNAL OF MISSISSIPPI HISTORY 13 (1951): 249-55.

_____. "Census of Jefferson County, 1810." JOURNAL OF MISSISSIPPI HISTORY 15 (1953): 33-46.

Hendrix, Mary Flowers. "Births, Deaths, and Aged Persons for Claiborne County, 1822." JOURNAL OF MISSISSIPPI HISTORY 16 (1954): 37-46.

_____. "Births, Deaths, and Aged Persons for Wilkinson County, Mississippi, 1822." JOURNAL OF MISSISSIPPI HISTORY 16 (1954): 121-50.

McCain, William D., ed. "Census of Baldwin County, Mississippi Territory, 1810." JOURNAL OF MISSISSIPPI HISTORY 11 (1949): 207-13.

Morgan, Madel Jacobs, ed. "Census of Claiborne and Warren Counties, Mississippi Territory, 1870." JOURNAL OF MISSISSIPPI HISTORY 13 (1951): 50-63.

_____. "Census of Wilkinson County, Mississippi Territory, 1805." JOURNAL OF MISSISSIPPI HISTORY 11 (1949): 104-10.

Owsley Charts, 1840-60 (T)

> Land and slave charts for all counties from the Federal Census Schedules. MS 64-1193

MISCELLANEOUS RECORDS

Cemetery Records

Greenwood Cemetery, Jackson, 1862-1938 (Ms-Ar)

> List of blacks buried. MS 62-1967

Church Records

All of the following include lists of black and white members:

Mississippi Baptist Church, 1819-1957 (MsSM) MS 66-888; 1837-68 (MsSM) MS 72-1569

Mississippi Church of Christ Records, 1900-1957 (MsSM) MS 66-889

Mississippi Methodist Church, 1833-1957 (MsSM) MS 66-890; 1843-85 (MsSM) MS 72-1570

Mississippi Presbyterian Church, 1823-1925 (MsSM) MS 66-1192; 1843-85 (MsSM) MS 72-1571

Mississippi Primitive Baptist Church, 1819-1957 (MsSM) MS 66-891

St. Philips Episcopal Church, Kirkwood. 1848-88

Records include vestry minutes; parish register; lists of communicants, baptisms, marriages, confirmations, and funerals of blacks and whites. This church is located near the governor's mansion (see Governor Alcorn's diary, below).

Diaries

Alcorn, Governor James L., 1859, 1879 (Nc-Ar)

Mississippi property and slave records.

Anonymous, 1828-32 (Ms-Ar)

Plantation account book and diary.

Capell, Eli J., 1842-50, 1867 (LU-Ar)

Pleasant Hill Plantation diary for Amite County. MS 71-240

Eggleston, Dick Hardeway, 1850 (LU-Ar)

Diary of the Learmont Plantation, near Woodville. MS 75-739

Gordon, Robert, and Gordon, James, 1851-76 (Ms-Ar)

Pontotoc County diaries. MS 60-741

Hilliard, Mrs. Isaac H., 1849-50 (Lu-Ar)

Vicksburg plantation life.

Justis, Horace Howard, 1857-59 (NcD)

>Mississippi law student and teacher's comments on slaves' behavior.

McCall, Duncan G., 1835-51; 1852-54 (NcD)

>Mississippi plantation journal and diary.

McGovern, Patrick Francis, and Charles Sauters, 1857 (Ms-Ar)

>Records work, treatment, punishment, food, clothing, illnesses, births, and deaths of slaves.

Shoemaker, Isaac, 1864 (NcD)

>Problems on Mississippi cotton plantation.

Wade, Walter, 1834-54 (Ms-Ar)

>Ross Wood Plantation diary from Jefferson County. Lists slaves. MS 60-205

Military Records

Availability not known.

Newspapers

FREE STATE (Brandon). 1898-1904? Weekly.

>Holdings: January 20, 1900; CSdS, CSS, CU, DLC, FTaSU, KHi, LU-NO, MdBMC, MiKW, TNF, WHi.

GOLDEN RULE (Vicksburg). 1898-1902? Weekly.

>Holdings: January 27, 1900; CSdS, CSS, CU, DLC, FTaSU, KHi, LU-NO, MdBMC, MiKW, TNF, WHi.

LIGHT (Vicksburg). 1891-1922? Weekly.

>Holdings: January 18, 1900; CSdS, CU, DLC, FTaSU, KHu, Lu-NO, MdBMC, MiKW, TNF, WHi.

Personal Papers

Clark, Charles, 1870-74 (Ms-Ar)

Book lists former slaves and accounts of Doro Planation in Bolivar County. MS 60-2583

Dupree, H.T.T., 1878-1900 (Ms-Ar)

Plantation account books, Hinds County. MS 60-747

Ross, Isaac, 1845-89 (MsSM)

Estate papers including will with slave manumissions. MS 69-342

Sizer, Henry E., 1844-67 (Ms-Ar)

Personal papers include bills of sale for slaves purchased in New Orleans, Richmond, and Nashville. MS 61-2724

Smith, A.F. Records, 1851-52 (OC1WHi)

Plantation accounts of births and deaths of slaves in Princeton.

Vick and Phelps Family Papers, 1810-1906 (Ms-Ar)

Includes list of blacks sold or mortgaged to the Bank of the United States, 1834-49. MS 60-1732

Slavery Records

Bills of sale and slave receipts can be found in several groups of papers:

Darden Family, 1835-1944 (MsSM) MS 66-881

Nannie Herndon Rice Papers, 1824-1963 (MsSM) MS 69-340

Manuscript Collection, 1803-1900 (MsVHi)

Plantation Records, 1818-65 (Ms-Ar) MS 61-2343

Adams County: Aventine, Artornish, and Loch Leven plantations

Amite County: Brooksdale Plantation

Claiborne County: Nailer and Belmont plantations

Hinds County: Learned Plantation

Percy, Mississippi: Panter Burn Plantation

Nanechehaw Plantation owned by Charles B. Allen (county not listed)

Washington, Marshall, and Jackson counties: unnamed plantation

Register of Freedmen's Contracts, 1865 (MsSM)

Located in Bertie Shaw Rollins Collection. MS 66-896

Chapter 20
TENNESSEE (South)

Tennessee, like Kentucky, was a gateway to the west and north from the coastal states. Consequently, many genealogical trails run through this state. The following books will be quite helpful for beginning research here:

Lamon, Lester C. BLACK TENNESSEANS, 1900-30. Knoxville: University of Tennessee Press, 1977.

> This recent book includes a bibliography and will be helpful for those who have trouble tracing ancestors back to the nineteenth century.

Mooney, Chase Curran. SLAVERY IN TENNESSEE. 1957. Reprint. Westport, Conn.: Negro University Press, 1971.

> Gives a good idea of the laws affecting the hiring and selling of blacks. Indicates what court records should be checked in each county for black genealogical information. Contains a list of slave owners in 1850 (p. 188), and a list of non-land-owning slave owners (pp. 203-42). Excellent bibliography which will give an idea of plantation records which exist.

Tennessee. State Library and Archives, Nashville. Manuscript Division. GUIDE TO THE MICROFILM HOLDINGS OF THE MANUSCRIPTS SECTION, TENNESSEE STATE LIBRARY AND ARCHIVES. Nashville, 1975.

> Research in Tennessee can be difficult because the records have not been centralized and many early records were lost. This guide will be essential in locating miscellaneous materials in this fine collection.

FEDERAL RECORDS

Mortality Schedules

> 1850-80 (DNA, DNDAR)

Population Schedules

>1820-80 and 1900 (DNA); 1820-80 (T, and Knoxville, Fayetteville, Chattanooga, and Memphis public libraries)

Special Census 1890 (DNA, T, TJoS)

Record Group 101 (DNA)

>For a description of these records see chapter 4, p. 27, under Freedmen's Bureau. Tennessee branches with deposits recorded: Memphis, Nashville.

Record Group 105 (DNA)

>For a description of these records see chapter 4, p. 27, Freedmen's Bureau. Records contain school report, letters sent and received (alphabetical), leases, indentures, labor contracts, and registers of plantations.

STATE AND COUNTY RECORDS

The resources at the University of Tennessee in Knoxville and the public library in Nashville are very helpful. There are fine collections at the Tennessee Historical Society and the Tennessee State Library and Archives in Memphis. In addition, the Negro Chamber of Commerce published a classified directory of blacks of Memphis and Shelby counties. Included among the records of the Tennessee State Library and Archives:

Owsley Charts

>Records of farms, slaves, and equipment in Davidson, DeKalb, Dickson, Dyer, Fayette, Fentress, Franklin, Gibson, Grainger, Greene, Hardin, Hawkins, Haywood, Henry, Johnson, Lincoln, Maury, Montgomery, Robertson, Stewart, Sumner, and Wilson counties from the Federal Census Schedules, I, II, IV of 1850.

>Charts for all counties for 1840 and 1860.

Petitions to Tennessee State Legislature, 1796-1869, including manumissions.

Voter Registration Rolls.

MISCELLANEOUS RECORDS

Cemetery Records

Confederate and Federal Papers, 1858-65 (T)
> Includes Civil War deaths and cemetery records.

Church Records

Cumberland Presbyterian Church, Negro, 1866-94 (T)

Disciples of Christ Historical Society (T)
> Collection of black churchmen including biographical sketches and some materials on black congregations; Archives of the Southern Christian Institute and Home Mission School for Negroes.

Mars Hill Presbyterian Church, Athens, McMinn County, 1823-1923 (T)

Methodist Episcopal Church, 1866-88; 1905-25 (T)
> Minutes of black-white conferences; may have names and vital statistics.

Mill Creek Baptist Church, Davidson County, 1797-1814. (T)
> List of black members.

St. Joseph Catholic Mission, Jackson, Madison County (T)
> Records of mission established for blacks.

Diaries

Cutchfield Family Papers, 1828-86 (T)
> Includes 1852 diary, settlement of estate, and slave deeds. Records treatment of blacks.

Perkins, Theresa Green (Ewen), date unknown (T)
> Discussion about blacks.

Porter, Nimrod, 1861-72 (T)

> Sheriff of Maury County's diary referring to blacks.

Reed, Seth, 1863 (MiU)

> Notes on slavery from U.S. Christian Commission with the Army of the Cumberland in Tennessee and Alabama. MS 65-506

Military Records

Confederate and Federal Papers, 1858-65 (T)

> In addition to the cemetery records listed above, these papers also contain many personal materials.

Military Records, 1861-75 (T)

> Ninety-nine reels of microfilm which include an index to service records of black Union veterans from Tennessee.

Tennessee Confederate Pension Application, 1891 (T)

> Personal and family history included for both black and white veterans.

Newspapers

COLORED TENNESSEAN (Nashville).   June 23?, 1865, to 1866.   Weekly.

> Continued by TENNESSEAN (1866-1867?)

> Holdings: August 12, 1865, to July 18, 1866 (incomplete); CSdS, CSS, CU, DLC, IHi, KHi, LU-NO, MdBMC, MiKW, TNF, WHi.

MARYVILLE REPUBLICAN.   October 26, 1867, to 1878.   Weekly.

> Title varies as REPUBLICAN.

> Holdings: October 7, 1876; CSS, CU, DLC, KHi, LU-NO, MdBMC, MiKW, TNF, WHi.

> November 2, 1867, to February 26, 1870; January 4, 1873, to October 27, 1877 (incomplete); T, US1GS.

Personal Papers

Berry, William Wells.   Papers, 1838-96 (T)

Includes slave records relating to Berry's activities in Davidson County. MS 70-723

Buckner Papers, 1818-1923

Includes slave lists.

Buell, George P., and Brien, John S. Papers, 1805-1943 (T)

Includes Brien's slaves and Brien and Buell's joint business pursuits. MS 61-1330

Dunlap, Hugh W., and John H. Papers, 1824-1905 (T)

These notes of two Henry County lawyers include over 200 documents related to slave sales, indentures, and deeds. MS 62-251

Eakin, William. Papers, 1841-46 (T)

Slave deeds included.

Harrison, William. Papers, 1840-90 (T)

Bills of sale for slaves.

McCutchen Family Papers, 1818-1958 (T)

Slave records included. MS 65-881

Pryor, Jackson. Papers, 1830-97 (T)

Bills of sale for slaves in Jasper, Marion County. MS 68-495

Sanford, Henry Shelton. Papers, 1796-1901

Large group of materials related to Barnwell Island, 1868-89, and Oakley, 1869-90, sugar plantations.

Westbrooks, Allie C. Collection, 1771-1935 (T)

Includes slave records of the Barton and Taylor families of Cannon and Rutherford counties. MS 73-872

Williamson Family Papers, 1833-74 (T)

Slave sales included.

Slavery Records

Bolton and Dickens Company Slave Traders, 1856–58 (NHi)

Extensive microfilm of the company's slave purchases and sales.

Cherokee Collection. Papers, 1775–1878 (T)

Many items relate to Cherokee ownership of slaves and their joint ownership of lands.

Fisk University Library.

The Anti-Slavery Collection has bills of sale and free papers. The Negro Collection includes estate papers, diaries, slave sales, biographies, birth records, certificates of freedom, and slave labor contracts.

Freedmen's Bureau. Papers, 73 reels of microfilm (T)

These papers may be the same as the National Archives records of the Freedmen's Bureau, discussed in chapter 4, p. 27.

Jackson, Andrew II. Account Books, 1845–77 (OC1WHi)

Includes purchase, sale, births, marriages, and deaths of slaves at Hermitage, 1845–77. MS 75–1849. Also available at (T).

Nichols–Britt Collection, 1771–1905 (T)

Extensive records of history and genealogy of Williamson and Davidson counties. Includes slave records and account books. MS 61–1854

Chapter 21

CONNECTICUT (North)

Connecticut's genealogical contribution to the black family is out of proportion to the state's size. Hundreds of black families emerged out of Connecticut during the colonial period. Because of this, a complete black genealogical study of Connecticut is necessary. Most of the records necessary for this study have been centralized at the state library in Hartford. Some of those of particular interest to blacks are outlined in the State and Town Records section below. In addition, there are some published books which will be of interest:

Bailey, Frederic William. EARLY CONNECTICUT MARRIAGES AS FOUND ON ANCIENT CHURCH RECORDS, PRIOR TO 1800. 1896-1906. Reprint. 7 vols. in 1. Baltimore: Genealogical Publishing Co., 1968.

Black marriages are included in this listing.

Greene, Lorenzo Johnston. THE NEGRO IN COLONIAL NEW ENGLAND, 1620-1776. 1942. Reprint. New York: Atheneum, 1968; Port Washington, N.Y.: Kennikat Press, 1966.

Excellent background reading and bibliography for blacks tracing New England ancestry.

Steiner, Bernard Christian. HISTORY OF SLAVERY IN CONNECTICUT. 1893. Reprint. New York: Johnson Reprint Corp., 1973.

Warner, R.A. NEW HAVEN NEGROES, A SOCIAL HISTORY. 1940. Reprint. New York: Arno Press, 1970.

Excellent book on blacks in this area. A "must" reading for fine genealogical leads.

FEDERAL RECORDS

Mortality Schedules

    1850–80 (Ct, USIGD)

Population Schedules

    1790–1880 and 1900 (DNA); 1790–1880 (Ct, CcRhW)

Special Census – none

STATE AND TOWN RECORDS

The following are located at the Connecticut State Library in Hartford:

General Assembly Records

    The Revolution, series 1, 2, and 3 contain military data and petitions concerning a variety of matters. Crimes and Misdemeanors, series 1 and 2, contain petitions for commutation of sentences and data on prisoners at Newgate Prison.

Justice Court Records

    These records deal largely with civil cases, a variety of criminal offenses, and frequently contain notices concerning the warnings of paupers. Available for a number of towns in Hartford area; also located at Connecticut Historical Society.

Land Records

    These records contain deeds, providing an index to residence and genealogical information. In addition, most towns recorded emancipations in the land records. The records are located at the town clerk's office.

Probate Court Records

    Original files, which are indexed.

Selectmen's Records

    Located at the state library, the Connecticut Historical Society, or in the town clerks' offices. They contain letters relating to black paupers, which furnish valuable genealogical data and information on transiency.

Superior Court Records

Include civil cases, some criminal cases, and pension applications and records of the Revolution.

Town Meeting Records

Blacks are often mentioned in cases as the object of court suits or as paupers. Records are at the town clerk's office.

Town Treasurer Reports

Some of these are available at the state library in addition to being housed at the town clerk's offices. These reports provide information on welfare, dates of death, and other genealogical information. They indicate monies paid to blacks for various services.

Vital Statistics

Birth, death, and marriage records which are located at the offices of the individual town clerks have been alphabetized and indexed. They can also be found in the Barbour Collection at the state library, and through the Genealogical Department and its branch libraries. The index identifies the people as "colored, Negro, mulatto or black," but the original statistics in the towns contain data on warnings, emancipations, and the like.

MISCELLANEOUS RECORDS

Cemetery Records

All cemeteries in the state have been indexed. Indexes are located at the Connecticut State Library; they are also available through the Genealogical Department's branch libraries.

Church Records

These include baptisms, births, deaths, and marriages of both free blacks and slaves, as well as whites. The originals, still extant, are almost all at the Connecticut State Library. The Congregational records have been indexed. The Connecticut Historical Society has copies of some church records not found in the state library. Vital records and minutes of church meetings constitute an important source of genealogical information.

Diaries

Availability not known.

Military Records

Marshall, Henry Grimes.   Letters, 1862–65 (MiU)

> Marshall was the captain of 29th Connecticut Volunteers, black regiment.   MS 63-226

Newspapers

The CONNECTICUT GAZETTE (New London) and the CONNECTICUT COURANT (Hartford) contain a considerable amount of genealogical material. Copies are held at the Connecticut State Library in addition to the holdings listed for them below.

CHRISTIAN FREEMAN (Hartford).   January 1843 to December 25, 1845. Weekly.

> Continues CHARTER OAK.

> Holdings: 1843–45; CtU, NIC, WHi.

CONNECTICUT COURANT (Hartford).   November 26, 1764, to October 29, 1914. Weekly, semiweekly.

> Subtitle varies.

> Holdings: 1764–1820; CFS, CNoS, CSdS, CSmH, CSt, CtY, CU, DeU, DLC, ICN, ICU, InNd, IU, KyU, LNT, McBJ, MeU, MH, MHi, MnU, NcD, NcGrE, NcU, NhD, NHi, NjP, NN, OC1, PEaS, PU, Readex, RPB, TNJ, TxHR, ViWI, WaU, WHi.

> 1820–37; NHi, McP.

> 1837–1914; McA.

CONNECTICUT GAZETTE (New London).   December 17, 1773, to February 26, 1823. Weekly.

> Subtitle varies.

> Holdings: 1773–1823; CU, DeU, ICU, InNd, LU-NO, MB, MBAt, MdBJ, MeU, NbOU, NcGrE, OKentU, OkS, OU, PBL, PEaS, PPiU, Readex, RPB, ScU, TrC.

Personal Papers

The manuscript collections at the Connecticut State Library and the Connecticut Historical Society contain extensive town records, correspondence, diaries, account books, and a variety of other useful material. These account books are of particular importance, for they frequently contain information not available elsewhere.

Donnan, Elizabeth. Papers, 1806-63 (CtU)

Manuscript notes taken from ships logs, etc. These notes were mostly used in her book on the slave trade (see chapter 2, p. 15, for citation).

Hempstead, Stephen. Papers, 1754-1927 (MoSHi)

Son of Joshua Hempstead of New London, Connecticut. Lists occupations of slaves and those who migrated to Missouri with him. MS 68-1287

Phillips, Elrich Bonnell. Papers, 1712-1923 (CtU)

Collection of documents used in editing the history of a Florida plantation, FLORIDA PLANTATION RECORDS FROM THE PAPERS OF GEORGE NOBLE JONES, cited in chapter 17, "Florida," p. 130.

Slavery Records

See discussion on pp. 151-52, State and Town Records.

Chapter 22

MASSACHUSETTS (North)

The records of all New England states, including Massachusetts, and especially New York, are similar to those records found in Connecticut. There are, however, additional records which will be uncovered as black genealogy becomes more widely established and researched. The following is a list of additional sources in Massachusetts:

American Antiquarian Society. Worcester, Mass. INDEX OF OBITUARIES IN SENTINEL AND COLUMBIA SENTINEL, 1784-1840. 5 vols. Boston: G.K. Hall, 1961.

> This index frequently designates blacks and covers the general New England area.

Bailey, Frederic William. EARLY MASSACHUSETTS MARRIAGES PRIOR TO 1800. 1897-1914. Reprint, 3 vols. in 1. Baltimore: Genealogical Publishing Co., 1968.

> Includes marriage records from Worcester, Plymouth, Middlesex, Hampshire, Berkshire, and Bristol counties.

Daniels, John. IN FREEDOM'S BIRTHPLACE: A STUDY OF THE BOSTON NEGROES. 1914. Reprint. New York: Arno Press, 1969; Johnson Reprint Corp., 1968; Negro University Press, 1968.

> Demographical and historical background.

Flagg, Charles Allcott, comp. A GUIDE TO MASSACHUSETTS LOCAL HISTORY: BEING A BIBLIOGRAPHIC INDEX TO THE LITERATURE OF THE TOWNS, CITIES AND COUNTIES OF THE STATE. Salem, Mass.: Salem Press, 1907.

> This book can still be purchased from the publisher and is an excellent bibliography of vital records, lists, census records, county histories, deeds, and wills of every town in Massachusetts.

Moore, George H[enry]. NOTES ON THE HISTORY OF SLAVERY IN MASSA-CHUSETTS. 1866. Reprint. New York: Negro University Press, 1968.

> Interesting because of its date of publication.

FEDERAL RECORDS

Mortality Schedules

> 1850-80 (DNA, DNDAR, M-Ar)

Population Schedules

> 1790-1880 and 1900 (DNA); 1790-1880 (MU)

Special Census 1890 (DNA)

STATE AND TOWN RECORDS

Boston. Registry Department. BOSTON BIRTHS, 1700-1800. Vol. 24, Report of the Record Commissioners of the City. Boston: Boston Municipal Printing Office, 1903.

> This volume contains some early black birth records in addition to those discussed under Vital Statistics, below.

Boston. Registry Department. BOSTON MARRIAGES, 1752-1809. Vol. 30, Records Relating to the Early History of Boston: Municipal Printing Office, 1903.

> This volume contains some black marriages.

Salem, Massachusetts

> List of blacks dated May 4, 1793 (NHi)

State Census Records, 1855, 1865 (M-Ar)

Vital Statistics

> Births, marriages, and deaths can be found at town and city clerks' offices. More than half of those records previous to 1850 have been published. Boston records are at the city registrar's office. The Commonwealth of Massachusetts Archives has copies from 1841 on file in its Vital Statistics Division.

MISCELLANEOUS RECORDS

Cemetery Records and Church Records

See Connecticut chapter, p. 152, and discussion of vital statistics, under State and Town Records, above.

Diaries

The Massachusetts Historical Society has published (Boston: G.K. Hall) a seven-volume folio catalog of their manuscript collection. For local availability of the catalog, write to the Historical Society, 1154 Boylston Street, Boston, Massachusetts 02215.

Military Records

Appleton, John W.M. Papers, 1861-1913 (WVUL)

Scrapbook and official papers of service in the 54th Regiment, Massachusetts Voluntary Infantry of Negro Troops.

Steward, Theophilus Gould. THE COLORED REGULARS IN THE UNITED STATES ARMY. 1904. Reprint. American Negro History and Literature Series, no. 2. New York: Arno Press, 1969.

Covers the service of blacks in the Spanish-American War.

Willis, George H. Papers, 1863-66 (MBU)

Orders, commissions and supply records for the 118th Colored Infantry Regiment while Willis was quartermaster. MS 66-399

Newspapers

BOSTON ADVOCATE. January 1885 to 1888? Weekly.

Holdings: 1885-86 (incomplete); MB, MHi.

THE LIBERATOR (Boston). January 1, 1831, to December 29, 1865. Weekly.

Holdings: January 1831 to December 1865; CFS, CtU, CU, DLC, GEU GStG, IHi, KyMoreU, LU-NO, MB, MiDW, MiYEM, MnU, MWiW, NHi, NN, OC, OKentU, PEaS, PPiD, WaSpC, WaU, WHi.

Personal Papers

Champion, Rev. George, 1834-37 (MH)

> Journal of a voyage from Boston to Cape Town, and missionary activities to the Zulus.

Slavery Records

America Freedmen's Inquiry Commission, 1862-63 (MH)

> Papers on ex-slaves' conditions.

Anti-Slavery Collection, 1820-1900 (MB)

> Account books, manuscripts, letters related to freedmen's school and fugitive slaves. There are also items involving slavery and the West Indies. This collection includes the Mather family papers, 1632-89.

Bates, William B. Journal, 1845 (MSaE)

> Mozambique trading conditions written by the captain of the RICHMOND.

Business records of firms trading with Africa (MH-B)

Collection of Account Books (MWA)

> Includes slave account books. MS 62-3523

Freedmen's Aid Society, 1869-71 (MH)

> Daily journal.

Hammond, Eli Shelby, 1895 (MH)

> A slave's recollections of his life on a pre-Civil War plantation.

Jacobs, Phillip (MWa1AJ)

> Bill of sale for slave. MS 68-139

Liberia College Collection, 1842-1927 (MHi)

Lincoln, William, 1770 (MH)

> Bill of sale for slave.

Massachusetts Anti-Slavery Society Records (NHi)
>   List of slaves aided. MS 1801

Massachusetts Colonization Society Papers, 1842-1911 (MHi)

Moore, Samuel Preston, 1776 (MH)
>   Manumission certificate.

New England Freedmen's Aid Society Papers (MHi)

Peabody, George Foster, 1830-57 (MSaE)
>   Extensive slave trading records for Massachusetts, Washington, D.C., and Maryland.

Sheftall, Mordecai, 1761-1873 (MWalAJ)
>   Bills of sale for slaves.

Ship Logbooks (MSaP)

Siebert, Wilbur Henry (MH, OHi)
>   This material was used to write THE UNDERGROUND RAILROAD. It is indexed by states (see Ohio, also). MS 68-1705

Slavery Papers (MH)
>   Sales, advertisements, apprenticeships, and certificates.

Slave Traders Papers, 1846-64 (MWA); 1759-69 (MMeHi)

Spanish Account Books; Account Books in Spanish and Relating to Spanish Enterprises, 1752-1803 (MH-B)
>   Includes records of the Spanish Royal Company of Cuba which was engaged in slave trading. MS 61-288

Chapter 23
NEW JERSEY (North)

The following publications will provide a good beginning for research in New Jersey:

New Jersey. Department of State. NEW JERSEY INDEX OF WILLS. 3 vols. Balitmore: Genealogical Publishing Co., 1969.

> A superior guide with a good index, usable for black genealogical research.

Rutgers University. Library. A GUIDE TO THE MANUSCRIPT COLLECTION OF THE RUTGERS UNIVERSITY LIBRARY. Compiled by Herbert F. Smith. New Brunswick, N.J.: Rutgers University Press, 1964.

> Supplements the information in the following entry.

_____. THE NEGRO AND NEW JERSEY: A CHECKLIST OF BOOKS, PAMPHLETS, OFFICIAL PUBLICATIONS, BROADSIDES AND DISSERTATIONS, 1754-1964, IN THE RUTGERS UNIVERSITY LIBRARY. New Brunswick, N.J.: Rutgers University Press, 1965.

> This checklist is available at Rutgers University Library and may be available at other large libraries.

_____. SLAVERY IN AMERICA: MANUSCRIPTS AND OTHER ITEMS, 1660-1865. Selected from the collection of Philip D. and Elsie O. Sang. New Brunswick, N.J.: Rutgers University Press, 1963.

> Materials from an exhibit prepared by Anthony S. Nicolosi.

Steward, William, and Steward, Theophilus Gould. GOULDTOWN, A VERY REMARKABLE SETTLEMENT OF ANCIENT DATE. Philadelphia: J.B. Lippincott Co., 1913.

> An unusual look at an early black family. The book deals specifically with the descendants of Elizabeth Fenwick, daughter of John Fenwick, one of New Jersey's founders. Elizabeth married a black

man named Adam, whose descendants, the Goulds, Pierces, and Murrays founded Gouldtown. Gouldtown exists today in the vicinity of Bridgetown (now Bridgeton), New Jersey.

FEDERAL RECORDS

Mortality Schedules

1850-80 (DNA, DNDAR, Nj)

Population Schedules

1830-80 (DNA, Nj); 1900 (DNA); several other public libraries and historical societies have schedules for some years available.

Special Census 1890 (DNA, Nj-Ar, NjRuF)

STATE RECORDS

In 1942, the Works Progress Administration conducted a survey of New Jersey counties and discovered some slave birth records. These are in Paterson, New Jersey, at the county clerk's office, along with one volume of manumissions. In addition, the following records are available:

Middlesex County

New Brunswick Register of Black Children, 1804-44 (NjR)

Slave Manumissions 1800-1825 (NjR)

Piscataway Township

Certificates of Abandoned Black Children, 1805-7 (NjR)

Residential Directories

List of Blacks Compiled and Held by New Jersey Historical Society in Newark (Nj-HS)

South Jersey Towns

List of Blacks, 1798-99. Compiled by New Jersey Abolition Society (NjGbS)

Vital Statistics

Card indexes for births, marriages, and deaths in the eighteenth and nineteenth centuries (Nj-Ar)

MISCELLANEOUS RECORDS

Cemetery Records

Availability not known.

Church Records

Quaker Collection (NjGbS)
  This collection contains Salem County manumissions, 1777.

Diaries

Allinson, Samuel, 1824–1883 (NjR)
  Quaker philanthropist's antislavery work. MS 65-1550

Military Records

Sherman, Adelbert C. Papers, 1864–1908 (NjR)
  Includes reports, rolls, and returns of personnel and equipment of
  Company G, 28th U.S. Infantry (Colored), 1864–66. MS 66-145

Whitney, Henry (NjR)
  Civil War journal includes recruitment of blacks from West Virginia and information on Whitney's students at Free Military School
  for Applicants for Command of Colored Troops.

Newspapers

THE SENTINEL (Trenton). January 26? 1880, to November 13? 1882. Weekly.
  Holdings: 1880–82 (incomplete); CSdS, CtY, CU, DLC, InNd,
  MB, MdBJ, MnU, MoSW, NcU, NjP, NjT, TNF, WHi.

Personal Papers

McKeag Family Papers, 1827–1939 (NjR)
  Includes slave bonds, releases, and indentures. MS 65-1679

Smith, Miles C. Papers, 1826–1930 (NjR)

    Includes slave certificates, 1821–25. MS 66–149

Still, Peter. Papers, 1798–1875 (NjR)

    Letters attempting to buy his wife and children who were Alabama slaves; genealogy included.

Van Liew–Voorhees. Papers, 1777–1859 (NjR)

    Includes bills of sale for slaves. MS 66–178

Slavery Records

African Association of New Brunswick Records, 1817–24 (NjR)

    Information on black and white members including owner's certificate permitting slave to join.

New Brunswick Colonization Society Records, 1838–54. (NjR)

    Members listed.

Chapter 24

NEW YORK (North)

New York is another primary area for the study of the black family. The Ethnic Genealogy Center at Queens College is in the process of gathering and indexing black primary source materials relating to New York. The following items are being compiled:

> Blacks in the Federal Census Schedules of New York, 1790–1850. To be published by Gale Research Company.

> Extracts of slave names found in New York City Surrogate Court Wills.

> Slave Ship Records for New York City, 1715–65.

The center has also compiled slave birth records for New York City, Brooklyn, and Staten Island, along with New York State manumissions, the latter to be published in the New York Genealogical and Biographical Society's RECORD. Death and tax assessments are being collected, also, in order to present a complete picture of blacks in New York State up to 1850.

In addition to the records listed above, there is black primary source material in the New York Historical Collection located at Queens College and directed by Dr. Leo Hershkowitz. Some of the materials available for inventory there are:

> Inventories of Estates for Albany and New York, 1690–1800.

> Letters and Extracts of Account of Her Majesty's Revenues in the Colonies: Massachusetts Bay Colony, Virginia, New York, Maryland, New England, Bermuda, Barbados Records filed in the Public Record Office, London, 1692–1706.

> > Slave ship records are found in these papers.

> Newspapers

> > Many of the papers listed in the Newspaper section below include arrival dates of slave ships, runaway slave advertisements, sales of slaves, and information on free blacks. Some of these have been inventoried, but the indexes do not indicate blacks, in most cases.

New York Chancery Court Papers, 1692-1820.

>   Manumission and registrations of free blacks are found
>   in these papers.

New York Colony Accounts of Her Majesty's Revenue of Customs
in the Province of New York, 1704.

New York Coroner's Reports, 1790-1850.

>   Racial designations given.

New York Mayor's Court Papers, prior to 1775.

New York Mayor's Court Papers, after 1775.

New York Supreme Court Minute Books, 1692-1840. 400 vols.

New York Town Records for Westchester, Jamaica, Newtown,
and Flushing, 1686-1800.

In addition to the above, the following published sources provide excellent
background reading and guidance:

Allen, James Egert. THE NEGRO IN NEW YORK. New York: Exposition
Press, 1964.

Bailey, Rosalie Fellows. GUIDE TO GENEALOGICAL AND BIOGRAPHICAL
SOURCES FOR NEW YORK CITY, (MANHATTAN), 1783-1898. New York:
The author, 1954.

>   This is one of the best guides to genealogical sources in New
>   York. While so many genealogical guides are not relevant to
>   black research, this one is an excellent overall research source
>   which contains information relevant to black family research.

Breton, Arthur J. A GUIDE TO THE MANUSCRIPT COLLECTIONS OF THE
NEW YORK HISTORICAL SOCIETY. Westport, Conn.: Greenwood Press,
1972.

>   An extensive guide which probably includes a number of materials
>   relevant to black genealogical research.

Davis, Thomas J. POPULATION AND SLAVERY IN NEW YORK. Master's
thesis, Columbia University, 1968.

>   Demographic, but good background material.

DOCUMENTS RELATIVE TO THE COLONIAL HISTORY OF THE STATE OF
NEW YORK. Vol. 1. Edited by E.B. O'Callaghan. Albany: Weed, Parsons
and Co., 1853-57.

>   This volume includes a New York census of 1755 giving names of

white slaveholders with names of their slaves; a list of all the
inhabitants of Dutchess, 1714; a census of New York City, 1703,
listing residents of the city with the number of slaves they owned;
a census of Long Island giving the names of white families and
names of blacks living in their households, 1698 (see part 2).

Foner, Phillip Sheldon. BUSINESS & SLAVERY. 1941. Reprint. New York:
Russell and Russell, 1968.

This book gives a general background of the business side of
slavery in New York. It is an excellent study of New York
slave merchants.

Harris, M.A. A NEGRO HISTORY TOUR OF MANHATTAN. Westport,
Conn.: Greenwood Press, 1968.

An excellent and interesting guide for locating early residential
areas of blacks in Manhattan.

Hershkowitz, Leo. WILLS OF EARLY NEW YORK JEWS, 1704–1799. New
York: American Jewish Historical Society, 1967.

This book contains a list of forty-eight wills and gives the names
of blacks mentioned in them.

Historical Records Survey. New York City. CALENDAR OF THE MANU-
SCRIPTS IN THE SCHOMBURG COLLECTION OF NEGRO LITERATURE, LO-
CATED AT 135TH STREET BRANCH, NEW YORK PUBLIC LIBRARY. 1942.
Reprint. New York: Andronicus Publishing Co., 1970.

This is a guide to the manuscript collection at the Schomburg
Center for Research in Black Culture, which contains extensive
material on black life both here and in Africa. The collection
has microfilm copies of all the Federal Census Population Schedules
for the United States from 1790 to 1880.

Horsmanden, Daniel. THE NEW YORK CONSPIRACY. 1810. Reprint. Boston: Beacon Press, 1971; New York: Negro University Press, 1969.

The names of blacks and whites involved in the "conspiracy" of
1741 are uncovered.

Korbin, David. THE BLACK MINORITY IN EARLY NEW YORK. Albany:
Office of State History, 1971.

Good background with indications of excellent sources.

McManus, Edgar J. A HISTORY OF NEGRO SLAVERY IN NEW YORK. Syracuse, N.Y.: Syracuse University Press, 1966.

The footnoting is of special interest for sources.

New York. State Library, Albany. Manuscript and History Section. AN INVENTORY OF NEW YORK STATE AND FEDERAL CENSUS RECORDS. Prepared by Edna L. Jacobsen. New York, 1937.

> This lists each county clerk's census records, in addition to other records.

Scheiner, Seth M. NEGRO MECCA: A HISTORY OF THE NEGRO IN NEW YORK CITY, 1865-1920. New York: New York University Press, 1965.

> Also available at Missouri Historical Society, St. Louis.

Stokes, Isaac Newton Phelps. THE ICONOGRAPHY OF MANHATTAN IS- LAND, 1498-1909. 6 vols. 1915-28. Reprint. New York: Arno Press, 1967.

> These six volumes contain a great deal of information on blacks in New York, making it very important reading.

Yoshpe, Harry B. "Record of Slave Manumissions in Albany, 1800-1828." JOURNAL OF NEGRO HISTORY 26 (1941): 499-522.

> Gives former slave's name, owner's name, place of residence, and date of manumission.

_____. "Record of Slave Manumissions in New York." JOURNAL OF NEGRO HISTORY 26 (1941): 78-107.

> See comment above.

FEDERAL RECORDS

Mortality Schedules

> 1850-80 (N)

Population Schedules

> 1790-1880 and 1900 (DNA); 1800-1860 (NNGB); 1800-1880 (NN-Sc, N). Also available at some public libraries and colleges throughout the state.

Special Census 1890 (DNA, NN, and a few other libraries).

Record Group 101 (DNA)

> For a description of these records see chapter 4, under Freedmen's

Bureau. New York branches with deposits recorded: New York City.

Record Group 21, "Records of District Courts of the United States" (DNA)

Southern District of New York and Eastern District of Pennsylvania. Records from 1789 include commercial aspects of slave trade and civil matters from Reconstruction to 1912.

STATE AND COUNTY RECORDS

In addition to the federal census for New York listed above, New York State conducted censuses in 1855, 1865, and 1875. The records for those in New York City are located at the Municipal Archives. The 1855 census takers used as census divisions the local election districts of each of the city wards. This enables the present-day searcher to find a desired household faster than in the federal census since, at the most, only two or three election districts need be searched rather than an entire ward. While the boundaries of the election districts were not defined in the census itself, the polling place of each of the 128 election districts in the 22 wards was published for the previous election (NEW YORK TIMES, November 7, 1854). The best procedure, according to Bailey (cited above) is to plot on a map (such as the 1855 Fire Insurance Companies Map by W. Perris) both the desired household's address, taken from the city directory of 1855-56 (available at the New York City Public Library, 42d Street) and the various polling places of the ward within which the family address was situated. Then the election district can be ascertained. The New York Public Library, 42d Street Branch, has maps and city directories which help in locating families on both the State and Federal Census Schedules.

In order to provide an idea of the types of records available on blacks in New York, a check was made of some of the various sources throughout the state. The following records, along with those already mentioned, are only a small part of the total resources:

Albany County--Courthouse

Miscellaneous Certificates (1810-90)

Slaves, Register of Manumitted (1800-1828)

Albany County--Secretary of State's Office

Extensive collection of bills of sale for slaves and other records on blacks.

Albany County--Institute of History and Art

Records of slave ownership, bills of sale, and inventories related to blacks, including a county census.

Albany County--(NYHS)

> Ledger of Mrs. Robert Sanders's sales of merchandise to blacks living in Albany.

Columbia County--Historical Society, Kinderhook

> Slave Sale Records, 1686-1836

Erie County--Grosvenor Library, Buffalo

> Anti-Slavery Society Records of West Aurora
>
> Bills of sale
>
> Certificates of Freedom of the Negro, 1804-11

Greene County--Historical Society, Coxsackie

> Blacks Born in Coxsackie
>
> > Gives name of owner, mother of child, name, age, and sex of child, date of birth.
>
> Free Children Born to Slaves, 1800-1823

Kings County--St. Francis College, Brooklyn

> Slave Births and Manumissions (extensive)

Montgomery County--Department of History and Archives, Fonda

> Town and Village Records, 1783-1934; includes assessment rolls and slave births.

Nassau County--Historical and Genealogical Society, Adelphi College

> Register of Black Residents.

Nassau County--Westbury Children's Library

> Manumission of Slaves, 1776-77; carried out by John Hicks, Esther Seaman, and Richard and Samuel Willis.

Nassau County--(NYHS)

> Oyster Bay, L.I. Negro Ledger, 1761-62
>
> > Records of sales of merchandise to blacks, probably kept by William Townsend.

New York County (NHi)

Association for the Benefit of Colored Orphans, 1836-Present

Indenture records, admissions, discharges, visitors, births, deaths, and marriages. There are more than 10,000 names of black children, and in some cases names of their parents. The records from 1900 to the present are restricted until 2000.

New York City 1741 Riot Records

List of volunteers and aides

New York Manumission Society Records, 1785-1845

Lists name of owner, manumitted black, county, and date of manumission.

New York Public School Society

Records include "colored" schools.

Slave Births, 1800-1818

More than 200 certificates of slave births, giving names of child, mother, and owner.

Richmond County--Town of Castleton (NHi)

New York Town Book, 1800-1927

Includes all children born to slaves after July 1, 1799.

Schoharie County--Historical Society

Slave Sales

Steubin County (NIC)

Slave Sales, 1808

Tompkins County (NIC)

"Early Settlers and Freemen of Tompkins County," written in 1862. Found in the Sydney Hollingsworth Galloway Collections.

Certificates of Manumission, 1722-1835, town of Beekman

New Born Slaves, 1722-1835, town of Beekman

OLD TOWN BOOK, 1773-1816. Found in the Brockett Collection.

Gives names of slave owners.

Westchester County--Thomas Paine Memorial House, White Plains

Certificates of Birth and Manumission of Slaves, dates not given

Westchester County--Historical Society, White Plains
    Business records of Westchester
    Manumissions
    Tax List, public records, and original wills
    Yonkers Tax List, 1822-30

MISCELLANEOUS RECORDS

Cemetery Records and Church Records

Availability not known.

Diaries

Brown, James F., 1829-44 (NHi)
    Black gardener of Fishkill, N.Y.

Military Records

Availability not known.

Newspapers

The Schomburg Center for Black Life and Culture has archives of more than 400 black newspapers. Some of these have been microfilmed and are available in other libraries outside the state. Little indexing of any of them has been done for genealogical purposes.

FREDERICK DOUGLASS' PAPER (Rochester). June? 1851 to February 17, 1860? Weekly.
    Continues the NORTH STAR (see below).
    Holdings: 1851-59 (incomplete); CtU, CtY, CU, DLC.
    1851-55 (incomplete); KyMoreU, MnU, MoJcL, NRU.
    February 1, 1856; September 17, 1858; July 8, 1859; February 17, 1860; CSdS, CSS, FTaSU, KHi, LU-NO, MdBMC, MiKW, TNF.

NATIONAL ANTI-SLAVERY STANDARD (New York). June 11, 1840, to December 1872. Weekly, monthly.

Holdings: 1840-71; CSdS, HU, LU-NO, MB, OKentU, TxHTSU, WaBeW, WHi.

NEW YORK AGE. October 15, 1887 to 1953. Weekly.

Continues NEW YORK FREEMAN (see directly below). Continued by NEW YORK AGE-DEFENDER.

Holdings: 1887-1900; CSdS, CSS, CtY, CU, DLC, InIB, InNd, MB, MdBJ, MoSW, NjP, TNF, TxU.

NEW YORK FREEMAN. November 22, 1884, to October 8, 1887. Weekly.

The title was FREEMAN from November 22 to December 6, 1884. Continues NEW YORK GLOBE (see directly below). Continued by NEW YORK AGE (see directly above).

Holdings: 1884-87; CSdS, CSS, CtY, CU, DLC, ICU, InIB, InNd, MB, MdBJ, MnU, MoSW, NcU, NjP, TNF, TxU.

NEW YORK GLOBE. 1880 to November 8, 1884. Weekly.

Continued by NEW YORK FREEMAN (see directly above).

Holdings: 1883-84; CSdS, CtY, CU, DLC, InIB, MB, MdBJ, MnU, MoSW, NcU, NjP, TNF, TxU.

NEW YORK GAZETTE. February 16, 1759, to December 28, 1767. Weekly.

Title varies as WEYMAN'S NEW YORK GAZETTE.

Holdings: 1759-67; CFS, CNoS, CSdS, InNd, LU-NO, MB, MBAt, MdBJ, MeU, NcGrE, NHi, NNC, OKentU, OU, PEsS, RPB, Readex, ScU.

NEW YORK GAZETTE AND WEEKLY MERCURY. February 1, 1768, to November 10, 1783. Weekly.

Continues NEW YORK MERCURY (see below).

Holdings: 1768-83; CFS, CNoS, CSdS, CSt, CU, DeU, InNd, LNT, MB, MBAt, MdBJ, MeU, MWA, NbOU, NcD, NcGrE, MdU, NN, OKentU, OU, PEsS, RPB, Readex, ScU, TNJ, ViWi, WaBeW, WvU.

NEW YORK GAZETTE OR WEEKLY POST-BOY. January 1, 1753, to March 12, 1759. Weekly.

Continues NEW YORK GAZETTE REVIVED IN THE WEEKLY POST-BOY (see below). Continued by PARKER'S NEW YORK GAZETTE

OR WEEKLY POST-BOY (see below).

Holdings: 1753-59; CSt, CU, CU-Riv, IU, MBAt, MdBJ, NhD, NHi, OKentU, RPB, TNJ, WaBeW.

NEW YORK GAZETTE OR WEEKLY POST-BOY. May 6, 1762, to August? 1773. Weekly.

Continues PARKER'S NEW YORK GAZETTE OR WEEKLY POST-BOY (see below).

Holdings: 1762-73; CSt, CU, CU-Riv, IU, MBAt, MdBJ, NhD, NHi, OKentU, RPB, TNJ, WaBeW, WaU.

NEW YORK GAZETTE REVIVED IN THE WEEKLY POST-BOY. January 19, 1747, to December 1752. Weekly.

Continues NEW YORK WEEKLY POST-BOY (see below). Continued by NEW YORK GAZETTE OR WEEKLY POST-BOY (1753-59, see above).

Holdings: 1747-52; CSt, CU, CU-Riv, IU, MBAt, MdBJ, MWA, NhD, NHi, OKentU, PPT, RPB, TNJ, ViWi, WaBeW, WaU.

NEW YORK JOURNAL OR GENERAL ADVERTISER. May 29, 1766, to August 29, 1776. Weekly.

Continues the volume numbering of NEW YORK GAZETTE OR WEEKLY POST-BOY (see above).

Holdings: 1766-76; CSmH, CoFS, CoU, CU, DeU, FU, InU, MBAt, MWA, NHi, NvU, PHarH, Phi, PSt, RP, ViWI, WaBeW, WHi.

NEW YORK MERCURY. August 3, 1752, to January 25, 1768. Weekly.

Continued by NEW YORK GAZETTE AND WEEKLY MERCURY (see above).

Holdings: 1752-68; CFS, CLS, CNoS, CSdS, CSt, CU, CU-Riv, DeU, DeWint, GStG, InMuB, InNd, LNT, LU-NO, MB, MBAt, McP, MdBJ, MeU, MWA, NbOU, NcD, NcGrE, NdU, NN, NSyU, OKentU, OU, PBL, PEsS, PPAmP, Readex, ScU, TNJ, ViU, ViWi, WaBeW, WaU, WvU, WvU-J.

NEW YORK WEEKLY POST-BOY. January 3, 1743, to January 12, 1747. Weekly.

Continued by NEW YORK GAZETTE REVIVED IN THE WEEKLY POST-BOY (see above).

Holdings: 1743-47; CU, IU, MBAt, MdBJ, MWA, NhD, NHi, OKentU, PBL, PPT, RPB, TNJ, ViWi, WaBeW.

PARKER'S NEW YORK GAZETTE OR WEEKLY POST-BOY. March 19, 1759, April 29, 1762. Weekly.

> Continues NEW YORK GAZETTE OR WEEKLY POST-BOY. Continued by NEW YORK GAZETTE OR WEEKLY POST-BOY (1762-73 see above).
>
> Holdings: 1759-62; CSt, CU, CU-Riv, ICU, IU, MBAt, MdBJ, NhD, NHi, OKentU, RPB, TNJ, WaBeW, WaU.

NORTH STAR (Rochester). November 1, 1847, to 1851. Weekly.

> Continued by FREDERICK DOUGLASS' PAPER (see above).
>
> Holdings: 1847-51 (incomplete); CtU, CtY, CU, DLC, KyMoreU, MnU.

Personal Papers

There are extensive collections at the Long Island Historical Society, the Schomburg Center, and the New York City and Albany State libraries which have not been surveyed for black genealogical source material.

Jay, John. Papers, 1715-1862 (NNC)

> Includes manumissions. MS 61-3334

National Council of Y.M.C.A. of U.S.A. Library

> Biographies of early black leaders from 1851.

Slavery Records

Ancient Documents of Saggaponeck, 1694-1771, Jermaine Memorial Library in Sag Harbor

> Dorcus Jones's slave sales and manumissions.

Bancker, Christopher, 1718-55 (NHi)

> Ledger of slave sales.

Brooklyn Public Library

> Fugitive slave pamphlets.

Carleton, Sir Guy. Papers (NN)

> "Book of Negroes"--blacks who left New York in 1783 for Nova

Scotia. Contains 3,000 first and last names.

Croesen, Cornelius, 1738-83 (NHi)

Staten Island slave sales.

Hammon, Isaac. Collection, 1859-65 (New Paltz State Normal School, Vi)

Letters and papers on suppression and release of slaves and free blacks. MS 65-988

Jones, Samuel. Papers, 1760-93 (WHi)

Lists slave manumissions, 1779. MS 62-2379

Joyce, John, 1785-90 (NHi)

Record of slaves bought at Kingston, Jamaica.

The Notorial Archives, Amsterdam, Holland

Records in New Amsterdam government, including large numbers of materials on slavery.

Pratt Family Papers, 1758-1903 (NIC)

Slave sales. MS 62-1657

Stillwell, John Edwin. Collection (NHi)

More than 1,000 manuscripts pertaining to blacks in Gravesend, Long Island, and Middletown, New Jersey. MS 60-2939

Van Cortlandt, Jacobus. 1658-1740 (NHi)

New York City slave sales.

Van Schaick Family Papers (NIC)

Slave deeds, 1732, 1758, 1784, Albany County. MS 64-943

Van Zandt, Gerrit. Papers, 1723-1831 (NA1I)

Slave deeds. MS 61-983

Young Family Papers, 1670-1846 (NGcA)

Slave sales and manumissions.

Chapter 25
PENNSYLVANIA (North)

Pennsylvania has some of the most unusual records with black genealogical information. To begin with, the following books are recommended:

THE BLACK BOOK: WHO'S WHO IN GREATER PHILADELPHIA IN THE NEGRO COMMUNITY. Philadelphia: Bricklin Press, 1972.

Good biographical sketches included.

Blockson, Charles L. PENNSYLVANIA'S BLACK HISTORY. Edited by Louise D. Stone. Philadelphia: Portfolio Associates, 1975.

Bibliography and index are included in this background reading.

Brown, Ira Vernon. THE NEGRO IN PENNSYLVANIA HISTORY. Pennsylvania History Studies, no. 11. University Park: Pennsylvania Historical Association, 1970.

Short article with illustrations. Good for background reading.

Oblinger, Carl D. "Ellipses the Black Masses and Local Elan: A Review of the Sources for the History of the Ante-Bellum Negro in Southeastern Pennsylvania." JOURNAL OF THE LANCASTER COUNTY HISTORICAL SOCIETY 74 (1970): 124-31.

An excellent source of records for this area. Lists dog tax records, 1800-1860, with names and addresses of all dog owners, including many blacks; records of State Supreme Court and Office of the Commissioner of Land which includes important information on migratory patterns, pleas and reviews of writs of habeus corpus involving indigent blacks who were reenslaved or illegally bound out as indentured servants.

_____. FREEDOMS FOUNDATIONS: BLACK COMMUNITIES IN SOUTHEASTERN PENNSYLVANIA TOWNS, 1780-1860. Northwest Missouri State University Studies, Vol. 33, no. 4. Maryville: Northwest Missouri State University, 1972.

Another fine article with good bibliographical references.

PENNSYLVANIA MAGAZINE OF HISTORY AND BIOGRAPHY. Vol. 1-- . 1877-- . Philadelphia: Historical Society of Pennsylvania.

Has a number of articles in its various publications which are relevant to black genealogical research. An index is available for vols. 1-7, 1877-1951.

Philadelphia. Library Company. AFRO-AMERICANA, 1553-1906: AUTHOR CATALOG OF THE LIBRARY COMPANY OF PHILADELPHIA AND THE HISTORICAL SOCIETY OF PENNSYLVANIA. Boston: G.K. Hall, 1973.

Excellent catalog of a large collection of materials. It would be another excellent research project, to uncover the genealogical material in these collections.

Turner, Edward Raymond. THE NEGRO IN PENNSYLVANIA: SLAVERY-SERVITUDE-FREEDOM, 1639-1861. 1911. Reprint. New York: Arno Press, 1969; Negro University Press, 1969.

This is an excellent history of blacks in Pennsylvania. The bibliography contains an excellent guide to some of the records available in the American Philosophical Society, Friends Meeting House, Historical Society of Pennsylvania, and the Pennsylvania State Library's Division of Public Records.

FEDERAL RECORDS

Mortality Schedules

1850-80 (P)

Population Schedules

1790-1880 and 1900 (DNA); 1800-1880 (P, PPiU, and several other libraries in the state which have schedules for a few of the years)

Special Census 1890 (DNA, PPiU, P, and a few other libraries)

Record Group 101 (DNA)

For a description of these records see chapter 4, p. 27, under Freedmen's Bureau. Pennsylvania branches with deposits recorded: Philadelphia.

Record Group 21, "Southern District of New York and Eastern District of Pennsylvania" (DNA)

> Records for 1789 including criminal matters related to slave trade and civil matters from Reconstruction to 1912.

STATE AND COUNTY RECORDS

Beginning in January 1782, the state of Pennsylvania began a septennial (every seven years) census. This census is of incomparable value since it was done in all the counties and lists free blacks and slaves, with first and last names. Some records which remain are maintained in Harrisburg at the Pennsylvania State Archives. Others may be in county offices.

There are prison records located at the Archives of the City and County of Philadelphia which sometimes have personal information as the following excerpt reveals:

> John Brown, 3rd, Black Man 5 feet 5 1/4, born in Chester County, Pennsylvania, aged 30 years, two small scars on the back of his left hand, one on the outside of his right knee. May 8th; a farmer; Chester County.

The extensive records in Pennsylvania contain an abundance of black genea-logical source material. For instance, the U.S. Works Progress Administration's INVENTORY OF COUNTY ARCHIVES OF PENNSYLVANIA (Gettysburg: Penn-sylvania Historical Records Survey, 1941) lists the following in county offices:

Delaware County

> Release of Slaves, dates unknown.

Fayette County

> Negro Birth Register, 1788-1826
>
> > With name of slave owner, date of birth, names of child, parents.

Lancaster County

> Slave Register, 1780-88
>
> > Shows dates, names and addresses of owners, names of slave mothers and children, dates of birth, sex, age, and date of manumission. Indexed.

Washington County

> Negro Register, 1782-1820

Records of Negro Slaves and Their Offspring

    Registered by owners; names and ages stated.

The following county records are located outside of the state:

Chester County (CtY)

    Register of Slaves, 1780-1815

Dauphin County (MiU)

    Slave Records, 1788-1825

        Records date of freedom.

Philadelphia County and City

    The innumerable sources at the Archives of the City and County of Philadelphia include some of the following materials. For a thorough survey of these records, see John Day's DESCRIPTIVE INVENTORY OF THE ARCHIVES OF THE CITY AND COUNTY OF PHILADELPHIA (Philadelphia: The author, 1970). Some of the following records, included in Day's inventory, are obviously relevant to blacks, while others may have genealogical material of importance to black families:

    Birth Register, 1860-1903

    Board of Health--City Hospital Register, 1840-54

        Lists patients names, ages, race.

    Cemetery Returns, 1803-6 (blacks identified by "B")

    Clerk of Court of Quarter Sessions and Oyer and Terminer Records

    Constable Returns to Assessors, 1762-80. 3 vols.; no index.

        Lists householder's name, occupation, blacks, and servants.

    Coroner Case Records, 1854-57, 1878-80, 1885-86, 1906

    County Tax Assessment Ledgers, 1779-1842

    Death Certificates, 1904-15

    Death Register, 1860-1903

    Deed Books, 1684-1969

    Enumeration of Taxables, Slaves, Deaf and Dumb Persons, 1821, 1828, 1835. 10 vols.; index.

Lists name, occupation, city ward or county township, and borough. Slaves are listed separately.

Marriage Records under Magistrate's Court No. 9, 1880-1908

Marriage Register, dates unknown

Mayor's Office--Record Group 60

Apprentice, Redemptioner Indentures, 1771-73; 1800-1806; index volume 1771-73 lists name of child, age, parents, (if living) and master; Marriage Records, 1841-44; 1857-1904, with index.

Midwife Register, 1920-34

Pauper Lists, 1821-29

Lists name, residence, age, sex, color, and country of origin.

Philadelphia City Directories, 1785-1935

Poor Tax Register, 1832-47

Prostitutes Register, 1863

Lists name, age, birthplace, length of time in Philadelphia, color, children's names, and name.

Record of Apprentice Indentures, 1800-1806

Records of the Prothonotary of the Court of Common Pleas

Register of Children's Asylum, 1819-87. 9 vols.

Register of Relief Recipients, 1814-15; 1828-32, with index.

MISCELLANEOUS RECORDS

Cemetery Records and Church Records

See Cemetery Returns, under Philadelphia County and city, above, and Slavery Records discussion, below.

Diaries

Allinson, William, 1804-5, 1809, 1827-28 (PHC)

Tour of Flemington in 1805 to attend Circuit Court trial of black slave's freedom.

Brown, Elijah, Jr., 1808 (PHi)

Philadelphia to West Indies trip for legal and commercial business. MS 62-1558

Jones, Rev. Morgan, 1795 (PCC)

Philadelphia to South Carolina sea voyage with notes on slave work.

Neilson, John, 1798-1832 (PSC-Hi)

Farm journal with notes on slaves and hired labor.

O'Bryen, Richard, 1789-91 (PHi)

Political and domestic affairs in Barbary states, cruel treatment of Christian slave. MS 62-1558

Pleasanton, August, 1838, 1841, 1844 (PHi)

Abolitionists and antislavery riots in Pennsylvania. MS 62-1558

Shaw, John, 1799 (PHi)

Trip to Mediterranean on the SOPHIA to Algiers, Bizerte, Tunis, and Tripoli. Records inhumane treatment of an American black held in Tunis. MS 62-1558

Still, William, 1852-7 (PHi)

Contains data on contraband, escaped slaves, and the Underground Railroad.

Military Records

Bates, Samuel Penniman. HISTORY OF PENNSYLVANIA VOLUNTEERS, 1861-5. 5 vols. Harrisburg: B. Singerly, State Printer, 1869-71.

Black volunteers are listed on the following pages for the designated units:

6th Infantry	V, 943-64
8th Infantry	V, 965-90
22d Infantry	V, 991-1010
24th Infantry	V, 1011-25
25th Infantry	V, 1026-46

32d Infantry	V, 1047-65
41st Infantry	V, 106-80
45th Infantry	V, 1106-24
127th Infantry	V, 1125-37

Johnson, Thomas S. Papers, 1839-69 (WHi)

Includes a handbook for 1864-65 of the 127th Regiment of U.S. Colored Troops. MS 68-2231

Mickley, Jeremiah Marion. THE FORTY-THIRD REGIMENT UNITED STATES COLORED TROOPS. Gettysburg: J.E. Wible, 1866.

Newspapers

STATE JOURNAL (Harrisburg). August 18, 1883, to 1885. Weekly.

Continues HOME JOURNAL.

Holdings: December 15, 1883, to January 24, 1883; January 24, 1885; CSdS, CSS, CU, DLC, LU-NO, MdBMC, MiKW, TNF, WHi.

Personal Papers

Chew, Benjamin, 1770 (ICHi)

Lists Chew's slaves in Whitehall, Pennsylvania.

Jenks, Michael Hutchinson. Papers, 1695-1909 (PDoBHi)

County papers, some related to blacks. MS 61-3174

Haverford College Library. Papers Related to Blacks, 1676-1937 (PHC)

Over 200 items including records of Friends Freedmen's Association of Philadelphia, 1864-65; considerable collection of Quaker and Anti-Slavery records. MS 62-4731

Historical Society of Pennsylvania. Miscellaneous Papers (PHi)

Sixteenth- to nineteenth-century personal account of slaves' lives, and letters and diaries related to or written by blacks.

Steinmetz, Mary Owen. Papers (PHi)

Includes Berks County cemeteries. MS 62-4050

Tallcott, Joseph. Family Papers, 1724-1857 (PHC)

    Letters related to the Wilberforce Colony of blacks. MS 67-429

Tilghman, William. Letters, 1772-1827 (PHi)

    Account of purchase and sale of slaves. MS 61-125

Wood, Anna Wharton. Collection of Quaker Papers, 1741-1853 (PHC)

    Letters related to transporting freed blacks to Haiti, 1826. MS 62-4377

Slavery Records

African Colonization Society. Papers, 1832-72 (PHi)

    Biographical sketches of members.

American Negro Historical Society, 1790-1901 (PHi)

    Roll books, lists of black organizations participating, including black colleges and churches. MS 60-2033

Dutilh and Wachsmuth, Philadelphia, Pa., 1704-1846 (PHi, WHi)

    Slave trade papers with bills of exchange, cargoes, and trade with West Indies. MS 60-1791; MS 62-2064

Pennsylvania Colonization Society, 1838-1913 (PLuL)

    Rosters of lifelong members, register of emigrants, 1834-64; Liberian applications, 1835-38.

Pennsylvania Society for Promoting the Abolition of Slavery, Papers (PHi)

    Over 6,000 manumission documents. The papers are of unusual value because they reveal information on African background of black slaves in Pennsylvania. These papers are another important prospective editing and publishing project. MS 61-425

Records of Clubs and Societies. Papers, 1775-1825 (PHi)

    Membership lists of diverse organizations, including burial societies, colonization societies, lodges, and churches.

Chapter 26

RHODE ISLAND (North)

Although Rhode Island is the smallest state, it holds a genealogical importance to blacks out of proportion to its size. The impact of black Rhode Islanders in the colonial period was felt particularly in New York, Vermont, and Pennsylvania during the nineteenth century. Thousands of black families emerged from Rhode Island. For background reading on black genealogical research in Rhode Island, the following sources are suggested:

Chapin, Howard M. RHODE ISLAND IN THE COLONIAL WARS: A LIST OF RHODE ISLAND SOLDIERS AND SAILORS IN OLD FRENCH AND INDIAN WAR, 1755-1762. Providence: Rhode Island Historical Society, 1918.

> Lists blacks from Rhode Island who fought in the war.

Jeters, Henry N. TWENTY-FIVE YEARS EXPERIENCE WITH THE SHILOH BAPTIST CHURCH AND HER HISTORY. Providence, Rhode Island: Remington Printing Co., 1901.

> Old manuscript available at Brown University, Rockefeller Library, recording the history of the first black church in Newport, Rhode Island. Has extremely valuable biographical accounts.

Woodward, Carl Raymond. PLANTATIONS IN YANKEELAND: THE STORY OF COCUMSCUSSOC, MIRROR OF COLONIAL RHODE ISLAND. Chester, Conn.: Pequot Press, 1971.

> Reports Wickford, Rhode Island, plantation life.

FEDERAL RECORDS

Mortality Schedules

1850-80 (R); 1860-80 (DNDAR)

Population Schedules

    1790-1880 and 1900 (DNA); 1800-1880 (R, RPPC)

Special Census 1890 (DNA)

STATE AND COUNTY RECORDS

The primary sources of information for Rhode Island are the Rhode Island Historical Society in Providence, the Newport Historical Society, and the Westerly Public Library. Rhode Island county records are, however, not centralized as was the case for Connecticut and Massachusetts. Each town kept its own deeds, and its own probate, town council, and town meeting records. As new towns were formed, they followed the same procedure. The law for recording births, marriages, and deaths was adopted in 1647. Those records before 1850 were gathered by J.N. Arnold and published by the state. The following is a list, by county and town, of where records are located:

Bristol County

    Barrington--Records are at town office.

    Bristol--Records are at town hall.

    Warren--Records are at town office.

Kent County

    Coventry--Records are in the village of Anthony.

    East Greenwich--Records are at the Kent County Courthouse and in East Greenwich.

    Warwick--Records are at Apponauq.

    West Greenwich--Probate, town council, and some land records are in the archives in Providence.

Newport County

    Jamestown--Records are at town hall.

    Little Compton--Records are at city hall.

    Middletown--Records are at city hall. Abstracts of four volumes of wills are printed in the July and October 1968 issues of the NEW ENGLAND HISTORICAL AND GENEALOGICAL REGISTER. It is best to use these only as an index and then go back to the originals.

    Newport--Saltwater damaged most of the early records before 1779, making some of them unreadable. The Newport Historical Society organized them in 1853 and has some fifteen thousand books and seventeen hundred manuscripts of log books, custom house papers, and mercantile records. The Newport County Courthouse has records of birth, deaths, and marriages.

Portsmouth--Records are at the town hall and the earliest records of the town have been printed in book form.

Tiverton--Records, at the town office, are in excellent condition.

Providence County

Cranston--Records are at city hall.

Cumberland--Records are at the town office in Lincoln.

Foster--Records are in the village of Foster Center.

Gloucester--Records are at Chepachet.

Johnston--Records are at town clerk's office. Early town council, town meeting, and probate records are at the Providence City Hall Probate Office.

North Providence--Records for the colonial period are at the clerk's office at Pawtucket City Hall.

Scituate--Records are at North Scituate.

Smithfield--Records are at Central Falls City Clerk's Office.

Washington County

Charleston--Records are at town office.

Hopkinson--Records are at town office.

New Shoreham--Part of Newport County until 1963. Records are at town office.

North Kingston--Fire damaged all of the town books. They have since been repaired and a great deal of information is still available, although vital records suffered serious damage. What remains is located in Wickford.

Richmond--Records are at town office.

South Kingston--Records are well kept and organized; located in the village of Wakefield.

Westerly--Town records are complete, but the Westerly Public Library is the best place to start here.

The census records found in the Rhode Island Historical Society are of excellent quality and very extensive. There is a cross-reference index file to all of the state censuses. The various censuses are listed below:

1747-54 Census--Lists names only.

1774 Census--Lists heads of household and whether they owned slaves or had free blacks and Indians living with them.

1776 Census--Same information as 1774 Census.

1777 Military Census--Lists all males 16-50 able to bear arms; all males 16-50 unable to bear arms; 50-60 able to bear arms; 50-60 unable to bear arms and all men over 60. It includes the names of blacks in these categories; however the towns of Exeter, Little Compton, Middletown, New Shoreham, Newport, and Portsmouth are missing.

1782 Census--Does not include Barrington, Johnston, North Providence, Richmond, and Smithfield.

MISCELLANEOUS RECORDS

Cemetery Records and Church Records

In addition to Jeters manuscript cited in introduction to Rhode Island further availability is not known.

Diaries

Allen, Eliza Harriet (Arnold), 1831, 1837, 1841 (RHi)

Describes trips to Savannah from Providence to live on brother's plantation.

Foster, Robert Watson, 1862-64 (RHi)

Plantation at Apalousas, Louisiana, describes blacks and whites.

Military Records

Chenery, William H. THE FOURTEENTH REGIMENT RHODE ISLAND HEAVY ARTILLERY (COLORED) IN THE WAR TO PRESERVE THE UNION, 1861-1865. Providence: Snow & Farnham, 1898.

A unit roster appears on pages 151-266.

Newspapers

No eighteenth- or nineteenth-century black newspapers are now available for this state.

Personal Papers and Slavery Records

The Rhode Island Historical Society has a tremendous collection of family papers and an index to them is located on the second floor of the society's building. Unfortunately, there is no published manuscript guide. Moreover, the records have not been inventoried for black genealogical materials. A check of the material located there revealed log books; bills of sale; records of the Providence Shelter for Colored Children with hundreds of names and excellent biographical information; lists of blacks who fought in the Revolution giving full names, place of enlistment, and sometimes date of birth; and the Providence directories of 1841 and 1844 with a list of "Colored Inhabitants."

The following records are located outside the state:

DeWolf, James, 1764–1837 (MH–B)

    Extensive personal papers of slave traders of Bristol.

Lopez, Aaron, 1752–93 (MWalAJ) MS 68–150; 1731–82 (MH–B) MS 60–1748; 1764–67 (MSaE) MS 73–563

    Extensive papers of a Newport slave trader.

Chapter 27

DELAWARE (North)

There are few genealogical resources available for Delaware. Nevertheless, the following book is basic although not too revealing for black genealogy:

National Society of the Colonial Dames of America. Delaware. Historical Reserve Committee. A CALENDAR OF DELAWARE WILLS, NEW CASTLE COUNTY, 1682-1800. 1911. Reprint. Baltimore: Genealogical Publishing Co., 1969.

FEDERAL RECORDS

Mortality Schedules

1850-80 (De-Ar)

Population Schedules

1790-1880 and 1900 (DNA, DeHi)

Special Census - None

MISCELLANEOUS RECORDS

Cemetery Records, Church Records, Diaries, Military Records

Availability not known.

Newspapers

ADVANCE (Wilmington). 1899-1901? Weekly.

Holdings: September 22, 1900; CSdS, CSS, CU, DeWI, DLC, FTaSU, KHi, LU-NO, McP, MdBMC, MiKW, TNF.

Personal Papers

Reese, Ann. Papers, 1715-1877 (De-Ar)

Collection of documents including land records, deeds, apprenticeships, indentures, and manumissions. MS 64-213

Slavery Records

African School Society. Papers, 1809-1916 (DeHi)

This collection from Wilmington organizations includes seven volumes of memos and records.

Delaware Association for the Moral Improvement and Education of the Colored People of the State, 1866-1909 (DeHi)

These accounts and minutes may contain genealogical information. MS 71-1638

Female African School Society. Papers, 1833-51 (DeHi)

Includes minutes and accounts which may contain genealogical information. MS 71-1639

Chapter 28

MAINE AND NEW HAMPSHIRE (North)

It is believed that, with further research, a study similar to that conducted by James M. Rose and Barbara Brown on New London, Connecticut, could be completed for Portland, Maine, and Portsmouth, New Hampshire. Like New London, these cities were strong nucleus areas for the beginnings of black families. Black ancestors can probably be traced there back to the nineteenth century.

Sargent, William Mitchell. MAINE WILLS, 1640-1760. 1877. Reprint. Baltimore: Genealogical Publishing Co., 1972.

> Contains every will proved in the province from 1640 to 1760.

Williamson, Joseph, "Slavery in Maine." COLLECTION OF THE MAINE HISTORICAL SOCIETY 7 (1867): 207-16.

> Good background reading; available through the Maine and Missouri Historical Societies.

FEDERAL RECORDS FOR MAINE

Mortality Schedule

> 1850-80 (Me-Vs); 1850-70 (US1GD)

Population Schedules

> 1790-1880 and 1900 (DNA); 1790-1860 (MeHi)

Special Census 1890-(DNA)

MISCELLANEOUS RECORDS FOR MAINE

Personal Papers

Howard, Oliver Otis, 1843-1910 (MeB)

> This collection contains sixty-two volumes of papers related to the founding of Howard University, and Howard's work with the Freedmen's Bureau.

Thurston, Charles Brown, 1843-1920 (GEU)

> Some papers relate to his service with the 13th Maine Infantry including information on the lives and activities of the black troops. MS 73-556

FEDERAL RECORDS FOR NEW HAMPSHIRE

Mortality Schedules

> 1850-80 (Nh); 1850-70 (US1GD)

Population Schedules

> 1790-1880 and 1900 (DNA); 1790-1880 (Nh)

Special Census 1890 (DNA, Nh)

MISCELLANEOUS RECORDS FOR NEW HAMPSHIRE

Newspapers

GRANITE FREEMAN (Concord). June 20, 1844, to April 23, 1847. Weekly.

> Holdings: 1844-47; NhHi.
>
> 1844-47 (incomplete); MiU-C, MWA, NhD.

HERALD OF FREEDOM (Concord). January 24, 1835, to October 23, 1846. Weekly, semimonthly.

> Title varies as ABOLISTIONIST. Suspended publication, June 14, to July 5, 1844; December 6, 1844, to March 14, 1845.
>
> Holdings: 1835-46 (incomplete); MiDW, PHC, PU.

Slavery Records

Hooper, William. Memorandum Book, 1780–83 (NN)

    Contains sales and purchases of blacks in New Hampshire.

Chapter 29
VERMONT (North)

Earliest blacks in Vermont were domestic servants, not slaves. In 1756 a bill was passed prohibiting sales of slaves after that date. Most blacks who came to the state migrated from Rhode Island, Massachusetts, and Connecticut after 1786. The following federal records should locate almost all blacks who lived in Vermont after that date.

FEDERAL RECORDS

Mortality Schedules
    1850–80 (Vt); 1850–60 (DNDAR); 1870 (DNA, Tx)

Population Schedules
    1790–1880 and 1900 (DNA); 1790–1880 (VtU)

Special Census 1890 (DNA)

STATE, COUNTY, AND MISCELLANEOUS RECORDS

No records of specific relevance to blacks have been found. All blacks who lived in the state should be found in the genealogical material available for all Vermont residents. In checking the newspaper union lists cited in chapter 2, pp. 19–20, it was ascertained that no eighteenth- or nineteenth-century black newspapers are now available for this state.

Chapter 30

ILLINOIS (Midwest)

Blacks began arriving in Illinois in great numbers around 1825 with the influx of white settlers to the Northwest Territory. As of December 8, 1812, free blacks and "mulattoes" were required to register six months after they arrived in the state. Such records still exist today.

Beginning September 1807, white slave owners with blacks aged fifteen and older were permitted to bring them to Illinois provided that they went before the clerk of the court of common pleas and registered them. The court records should document when a black ancestor arrived in Illinois, if he or she were registered by the owner, as required by law.

There is an indication (see Harris reference below) that free blacks were issued freedom certificates after January 17, 1829, which they were required to carry. These certificates may also be listed in the old common pleas court records.

The following are suggested sources for research in Illinois:

Harris, Norman Dwight. THE HISTORY OF NEGRO SERVITUDE IN ILLINOIS AND OF SLAVERY AGITATION IN THAT STATE, 1719-1864. 1904. Reprint. New York: Haskell House, 1969; Negro University Press, 1969.

> This book starts by giving a background on the beginning of slavery in Illinois, reporting that on June 6, 1719, five hundred slaves arrived in Lower Louisiana from Guinea. Many of these slaves migrated up the Mississippi River with their masters to Illinois Territory. The book's footnoting is superior and gives excellent indications of location of records. Examples include bills of sale (p. 258) and registers of free Negroes for many counties (pp. 245-57) as well as numerous other sources on blacks. An essential book for research in Illinois.

Hodges, Carl G. ILLINOIS NEGRO HISTORYMAKERS. Chicago: Illinois Emancipation Centennial Commission, 1964.

Norton, Margaret C. ILLINOIS CENSUS RETURNS, 1810 AND 1818. Illinois State Historical Library Historical Collections, no. 24. 1935. Reprint. Baltimore: Genealogical Publishing Co., 1969.

See annotation below.

_____. ILLINOIS CENSUS RETURNS, 1820. Illinois State Historical Library Historical Collections, no. 26. 1934. Reprint. Baltimore: Genealogical Publishing Co., 1969.

Both of these books by Norton are excellent census reproductions, giving listings of free blacks and white slave owners, in addition to the usual information. They can be purchased through the publishing house if not available at a local library.

FEDERAL RECORDS

Mortality Schedules

1850-80 (DNA, I-Ar)

Population Schedules

1810-80 and 1900; 1818 Territorial Census (DNA); numerous public and college libraries have schedules for some years available.

Special Census--none

Record Group 21, "Records of District Courts of the United States" (DNA, and the Federal Records Center, Chicago)

This record group contains U.S. District Court Records, 1789-1959, for Region 5. Many records deal with slave trade.

STATE AND COUNTY RECORDS

The Illinois State Historical Library at Springfield has in its collection a few Slave Record Books from various counties which are lists of indentured French slaves and freedmen before 1860. Most of such lists, however, are still in the county courthouses as described in the following two articles:

Bridges, Roger D. "Illinois Manuscript and Archival Collections: A Checklist of Published Guides." JOURNAL OF THE ILLINOIS STATE HISTORICAL SOCIETY 66 (1973): 412-27.

An important supplement to the Pease article (below). The collection has not been adequately surveyed for black genealogical information.

Pease, Theodore Calvin. THE COUNTY ARCHIVES OF THE STATE OF ILLI-
NOIS. Springfield, Ill.: Trustees of Illinois State Historical Library, 1915.
Bibliographical Series, no. 3. 12 (1915).

> Some of these records were used by Harris for his book (cited
> above).

MISCELLANEOUS RECORDS

Cemetery Records

Availability not known.

Church Records

Immaculate Conception Parish, Kaskaskia, Randolph County, Ill., 1695-1844
(ICHi)

> Baptisms, marriages, and deaths of blacks recorded.

St. Anne's Parish, St. Charles, 1721-65 (ICHi)

> Same as above.

St. Joseph's Parish, Prairie du Rocher, 1761-99 (ICHi)

> Same as above, but in French.

Diaries

Franklin, John Hope, ed. "The Diary of James T. Ayers, Civil War Recruiter."
OCCASIONAL PUBLICATIONS OF THE ILLINOIS STATE HISTORICAL SOCIETY
50 (1947).

Military Records

Griffin, John A. Papers, 1860-69 (IHi)

> Diary written in 1862-63 when Griffin was a private in Company
> D, 17th Illinois Infantry. Includes letters from soldiers in the 53d
> U.S. Colored Infantry.

Griffith, Dr. David J., 1862-64 (ICHi)

> Civil War medical records, reporting the care of black troops, and

employment of black personnel.

Kendrick, John F. Papers, 1959 (ICHi)

Manuscript papers for MIDSUMMER PICNIC OF '98. Describes and evaluates work of Negro Troops of 24th U.S. Infantry and 8th Illinois Infantry in Cuba.

Newspapers

The Northern Illinois University Library has archives of the titles listed below, plus a large microfilm collection of other black newspapers. Current major black newspapers are located at the Johnson Publishing Company, Chicago.

BROADAX (Chicago). July 15, 1899, to 1927? Weekly.

Holdings: 1899 to September 10, 1927; CSdS, CtY, CU, DLC, FTaSU, ICU, IHi, MB, MnU, MoSW, NcU, TNF, WHi.

ILLINOIS RECORDS (Springfield). 1897?–1899? Weekly.

Holdings: November 8, 1897, to April 23, 1899; CSdS, CSS, CtY, DLC, FTaSU, IHi, InNd, MB, MdBJ, MnU, MoSW, NcU, NjP, TNF, WHi.

STATE CAPITAL (Springfield). 1886–1910? Weekly.

Holdings: March 13, 1891, to December 3, 1892 (incomplete); January 13, 1899; CSdS, CSS, CU, DLC, IHi, KHi, LU–NO, MdBMC, MiKW, TNF, WHi.

Personal Papers

Brotherhood of Sleeping Car Porters. Papers, 1925–69 (ICHi)

Membership records and letters. MS 71–41

Chew, Benjamin. Papers, 1770 (ICHi)

List of blacks in Whitehall, Pennsylvania.

Hector Davis and Company Account Books, 1857–65 (ICHi)

Richmond, Virginia, company, with superior ledgers of slave sales and food and doctor bills. Also at the Ethnic Genealogy Center at Queens College.

WPA Illinois Writers' Project (IC-H)

Files for "The Negro in Illinois," including interviews with early black settlers conducted in 1938-40.

Slavery Records

Chicago Historical Society Library

Large manuscript collection including bills of sale (some in French), marriage certificates, manumissions, and indentures. See THE DIRECTORY OF AFRO-AMERICAN RESOURCES described in chapter 2, pp. 16-17, for a partial listing of the library's relevant holdings.

Slavery Collection (ICIU)

Includes account and personal narratives.

Chapter 31
INDIANA (Midwest)

The earliest mention of blacks in Indiana concerned a post on the Wabash River in 1746 which had forty white men and five blacks. Later, in 1763, a cargo of blacks was purchased in Jamaica and brought to Kaskaskia, Illinois, which is located on the Mississippi River. However, most blacks arrived in Indiana in three other ways: (1) as free persons, recently emancipated in the South, particularly North Carolina; (2) as slaves coming with white owners; and (3) as fugitive slaves on the Underground Railroad.

Slaves began arriving with white settlers around 1810, coming mainly from Kentucky, South Carolina, Tennessee, and Virginia. Most settled in Knox County, Indiana, before moving to other areas of the state. As in Illinois, blacks were required to register with the courts upon emigration to the Northwest Territory after 1831. Apparently these records are not complete. In addition, many free blacks acquired land upon arrival and their names were, consequently, entered into land records. In most cases there are no racial designations, but knowing the name will then make it possible to trace the ownership of land. These land entries have been copied by Margaret R. Walters and are available at the Indiana State Library.

The black population increased rapidly between 1816 and 1860. By 1860 a total of 11,428 blacks were in the state, with the largest group coming from North Carolina, followed by Virginia, Kentucky, Ohio (with 826), Tennessee (with 600), and a low total of 329 from South Carolina, Georgia, Mississippi, Alabama, and Louisiana combined.

In the 1870s, the Emigrant Aid Society, sponsored by the Society of Friends, helped thousands of blacks from North Carolina migrate to Indianapolis. It would be of great value to locate the society's records for possible genealogical data. By the 1880s more blacks were migrating from Kentucky and Tennessee, but some Indiana counties barred their entry. Consequently, research will necessarily be concentrated around the most heavily black-populated areas.

The following books will be helpful for research in Indiana:

Lyda, John W. THE NEGRO IN THE HISTORY OF INDIANA. Terre Haute, Ind.: The author, 1953.

Thornbrough, Emma Lou. THE NEGRO IN INDIANA: A STUDY OF A MINORITY. Indiana Historical Collections, vol. 37. Indianapolis: Indiana Historical Bureau, 1957.

> The population data reported above was taken from this book, which is demographic in nature, but still helpful for genealogical purposes.

Finally, some blacks will find that their ancestors in Indiana may have intermarried with native Americans in that territory. Such intermarriage was prevalent especially along the western frontier; consequently, some research into tribal patterns and the history of Indiana tribes might be helpful.

FEDERAL RECORDS

Mortality Records

1850–80 (In)

Population Schedules

1820–80 and 1900 (DNA); 1820–80 (InFw, In, and Valparaiso, Rockville, La Porte public libraries). Other libraries in the state have schedules for a few years.

STATE AND COUNTY RECORDS

The Order Book of the General Court of Indiana Territory, the Order Book of the court of common pleas, and the circuit court records of Knox, Harrison, and Clark counties all contain manumission records and other matters pertaining to slaves and free blacks. These records, like most Indiana county records, have been microfilmed. For a list of those available see:

Childs, Sergeant Burrage, and Holmes, Dorothy P. CHECKLIST OF HISTORICAL RECORDS SURVEY PUBLICATIONS. WPA Technical Service, Research and Records Bibliography, no. 7. 1943. Reprint. Baltimore: Genealogical Publishing Co., 1969.

Knox County

> Barekman, June Beverly. REGISTER OF NEGRO SLAVES AND MASTERS FOR 1805-7 KNOX COUNTY: INDIANA TERRITORY. Abstracted by June and Ruth Barekman. Chicago: Bar(r)ackman-Bar(r)ickman-Barkman-Barekman Family Association, 1970.

The original is also available (In).

Indentures

These records give information on place of origin. In some cases blacks signed themselves over for indenture because of lack of support or because of the desire to migrate to Indiana.

Clark County

Register of Negroes, 1805–10 (In)

Indentures (see note for Barekman, above)

MISCELLANEOUS RECORDS

Cemetery Records

Indiana State Library has some cemetery records. Other availability not known.

Church Records

Quaker Archives--Earlham College Library

Includes material on Underground Railroad activities and Society of Friends Indiana Yearly Meetings, 1826–1920. Contains minutes of the Committee on the Concerns of People of Colour, 1821–68, and the Executive Committee on Freedmen, 1864–65.

St. Francis Xavier Parish Records, 1749–1838 (In)

Six volumes of records with some baptisms of blacks, from the period beginning 1753.

Diaries

Availability not known.

Military Records

Availability not known.

Newspapers

In addition to the collections cited below for the FREEMAN, the Public Library of Fort Wayne and Allen County also has a large microfilm collection of black newspapers.

FREEMAN (Indianapolis). 1884-1926? Weekly.

    Holdings: December 2, 1886, to 1916 (incomplete); CSdS, CSS, CtY, DLC, InNd, MB, MdBJ, MnU, MoSW, NcU, NjP, TNF, TxF, TxFS.

    July 21, 1888, to 1916 (incomplete); CU, FTaSU, ICU, McP, WHi.

    February 1892 to November 1, 1924 (incomplete); In.

Personal Papers and Slavery Records

Indiana Historical Society Library, Indianapolis.

    Card file references on material on blacks in Indiana.

Indiana State Library, Indianapolis.

    Fugitive Slave Cases.

Chapter 32

IOWA (Midwest)

In many midwestern states, as was the case in Iowa, restrictions were placed on black migration. Beginning April 1, 1839, no black or "mulatto" was to be permitted to settle in Iowa unless he or she could present "a fair certificate of actual freedom under a seal of a judge and give bond of $500 as surety against becoming public charges." This obviously prevented many free blacks from coming to Iowa. By the 1840s only 333 free blacks were living in this state, while after 1865, the black population in Iowa tripled. Most of those coming into Iowa came from Missouri and other points down the Mississippi and Ohio rivers.

The following collection may contain black genealogical information: Iowa. State Historical Society. GUIDE TO MANUSCRIPTS. Compiled by Katherine Harris. Iowa City, 1973.

FEDERAL RECORDS

Mortality Schedules

> 1850-80 (IaHi)

Population Schedules

> 1840-80, 1900, 1844, 1846 Territorial Census (DNA); 1840-80 (IaCfT)

Special Census--none

STATE RECORDS

The Department of Archives and History in the Iowa Historical Library has all the census records for Iowa, in addition to the mortality schedules. There is also a state census for 1856 which lists free blacks. Availability of any additional state or county records related specifically to blacks is not known.

MISCELLANEOUS RECORDS

Cemetery Records

Availability not known.

Church Records

Iowa Conference Historical Society of the United Methodist Church. Records, 1844-? (IaU)

> Records of freedmen's organization.

Diaries

Availability not known.

Military Records

Iowa. Adjutant-General's Office. ROSTER AND REGISTER OF IOWA SOLDIERS IN THE WAR OF THE REBELLION. 32D-48TH REGIMENTS-INFANTRY, 1ST REGIMENT AFRICAN INFANTRY AND 1ST-4TH BATTERIES LIGHT ARTILLERY. Vol. 5. Des Moines: E.H. Engist, State Printer, 1908-11.

> Lists the members of the only black regiment in the Civil War from Iowa. (IaHi)

Strong, George W. Papers, 1863-1908 (IaU)

> Collection includes letters, memos, orders, and supplies of Strong as Commander of Company H, 1st Regiment of Tennessee Infantry, African Descent and 59th Colored Infantry, Regiment 16th Corps, 1863-65.

Newspapers

IOWA BYSTANDER (Des Moines). 1894-- . Weekly.

> Title varies as BYSTANDER; IOWA STATE BYSTANDER.
> Holdings: 1896-- ; IaDH.

1896–1900; CSdS, CtY, DLC, FTaSU, IaDM, InNd, MB, MdBJ, MnU, MoSW, NcU, NjP, TNF, WHi.

Personal Papers

Iowa Wesleyan College Archives, Mt. Pleasant (IaMpl)
First black students' graduation, 1885; 1887; 1891.

Slavery Records

Not available.

Chapter 33

MICHIGAN (Midwest)

County histories for most counties of Michigan have been published and are of special importance for background reading. Many of the records for these counties are listed in the U.S. Works Progress Administration's INVENTORY OF THE COUNTY ARCHIVES OF MICHIGAN (Detroit: Historical Records Survey Project, 1940).

The following books provide a good sense of the role blacks played in history of Michigan and are, therefore, recommended for background reading:

Banner, Melvin E. THE BLACK PIONEER IN MICHIGAN. Midland, Mich.: Pendell Publishing Co., 1973.

   See annotation directly below.

Larrie, Reginald. BLACK EXPERIENCES IN MICHIGAN HISTORY. Lansing: Michigan History Division, Michigan Department of State, 1975.

   Both of the above are short, but contain good bibliographical references.

Michigan. Department of State. ALPHABETICAL GENERAL INDEX TO PUBLIC LIBRARY SETS OF 85,271 NAMES OF MICHIGAN SOLDIERS AND SAILORS INDIVIDUAL RECORDS. Lansing: Wynkoop Hallenbeck Crawford Co., 1915.

   This index is available at the Michigan State Archives (Mi-HC) and the Genealogical Department (Microfilm Order # USIGD 915, 948). Blacks are identified in this index by "1st Mich. Col. Inf.," the First Michigan Colored Infantry which is also known as the 102d U.S. Colored Infantry.

Woodson, June Baber. "A Century with the Negroes of Detroit, 1830-1930."

   Master's thesis, Wayne University, 1949.

Michigan

FEDERAL RECORDS

Mortality Schedules
      1860-80 (DNDAR, MiHi)

Population Schedules
      1820-80 and 1900 (DNA); 1820-80 (MiU, MiD, Mi, MiMtpt)

Special Census 1890 (DNA, Mi, MiMtpt, MiD)

STATE AND COUNTY RECORDS

Two good places for beginning research are the Burton Historical Collection of
the Detroit Public Library, which is a collection of genealogy and local history
resources; and the Michigan State Archives and Library at the Michigan History
Division, which has state, municipal, and county records on microfilm.

In addition, the Michigan Historical Commission, now the Michigan History
Division, located in Lansing, has state census records for 1864-94. They list
individuals, indicating race and place of origin. A second group of records
found here are the Executive Office Records, 1810-1910, which include material
on criminal cases concerning minorities.

Records for the French period in Michigan can be found in the Canadian Archives and Paris Archives.

MISCELLANEOUS RECORDS

Cemetery Records

Availability not known.

Church Records

American Home Missionary Society Records, 1825-47 (MiU)
      Five reels of microfilm dealing with the mission's work. Genea-
      logical material on blacks is probably included.

Diaries

Bell, Sir William, 1830-33 (MiU)

Notes on Barbados, slavery, and Gibraltar. MS 62-2076

Perry, Mr. (MiU)

Undated diary of a black who escaped and settled in Cass County, Michigan. MS 65-1355

Reed, Seth, 1863 (MiU)

U.S. Christian Commission with the Army of the Cumberland in Tennessee and Alabama; observations of slavery, guerillas, hospitalization, etc. MS 65-506

Military Records

Hopper, George C. FIRST MICHIGAN INFANTRY, THREE MONTHS AND THREE YEARS. PROCEEDINGS OF 1891 REUNION AT DETROIT. BRIEF HISTORY OF THE REGIMENT. ROSTER OF SURVIVING MEMBERS. Coldwater, Mich.: Coldwater Courier Printing, 1891.

Michigan. Adjutant General's Office. 1ST MICHIGAN COLORED INFANTRY (102ND UNITED STATES COLORED INFANTRY). Vol. 46. Record of Service of Michigan Volunteers in the Civil War, 1861-65. Kalamazoo, Mich.: Ihling Bros. & Everard, 1905.

Includes roster.

Warren, Francis H., comp. MICHIGAN MANUAL OF FREEDMEN'S PROGRESS. 1915. Reprint. Detroit: J.M. Greene, 1968.

Pages 217-56 include a roster of the 1st Michigan Colored Infantry.

Newspapers

MICHIGAN LIBERTY PRESS (Battle Creek). April 13, 1848, to 1849. Weekly.

Continues SIGNAL OF LIBERTY (see below).

Holdings: April to August 1848; MiD-B

PLAINDEALER (Detroit). May 16, 1883, to 1895? Weekly.

Holdings: September 1889 to May 1893; CSdS, CtY, DLC, InNd,

KHi, MB, MdBJ, Mi, MnU, NcU, NjP, TNF, WHi.

SIGNAL OF LIBERTY (Ann Arbor). April 26, 1841, to February 5, 1848. Weekly.

> Continued by MICHIGAN LIBERTY PRESS (see above).

> Holdings: 1841-48 (incomplete); MiD-B.

Personal Papers and Slavery Records

Gregg, Phineas. Papers, 1849-1925 (MiU)

> Records of the Saunders Colony of freed slaves in Calvin Township in Cass County. MS 65-286

Historical Records Survey, 1936-41 (MiU)

> Material used in compiling the WPA's INVENTORY OF THE COUNTY ARCHIVES (cited above), and HISTORY OF NEGROES IN MICHIGAN (MiD).

Burton Historical Collection, Detroit

> This collection contains extensive holdings of newspapers, diaries, manuscripts, and papers on the history of blacks in Michigan and the Old Northwest. Included are the papers of Fred Hart Williams, descendant of a black who was an early Detroit settler. Hart's papers include the manuscript of DETROIT HERITAGE: A HISTORY OF NEGROES IN DETROIT, written in 1957 with Hoyt Fuller; includes biographies.

Niles Public Library, Niles

> Underground Railroad source material, with list of slaves who traveled on it.

Chapter 34

MINNESOTA (Midwest)

Some of the first blacks to come to Minnesota were engaged in fur-trading activities during the early nineteenth century. Many of these blacks came from St. Louis and were hired by fur companies for the work in Minnesota. Other blacks came from Ohio, Maryland, New England, and Canada as servants of army officers. Those who came from the South were usually brought by white southerners on visits to the North. Very few blacks, however, entered Minnesota in the period preceding the Civil War because of the limited economic opportunities. After 1860, the black population doubled, and by 1880 it had tripled. All but one of the counties with black residents were located along the Mississippi River, which shows the great influence of the river as a highway for black migration.

One of the largest migrations of blacks ended on May 6, 1863, when about three hundred men, women, and children arrived in St. Paul by steamboat from St. Louis. The second largest group had arrived the previous day when 218 blacks arrived aboard the steamboat DAVENPORT from St. Louis. The following books are sources of this information and present a good view of blacks in Minnesota:

Spangler, Earl. BIBLIOGRAPHY OF NEGRO HISTORY: SELECTED AND AN-NOTATED ENTRIES, GENERAL AND MINNESOTA. Minneapolis: Ross and Haines, 1963.

A 101-page annotated bibliography about blacks in Minnesota.

_____. THE NEGRO IN MINNESOTA. Minneapolis: T.S. Denison, 1961.

See pages 186-213 for a fine bibliography.

Taylor, David Vassar. BLACKS IN MINNESOTA: A PRELIMINARY GUIDE TO HISTORICAL SOURCES. Publications of the Minnesota Historical Society. St. Paul, 1976.

FEDERAL RECORDS

Mortality Schedules

1850-70 (DNDAR, USIGD); 1870 (DNA)

Population Schedules

1850-80 and 1900; 1849 and 1857 Territorial Census (DNA); 1850-80 (MnHi, Mn-Ar)

Special Census 1890 (DNA and Gustavus Adolphus College, St. Peter)

STATE RECORDS

The Minnesota Historical Society in St. Paul is the place to begin Minnesota research. It has, among other things, a full alphabetical biographical file of current information on early Minnesotans and a name index for the federal censuses of 1850, 1857, and 1860.

MISCELLANEOUS RECORDS

Cemetery Records

Availability not known.

Church Records

Pilgrim Baptist Church (MnHi)

Records of this and other churches are available at the historical society and do contain genealogical information.

Diaries

Availability not known.

Military Records

Montgomery, Thomas. Letters, 1862-67 (MnHi)

Captain of Company I, 65th Regiment, and Company B, 67th Regiment, of U.S. Colored Infantry. Includes information on a black farming community in St. Peter Land District, Minnesota. MS 60-1360

Newspapers

AFRO-AMERICAN ADVANCE (Minneapolis). 1899-1903? Weekly.

Continues TWIN CITY AMERICAN.

Holdings: May 27, 1899, to November 17, 1900; CSdS, CSS, CU, DLC, FTaSU, KHi, LU-NO, MdBMC, MiKW, MnHi, TNF.

APPEAL (St. Paul). 1899-1923. Weekly.

Continues WESTERN APPEAL (see below). Merged with NORTH-WESTERN BULLETIN and became NORTHWESTERN BULLETIN-APPEAL.

Holdings: February 23, 1889, to December 3, 1892 (incomplete); September 1894 to June 1897 (incomplete); July 1897 to November 24, 1923; CSdS, CtY, DLC, InNd, MB, MnHi, NcU, NjP, TNF.

BROAD AXE (St. Paul). 1891-1903. Weekly.

Holdings: September 17, 1891, to June 11, 1903; CSdS, CtY, DLC, FTaSU, ICU, InNd, MB, MnHi, NcU, NjP, TNF.

NEGRO WORLD (St. Paul). 1892-- . Weekly.

Holdings: July 23 to September 10, 1892 (incomplete); March 10 to June 2, 1900 (incomplete); CSdS, CSS, CU, DLC, FTaSU, KHi, LU-NO, MdBMC, MiKW, TNF.

WESTERN APPEAL (St. Paul). 1885-88. Weekly.

Continued by APPEAL (see above).

Holdings: June 13 to July 18, 1885; March 1887 to 1888; CSdS, CtY, DLC, FTaSU, InNd, MB, MnHi, NcU, NjP, TNF.

Personal Papers and Slavery Records

Bailey, Everett Hoskins. Family Papers, 1839-1954 (MnHi)

Boxes of material on black education. MS 62-1613

Bishop, Judson Wade. Family Papers, 1856-1917 (MnHi)

Contents of these papers are available on an inventory sheet at the Minnesota Historical Society.

Gilman, Robbins. Family Papers, 1699-1952 (MnHi)

Large collection of information on blacks in Minneapolis.

Keckley, Elizabeth, 1868-1936 (MnHi)

Items related to her are listed on an inventory sheet at the Minnesota Historical Society.

Minnesota Annals (MnHi)

Material covering 1852-87, assembled by Works Progress Administration writers' project. Reports early life of blacks in Minnesota. Contains oral histories of four blacks who migrated to Minnesota.

Persons, Irene (MnHi)

Reports an interview with Mrs. Sally Dover, nee Sally Brown, Minneapolis, 1937. Mrs. Dover was a descendant of a white man and black woman slave of Virginia.

Chapter 35
MISSOURI (Midwest)

There is considerable historical material for the study of black ancestry in Missouri. It would be best to begin at the State Historical Society of Missouri in Columbia, where tax books, probate records, and court records are available.

The following articles all appeared in the MISSOURI HISTORICAL REVIEW, which should be available at most research libraries:

Blassingame, John W. "The Recruitment of Negro Troops in Missouri during the Civil War." MISSOURI HISTORICAL REVIEW 58 (1964): 326-38.

Bowen, Elbert R. "Negro Minstrels in Early Rural Missouri." MISSOURI HISTORICAL REVIEW 47 (1953): 103-9.

DeArmond, Fred. "Reconstruction in Missouri." MISSOURI HISTORICAL REVIEW 61 (1967): 364-77.

_____. "The Underground Railroad and the Missouri Borders." MISSOURI HISTORICAL REVIEW 37 (1943): 271-85.

Nelson, Earl J. "Missouri Slavery, 1861-1865." MISSOURI HISTORICAL REVIEW 28 (1934): 260-74.

Sampson, F.A., and Breckenridge, W.C. "Bibliography of Slavery and Civil War in Missouri." MISSOURI HISTORICAL REVIEW 2 (1908): 320-32.

Slavens, George Everett. "The Missouri Negro Press, 1875-1920." MISSOURI HISTORICAL REVIEW 65 (1971): 505-26.

Trexler, Harrison A. "Slavery in Missouri Territory." MISSOURI HISTORICAL REVIEW 3 (1909): 179-98.

Wamble, Gaston Hugh. "Negroes and Missouri Protestant Churches before and after the Civil War." MISSOURI HISTORICAL REVIEW 61 (1967): 321–47.

In addition, the State Historical Society of Missouri has a superior bibliography of background books relevant to black genealogical research in many states, which are available for research at the society. The few listed below are only a small sample of those about Missouri and are all located at the society. Most, however, are not available in New York City libraries and are likely to be difficult to locate except through the historical society itself. In most cases their contents and publishers are not listed by the society, and they may represent a variety of attitudes about blacks and slaves. For further information write directly to the society.

Bundsche, Henry A. SOME ASPECTS OF SLAVERY IN JACKSON COUNTY, MISSOURI. Kansas City, 1962.

Campbell, Rex Randall, and Robertson, Peter C. "Negroes in Missouri." Unpublished manuscript held by the Historical Society of Missouri, Columbia.

Fuller, Bernice Morrison. PLANTATION LIFE IN MISSOURI. St. Louis, 1935.

Lansdown, Albert Young, and Lansdown, William LeRoy, comps. THE GENERATIONS OF ANDREW THOMPSON AND SILVEY WILLIAMSON (THE STORY OF THE WILLIAM HENRY LANSDOWN FAMILY). White Plains, N.Y., 1972.

This should be read for more pointers on tracing your own family.

PORTRAITS AND BIOGRAPHICAL SKETCHES OF THE REPRESENTATIVE NEGRO MEN AND WOMEN OF MISSOURI AND KANSAS FOR DISTRIBUTION AT THE COTTON STATES AND INTERNATIONAL EXPOSITION TO BE HELD AT ATLANTA, GEORGIA, SEPT. 18 TO DEC. 31, 1895. Kansas City, Mo.: Charles W. Lee, 1895.

St. Louis. Public Library. THE JULIA DAVIS COLLECTION: NEGRO AND AFRICAN LITERATURE AND CULTURE, A BIBLIOGRAPHY. St. Louis, 1971.

FEDERAL RECORDS

Mortality Schedules
    1850–80 (MoSHi)

Population Schedules
    1830–88 and 1900 (DNA); 1830–80 (MoHi, MoS, MoIG)

Special Census 1890 (DNA, MoS, MoHi, MoIG)

Record Group 101 (DNA, MoHi)

> See chapter 4, p. 27, under Freedmen's Bureau, for a description of these records Missouri branches with deposits recorded: St. Louis.

Record Group 105 (DNA)

> See chapter 4, p. 27, under Freedmen's Bureau, for a description of these records. Missouri records contain school records.

STATE AND COUNTY RECORDS

Missouri county records are published and available in most genealogical libraries. In addition, the following are available at the State Historical Society of Missouri in Columbia:

Clay County

> Freed Negro Registry, 1836-56
>
>> Lists slaves freed between February 8, 1836, and January 7, 1856. There may be similar registers for other counties located elsewhere in the state.

Columbia, Missouri

> Social and Economic Census of the Colored Population, 1901
>
>> Consists of family reports listing members with ages, income, and living conditions.

Eldridge, William. MARRIAGE LICENSES INDEX, "COLORED," 1865-1891, INCLUSIVE. Liberty, Mo.: The author, 1971.

French and Spanish Archives, 1766-1803

> These St. Louis records of sales are on microfilm and indexed. They are similar to present-day recorder's office records and are in French and Spanish. Occasionally there is a record of a slave sale.

MISCELLANEOUS RECORDS

Cemetery Records

Many cemetery records have been published. However, it is not known whether any of these records indicate whether persons buried were black or not. Further work needs to be done in this area.

Church Records

African Methodist Episcopal Church Records (MoHi)

Baptist Association Records (MoHi)

Christian Church of Missouri, Annual Meetings (MoHi)

> All of the above are from the late nineteenth and early twentieth century period. The historical society indicates that the records are of relevance to blacks, but does not state their contents specifically.

Concordia Historical Institute, Concordia, Missouri

> Extensive records on Lutheran Church in Missouri, and its Synod missions in the South and Africa are held in this institute. The records are under restrictive usage.

Military Records

See MISSOURI HISTORICAL REVIEW articles listed above.

Newspapers

RISING SUN (Kansas City). 1869?-1919? Weekly.

> Holdings: January 27, 1900; January 16, 1903, to 1907 (incomplete); CSdS, CSS, DLC, FTaSU, TNF, WHi.

SEDALIA TIMES. 1894-1905? Weekly.

> Holdings: August 31, 1901, to December 19, 1903; January 21 to February 4, 1905; CSdS, CtY, DLC, InNd, MB, MdBJ, MnU, MoHi, MoSW, NcU, NjP, TNF, WHi.

See also the following:

Lincoln University. School of Journalism. NEGRO NEWSPAPERS IN THE UNITED STATES. Jefferson City, Mo.: 1962, 1964, 1966, 1970.

Personal Papers and Slave Records

Applegate, Lisbon. Papers, 1819-99 (MoHi)

Surveyor and county judge of Chariton County. Includes letters from the Civil War period and records the hiring and selling of slaves. MS 64-26

Bills of Sale for many families (MoHi)

Breckenridge Family Papers, 1750-1960 (MoHi)

Accounts of slave sales are included. MS 68-1310

Burt, Franklin. Papers, 1843-1903 (MoU)

Contains Calloway County tax records with an 1858 list of landowners and slaves. MS 60-1979

Conway, Joseph. Papers, 1798-1922 (MoSHi)

Conway was a St. Louis County pioneer. Bills of slave sales are included. MS 64-322

Corby Family Papers, 1801-1905 (MoU)

St. Joseph, Missouri, pioneers. Includes some bills of sale for slaves. MS 60-1993

Diamant, Henry A. Collection, 1805-75 (MoSHi)

Records emancipations and sale of slaves. MS 64-337

Elliott, Newton G. Papers, 1834-1909 (MoSHi)

Contains slave papers of Elliott of Howard County. MS 65-682

Emmons Family Papers, 1796-1938 (MoSHi)

Includes land and slavery papers. MS 65-683

Givens, Spencer H. Papers, 1816-1911 (MoU)

Givens was from Cooper County. Contains a bill of slave sale.

Hempstead, Stephen. Papers, 1754-1927 (MoSHi)

Includes four letters from Manuel Lisa. Farm tasks, occupation of Hempstead's slaves, and vital records are recorded. MS 68-1287

Hickman-Bryan. Papers, 1796-1920 (MoU)

Missouri, Louisiana, and Kentucky families with land and slave records. MS 60-1817

McCanse, William A. Papers, 1856-68 (MoHi)

Contains a letter and an agreement regarding ownership of slaves.

McKenzie, Kenneth. Papers, 1796-1918 (MoSHi)

Bills of sale for slaves, 1828-57. MS 65-695

Negro Association Collections (MoHi)

Includes over 200 groups of records and proceedings for black organizations in Missouri, such as Knights and Daughters of Tabor, Ancient Order of United Workmen, Independent Order of Odd Fellows, and Royal Sons and Daughters of Douglass.

Slavery Papers (MoHi)

Letters, manumissions, bills of sale, and records of hirings have been collected.

Smith, Thomas Adams. Papers, 1777-1919 (MoU)

Saline County landowners' and doctors' records of births, deaths, and sales of 180 slaves from 1777 to 1864. MS 62-4788

Snoddy, Daniel F. Papers, 1817-61 (MoU)

Includes Saline County bills of sale for slaves. MS 60-3103

Sublette Family Papers, 1848-54 (MoSHi)

Contains documents on runaway slaves and accounts with B.M. Lauch, slave dealer.

Tiffany, P. Dexter. Papers (MoSHi)

Many St. Louis County documents, including bonds of free negroes, fines on unlicensed free blacks, and an 1841-59 list of licensed free blacks in St. Louis.

Tucker, D.M., and Tucker, J.H.   Records, 1833–1902 (MoU)
   Fulton, Missouri slave sale records.   MS 60–2476

White, John R.   Record Book, 1846–60 (MoU)
   Names and relevant information on slaves.

Chapter 36

OHIO (Midwest)

The following published sources should provide good background reading in Ohio:

Alilunas, Leo. "Fugitive Slave Cases in Ohio Prior to 1850." OHIO STATE ARCHAEOLOGICAL AND HISTORICAL QUARTERLY 69 (1940): 160-84.

> This is one of a number of excellent articles published in this periodical which are of relevance to genealogical research of black families.

Davis, Russell H. BLACK AMERICANS IN CLEVELAND FROM GEORGE PEAKE TO CARL B. STOKES, 1796-1969. Washington, D.C.: Associated Publishers, 1972.

> Biographical in nature.

GUIDE TO MANUSCRIPTS COLLECTIONS AND INSTITUTIONAL RECORDS IN OHIO. Edited by David R. Larson. Columbus: Society of Ohio Archivists, 1974.

> Excellent resource which includes bibliographical references and an index of many Ohio records.

Hickok, Charles Thomas. THE NEGRO IN OHIO, 1802-1870. 1896. Reprint. New York: AMS Press, 1975.

> A bibliography is on pages 180-82.

Pih, Richard W. THE NEGRO IN CINCINNATI, 1802-1841. Oxford, Ohio: Miami University Press, 1968.

> Available at the Cincinnati Historical Society.

Wilson, C.J. "The Negro in Early Ohio." OHIO STATE ARCHAEOLOGICAL AND HISTORICAL QUARTERLY 39 (1930): 717-68.

Descriptive article; good background reading.

FEDERAL RECORDS

Mortality Schedules

1850-60 and 1880 (DNA)

Population Schedules

1820-80 and 1900 (DNA); 1820-80 (OHi, OC1WHi, and many other public and college libraries throughout the state)

Special Census 1890 (DNA, OU, OC1WHi, OOxM)

STATE AND COUNTY RECORDS

One of the first places to stop in Ohio is the Ohio Historical Society in Columbus. The society has several record books of Negroes that were maintained by several counties in the early nineteenth century. The record book for Ross County is on microfilm. In addition, the following sources are available at the society:

City Directories

Most major Ohio cities, from approximately 1850.

Columbus State Hospital Admissions Registers, 1838-1923; not indexed.

County History Collection

Published county histories and some transcripts of cemeteries and other Ohio county records. The Surname Index covers many of the published histories, while other books have their own indexes.

Franklin and Licking County Records

Some of these county records have been transferred to the State Archives. They are incomplete, and there are few indexes.

Naturalization Records

Some indexed, mostly for Franklin and Licking Counties.

Ohio Historical Society Guides

Lentz, Andrea D. A GUIDE TO MANUSCRIPTS AT THE OHIO HIS-

TORICAL SOCIETY. Columbus: Ohio Historical Society, 1972.

Yon, Paul D. GUIDE TO OHIO COUNTY AND MUNICIPAL RECORDS FOR URBAN RESEARCH. Columbus: Ohio Historical Society, 1973.

Published Genealogies

A very large collection of Ohio family histories.

State Penitentiary Register of Prisoners, 1834-1900; indexed by year.

State Property Tax Lists, 1801-38

Organized by county; only the 1812 list has an index. Microfilm copies of rolls can be purchased from the society.

Transcripts of County Records

Microfilm copies of records, completed by the Daughters of the American Revolution; not indexed.

The following materials are not held by the Ohio Historical Society:

Deeds

Mostly for land transactions; available at the various county seats.

Land Grant, Bounty Land, and Land Purchase Records

The earliest ones for Ohio are located at the Auditor of the State, Statehouse, Columbus, Ohio 43215.

Naturalization Records

Filed in the probate court of the county where the action took place, or in federal district courts.

MISCELLANEOUS RECORDS

Cemetery Records

Cemetery location lists are presently being compiled by the Ohio Genealogical Society.

Graves Registration File (OH)

Compiled by the adjutant general's office; includes all veterans, regardless of state of service, buried in Ohio.

Church Records

African Methodist Episcopal Church Records (OWibfU)

Records of the following former bishops have been retained:

Arnett, Benjamin William. Papers, 1860-1900. MS 60-886
Coppin, Levi Jenkins. Papers, 1888-1920. MS 60-884
Payne, Daniel Alexander. Collection of Negro Life and History, 1811-93.
Ransom, Reverdy Cassius. Papers, 1893-1951. MS 60-885

Allen's Chapel African Methodist Episcopal Church, 1854 (OCHP)

Williams, Samuel Wesley. Papers. MS 63-202

Contains a memorial of members.

Free Will Baptist Church. Records, 1819-1916 (OH). MS 68-1384

Society of Friends Papers, 1688-1937 (OH)

Mostly topical material, but may include some black genealogical sources.

Diaries

Birchard, Sardis, 1832-33; 1842-43; 1852 (OFH)

Travel diaries of trips to the South, Barbados, and the Caribbean. MS 61-1988

Brice, Albert G., 1858 (OCX)

Records the culture and accomplishments of American blacks.

Military Records

Clark, Peter H. THE BLACK BRIGADE OF CINCINNATI. New York: Arno Press, 1969.

Curry, William Leontes. Papers, 1832-1926 (OH)

Extensive microfilm collection of the Civil War in Ohio, including

Ohio U.S. Colored Troops. MS 75-966

Lyman, Carlos Parsons. Papers, 1795-1915 (OC1WHi)

Letters and diaries of officers of 100th U.S. Colored Infantry, 1861-65. MS 75-1608

Ohio Militia Records, 1807-67 (OHi)

Very fragile records arranged by numerical designation of units; not indexed and not complete. MS 75-1660

Palmer, William Pendleton. Collection, 1861-1927, (OC1WHi)

Letters on plantation life, and the Underground Railroad. The collection contains military records including casualty lists and lists of black regiments in the South. MS 62-438

Regimental Papers of Civil War, 1861-65

Extensive material on Ohio regiments. Contains papers of H.G. Crickmore and J.W. Paine of the 4th U.S. Colored Cavalry.

Risdon, Orlando Charles. Papers, 1861-72 (OC1WHi)

Organizer of the 53d U.S. Colored Infantry. MS 75-1698

Service Records (OC1WHi, OHi)

Ohio adjutant general's records of servicemen for the War of 1812, Mexican War, Civil War, Spanish-American War, and World War I. Indexed. MS 75-1858

Service Records (Soldiers Claims Division, Office of Adjutant General, State-house, Columbus)

Service records of all Ohio men who enlisted after World War I, and National Guardsmen since 1902.

Wesley, Charles Harris. OHIO NEGROES IN THE CIVIL WAR. Publications of the Ohio Civil War Centennial Commission, no. 6. Columbus: Ohio Historical Society, 1962.

Newspapers

In addition to those listed below, there are extensive collections of black newspapers at Kent State University, the Ohio Historical Society, and the Bell and Howell Corporation in Wooster. They cover many states and some from the latter two collections are available on microfilm.

FAMILY VISITOR (Cleveland & Hudson). January 3, 1850, to 1858? Weekly, biweekly.

Holdings: 1850 to May 10, 1853; McP.

GAZETTE (Cleveland). August 25, 1883, to May 20, 1945. Weekly.

Holdings: 1883-1945; CtY, CU, DLC, InNd, MB, MdBJ, MnU, NcU, NjP, OClWHi, TNF, TxFS, WHi.

UNION (Cincinnati)

Dabney, Wendell Phillips. Papers, 1905-64 (OCHP)

This collection contains material related to the fifty-year publication of the UNION, a Cincinnati black newspaper. Some issues from 1918-52 are included in Dabney's papers. MS 71-1532

Personal Papers and Slavery Records

Ashtabula County Female Anti-Slavery Society Records, 1835-37 (OClWHi)

List of members and memorialists for 1836. MS 75-1880

Bowen, George Washington. Notebook, 1851-62 (OClWHi)

Written at Cleveland Institute of Homeopathy. Bowen served in the 5th U.S. Colored Cavalry, 1864. MS 75-1861

Brown, John, Jr., and Brown, John., Sr.

The Ohio Historical Society has an extensive collection of papers of both John Brown, Jr., and John Brown, Sr., with many newspaper clippings, diaries, and letters (some written to fugitive slave Thomas Thomas). There are many other places in the country where John Brown's papers can be found. For a complete listing see DIRECTORY OF AFRO-AMERICAN RESOURCES described in chapter 2, pp. 16-17.

Cranch, William. Papers, 1790-1855 (OCHP)

Cranch was a Washington, D.C., jurist. Some material is related to slave trade. MS 63-166

Gholson, William Yates. Papers, 1795-1870 (OCHP)

Includes letters from Frances Wright (1795-1852), founder of the

Nashoba Colony of freedmen. MS 71-1538

Ladies Aid Society, Brocton, Ohio (OC1WHi)

Records for January 14 to February 15, 1866: The society was an auxiliary of the New York National Freedmen's Relief Association. MS 75-1880

Miscellaneous Legal Documents Collection, 1800-1860 (OHi)

Includes slave receipts and manumission papers. MS 75-1104

Peyton, Polly. Papers, 1850-61 (OHi)

Legal papers and letters concerning the kidnapping of Polly's eight children from Lawrence County, Ohio. She was a free black.

Pitkin, Perley Peabody. Papers, 1861-68 (OC1WHi)

Records wages of "contraband" slaves.

Rankin, John, 1798-1886 (OHi)

Recollections by members of Rankin's family of fugitive slaves who stayed at their home on the Underground Railroad in Ripley, Ohio.

Siebert, Wilbur Henry. Papers, 1866-1961 (OHi)

Notes and official documents relative to his book on the Underground Railroad. MS 68-1705

Walker, Timothy. Papers, 1806-56 (OCHP)

Information on African Education and Civilization Society and participants. MS 63-198

Chapter 37

WISCONSIN (Midwest)

There have been three periods in Wisconsin history: the French period, 1634–1760; the British period, 1760–83; and the federal period, from 1783 to the present. During the federal period, white families arrived in Wisconsin from Kentucky, Virginia, including what is now West Virginia, and North Carolina. As with other cases of migration, these families brought their slaves with them.

Davidson, John Nelson. NEGRO SLAVERY IN WISCONSIN AND THE UNDERGROUND RAILROAD. Parkman Club Publications, no. 18. Milwaukee: Printed for the Parkman Club by E. Keogh, 1897.

> Has an excellent presentation of the migration of slaves with their owners.

FEDERAL RECORDS

Mortality Schedules

> 1850–80 (WHi); 1850–70 (DNDAR); 1860–70 (WM)

Population Schedules

> 1820–80 and 1900 (DNA); 1820–80 (WHi); 1830–80 (WM); Territorial Censuses 1836, 1842, 1846, 1847 (DNA)

Special Census 1890 (DNA, WM, WU)

STATE AND COUNTY RECORDS

Vital records are located in each county, with duplicates at the Bureau of Vital Records in Madison. Two additional sources for state and county records are the Detroit Society for Genealogical Research's publication of PRINTED RESOURCES FOR GENEALOGICAL SEARCHING IN WISCONSIN, completed in 1964, and the WISCONSIN MAGAZINE OF HISTORY published quarterly by the State Historical Society of Wisconsin in Madison and available at most research libraries. The Rock County Historical Society in Janesville has a fine collection of materials on blacks in their area covering the years 1895–1950.

MISCELLANEOUS RECORDS

Cemetery Records, Church Records, and Diaries

Availability not known.

Military Records

Gilson, Norman Shepard. Papers, 1860–1901 (WHi)

> Muster rolls for the 58th Infantry Regiment of U.S. Colored Troops from Wisconsin. MS 62–2651

Newspapers

NORTHWESTERN RECORDER (Milwaukee). 1892–93. Weekly, monthly, and irregular.

> Continues WISCONSIN AFRO-AMERICAN (see below).

> Holdings: December 3, 1892; January 14, 1893; February–March 1893; CSdS, CSS, CU, DLC, KHi, LU-NO, MdBMC, MiKW, TNF, WHi.

WISCONSIN AFRO-AMERICAN (Milwaukee). April to November, 1892. Weekly, monthly, and irregular.

> Continued by NORTHWESTERN RECORDER (see above).

> Holdings: August 13 to November 19, 1892 (incomplete); CSdS, CSS, CU, DLC, KHi, LU-NO, MdBMC, MiKW, TNF.

WISCONSIN WEEKLY ADVOCATE (Milwaukee). 1898–1915. Weekly.

> Holdings: May 1898 to September 19, 1907; CSdS, CtY, DLC, FTaSU, InNd, MB, MdBJ, MnU, MoSW, NcU, NjP, TNF, WHi.

The State Historical Society of Wisconsin has a collection of black newspapers, but its contents are not stated. See also Donald E. Oehlerts's GUIDE TO WISCONSIN NEWSPAPERS, 1833–1957 (Madison: Wisconsin State Historical Society, 1958), which should be available in large libraries.

Personal Papers and Slavery Records

Remsen, Peter A.   Papers, 1817–52 (WHi)

>   Letters in 1820s concerning rescue of Henry Hicks, an indentured
>   black apprentice.   MS 62–2876

Shepard, Charles.   Papers, 1850–1958 (WHi)

>   Shepard was a freed slave and farmer of Beetown Township in
>   Grant County.   The collection includes family letters and manu-
>   scripts containing Grant County history.   MS 61–1057

The State Historical Society of Wisconsin has published a GUIDE TO MANU-
SCRIPTS, edited by Alice E. Smith (1944), which should be available in most
research libraries.   In addition, the society houses the extensive Draper Collection of Manuscripts.   While the published guide is presently out of print,
Dr. Josephine L. Harper, Reference Curator, is working on a revision of its
descriptive list which will include references to blacks.   She notes that there
are few such references in this vast collection, but those found may be important clues for tracing black ancestors.

Chapter 38

WESTERN STATES

Most of the states west of the Missouri were admitted to the Union after the Emancipation Proclamation. This historical fact changes both the quantity and quality of records available for black genealogical research. For the most part, the records relating to blacks are located in the usual genealogical sources-- federal and state records, vital statistics, wills, deeds, and county records. There are, however, two sources which are essential for western research on black families:

Abajian, James de T., ed. BLACKS AND THEIR CONTRIBUTIONS TO THE AMERICAN WEST: A BIBLIOGRAPHY AND UNION LIST OF LIBRARY HOLD-INGS THROUGH 1970. Boston: G.K. Hall, 1974.

> Lists individual biographies and autobiographies of black pioneers, tape recordings of blacks, books that detail the migration trails of blacks, list of residential directories in the West which designate blacks by name, bibliography of books on black churches and fraternal organizations, lists of newspapers and periodicals relating to blacks in Colorado, Montana, Nevada, Oregon, Utah, Washington, and other western states.

Davis, Lenwood G. BLACKS IN THE AMERICAN WEST: A WORKING BIBLI-OGRAPHY. 2d ed. Council of Planning Librarians, Exchange Bibliography, no. 984. Monticello, Ill.: 1976.

Durham, Philip, and Jones, Everett L. THE NEGRO COWBOYS. New York: Dodd, Mead, 1965.

> An interesting and often overlooked aspect of blacks in the West.

Katz, William Loren. THE BLACK WEST. Rev. ed. Garden City, N.Y.: Anchor Press, 1973.

> Excellent for information on blacks who went west; gives ideas on migratory patterns and early settlements of blacks.

Savage, William Sherman. BLACKS IN THE WEST. Contributions in Afro-American and African Studies, no. 23. Westport, Conn.: Greenwood Press, 1976.

> Descriptive and bibliographical.

The states included in this chapter have few sources for black genealogical research. The headings which follow represent western states with published sources, federal records, state records, or miscellaneous records. Abajian's and Katz's books (see above) should be consulted for additional sources.

ALASKA

Federal Records

Mortality Schedules--none

Population Schedules

> 1870-80 and 1900 (DNA)

Special Census--none

Newspapers

No eighteenth- or nineteenth-century black newspapers are now available for this state.

ARIZONA

The Arizona Pioneers Historical Society in Tucson has a limited group of materials on black pioneers, including the following:

Culin, Beppie. Papers, 1850-1900 (AzTP)

> Over 324 items of correspondence regarding bills of sale for slaves. MS 61-3576

Federal Records

Mortality Schedules

> 1870, 1880 (DNA, DNDAR)

Population Schedules

    1870-80 and 1900 (DNA); 1870-80 (AzML, Az); Territorial Censuses
1864, 1866, 1867, 1869 (DNA, Az)

Special Census--none

Newspapers

No eighteenth- or nineteenth-century black newspapers are now available for
Arizona.

COLORADO

Federal Records

Mortality Schedules

    1870-80 and 1885 (DNA); 1870-80 (DNDAR)

Population Schedules

    1860-80, 1885, and 1900 (DNA); 1860-80 (CoD); 1860-80 and
1885 (CoU)

Special Census--none

Miscellaneous Records

NEWSPAPERS

Oehlerts, Donald E. GUIDE TO COLORADO NEWSPAPERS, 1859-1963.
Denver: Bibliographical Center for Research, Rocky Mountain Region, 1964.

    Lists black newspapers and the locations of some files.

DENVER STAR. 1889-- . Weekly.

    Holdings: January 27, 1900; December 10, 1910, to January 3,
1914; WHi.

    November 23, 1912 to October 1918; CoHi.

PERSONAL PAPERS AND SLAVERY RECORDS

The State Historical Society of Colorado Library and Museum in Denver has some materials relating to contributions blacks made to Colorado's growth. Also, the Works Progress Administration papers for 1930-35, containing unpublished interviews with early black pioneers, are available at the society.

Atkins, James A., 1890-1968 (CoHi)

> Pioneer black educator's personal papers. MS 74-83

Lewis, Junius R. Papers (CoHi)

> A Boulder County, Colorado, black miner. MS 71-1592

IDAHO

Federal Records

Mortality Schedules
> 1870-80 (IdHi)

Population Schedules
> 1870-80 and 1900 (DNA); 1870-80 (IdHi)

Special Census--none

Newspapers

No eighteenth- or nineteenth-century black newspapers are now available for this state.

MONTANA

Thompson, Lucille Smith, and Jacobs, Alma Smith. THE NEGRO IN MONTANA, 1800-1945: A SELECTIVE BIBLIOGRAPHY. Helena: Montana State Library, 1970.

> One of a very few sources which has information on blacks in Montana.

Federal Records

Mortality Schedules
> 1870-80 (DNA, MtHi)

Population Schedules
> 1860-80 and 1900 (DNA)

Special Census 1890 (DNA)

Newspapers

No eighteenth- or nineteenth-century black newspapers are now available for this state.

NEBRASKA

Nebraska. State Historical Society. A GUIDE TO THE ARCHIVES AND MANUSCRIPTS OF THE NEBRASKA STATE HISTORICAL SOCIETY. Compiled by Douglas A. Bakken, Duane J. Reed, and Harold E. Kemble. Historical Society Bulletin, no. 3. Lincoln, 1967.

Federal Records

Mortality Schedules
> 1860-80, 1885 (DNA); 1860-80 (NbHi)

Population Schedules
> 1860-80*, 1885, and 1900 (DNA); 1860-85 (NbHi)

Special Census 1890 (DNA)

*The 1860 Census for Kerney County names five slaves; Oteo County lists ten slaves, but they are not named.

Miscellaneous Records

NEWSPAPERS

AFRO-AMERICAN SENTINEL (Omaha). October 1896 to March? 1899. Weekly.

> Holdings: February 1896 to March 1899 (incomplete); CSdS, CtY, DLC, InNd, MB, MdBJ, MnU, MoSW, NcU, TNF, WHi.

ENTERPRISE (Omaha). January 1893 to 1914? Weekly.

> Holdings: August 1895 to July 1897 (incomplete); January 12, 1900; DLC, TNF, WHi
>
> August 1895 to July 1897 (incomplete); CSdS, CSS, CtY, InNd, MB, MdBJ, MnU, MoSW, NcU, NjP.

PERSONAL PAPERS AND SLAVERY RECORDS

Day, Mrs. Lee. Letters (NbHi)

> Experiences of early black homesteaders in Nebraska.

Delta Sigma Theta Collection of Negro History and Culture (NbO)

> Fine collection of life and history of blacks; mostly books.

Nebraska Negro Historical Society Library, Lincoln.

> The library has collections of material related to blacks in Nebraska.

Nebraska State Farmers Alliance Records, 1874-1920 (NbHi)

> Includes mailing lists, petitions, letters, and biographical sketches of members.

NEVADA

Federal Records

Mortality Schedules

> 1860-80 (NvHi); 1870 (DNDAR)

Population Schedules
>1870–80 and 1900 (DNA, NvL); 1870–80 (NvU) and a few others.

Special Census 1890 (DNA, NvL, NvU)

Newspapers

No eighteenth- or nineteenth-century black newspapers are now available for this state.

NEW MEXICO

Federal Records

Mortality Schedules
>1885 (DNA, NmU)

Population Schedules
>1850–80, 1885, and 1900 (DNA); 1850 and 1880 (NmU)

Special Census 1890 (DNA, NmU)

Newspapers

No eighteenth- or nineteenth-century black newspapers are now available for this state.

NORTH AND SOUTH DAKOTA

Federal Records

Mortality Schedules
>1880 (USIGD); 1885 (NdHi, SdHi)

Population Schedules
>1860–80 and 1885 (DNA, SdHi); 1900 (DNA); 1880–85 (NdHi)

Special Census 1890 (DNA, SdHi)

Newspapers

No eighteenth- or nineteenth-century black newspapers are now available for this state.

OREGON

Two bibliographies are helpful for research in Oregon:

Brownell, Jean B. "Negroes in Oregon before the Civil War." Unpublished manuscript. Oregon Historical Society Library, n.d.

    Contains a twenty-five-page bibliography.

Davis, Lenwood G. BLACKS IN THE STATE OF OREGON, 1788-1971: A BIBLIOGRAPHY OF PUBLISHED WORKS AND UNPUBLISHED SOURCE MATERIALS ON THE LIFE AND ACHIEVEMENTS OF BLACK PEOPLE IN THE BEAVER STATE. 2d ed. Council of Planning Librarians, Exchange Bibliography, no. 616. Monticello, Ill.: 1974.

Federal Records

Mortality Schedules
    1850-80 (Or-Ar)

Population Schedules
    1850-80* (DNA, Or-Ar, OrHi); and 1900 (DNA)

Special Census 1890 (DNA, Or-Ar, OrHi)

*There were a few black families who were living in Oregon by the 1850 census. In addition, there were several blacks listed who apparently had no family ties in Oregon.

Miscellaneous Records

NEWSPAPERS

PORTLAND NEW AGE. 1896-1907. Weekly.
    Holdings: November 25, 1899, to May 4, 1907; OrU.

January 27, 1900 to April 20, 1907 (incomplete); CSdS, CSS, CtY, DLC, MB, MdBJ, MnU, MoSW, NcU, NjP, TNF, WHi.

PERSONAL PAPERS

Shannon, Wesley. Correspondence, 1850–84 (OrHi)
Some letters relating to free blacks. MS 72–1676

UTAH

There are three excellent but short sources for research in black genealogy in Utah:

Carter, Kate B. THE NEGRO PIONEER. Salt Lake City: Utah Printing, 1965.

Davis, Lenwood G. BLACKS IN THE STATE OF UTAH: A WORKING BIBLIOGRAPHY. Council of Planning Librarians, Exchange Bibliography, no. 661. Monticello, Ill.: 1974.

Lythgoe, Dennis Leo. "Negro Slavery in Utah." Master's thesis, University of Utah, 1966.

Federal Records

Mortality Schedules
   1850–80 (DNA); 1870 (Tx)

Population Schedules
   1850–80* and 1900 (DNA); 1850–80 (US1GD, UPB, UL)

Special Census 1890 (DNA, US1GD, UL)

*The Slave Schedules for Davis and Salt Lake counties list twenty-nine slaves by name in 1850. The 1860 Slave Schedules enumerate twenty-six slaves living in Utah County, but they are not named; one was en route to California.

Newspapers

BROADAX (Salt Lake City). 1895 to June 6, 1899. Weekly.
   Holdings: August 31, 1895, to 1899; CSdS, CtY, DLC, FTaSU, ICU, MB, MdBJ, MnU, NcU, TNF, WHi.

WASHINGTON

Three sources for Washington are:

Davis, Lenwood G. BLACKS IN THE PACIFIC NORTHWEST, 1788-1974: A BIBLIOGRAPHY OF PUBLISHED WORKS AND OF UNPUBLISHED SOURCE MATERIALS ON THE LIFE AND CONTRIBUTIONS OF BLACK PEOPLE IN THE PACIFIC NORTHWEST. 2d ed. Council of Planning Librarians, Exchange Bibliography, nos. 767 and 768. Monticello, III., 1975.

Hanford, Cornelius Holgate, ed. SEATTLE AND ENVIRONS: 1852-1924. 3 vols. Chicago: Pioneer Historical Publishing Co., 1924.

> Contains a list of blacks who served in World War I from that area (p. 664).

Washington. State Library, Olympia. THE NEGRO IN THE STATE OF WASHINGTON, 1788-1969: A BIBLIOGRAPHY OF PUBLISHED WORKS AND OF UNPUBLISHED SOURCE MATERIALS ON THE LIFE AND ACHIEVEMENTS OF THE NEGRO IN THE EVERGREEN STATE. Olympia: The author, 1968. (Microfiche).

> One of the few bibliographies on blacks in Washington. It covers much of the manuscript sources in the library.

Federal Records

Mortality Schedules

> 1860-80 (DNDAR, Wa)

Population Schedules

> 1860-80 (DNA, Wa, WaSp, WaHi); 1900 (DNA)

Special Census 1890 (DNA, Wa, WaHi, WaSp)

Newspapers

SEATTLE REPUBLICAN. 1894-1915? Weekly.

> Holdings: February 26, 1896, to 1907 (incomplete); Wa, WaU.

WYOMING

Federal Records

Mortality Schedules
    1870–80 (DNDAR)

Population Schedules
    1860–80 and 1900 (DNA); 1860–80 (Wy–Ar)

Special Census 1890 (DNA, Wy–Ar)

Newspapers

No eighteenth- or nineteenth-century black newspapers are now available for this state.

Chapter 39
CALIFORNIA (West)

Many blacks, whether slave or free, followed the same pioneer trails as white families across the western plains. Some came by way of the great port of San Francisco from the port states in the East, particularly New England.

Beasley, Delilah Leontium. THE NEGRO TRAIL BLAZERS OF CALIFORNIA. New York: Negro Universities Press, 1969.

> Gives many hundreds of names of blacks in California from the pioneer period to the late nineteenth century.

Bowman, Alan P. INDEX TO THE 1850 CENSUS OF CALIFORNIA. Baltimore: Genealogical Publishing Co., 1972.

> Lists blacks who were heads of family or living in households where the head had a different surname. The original census schedules must be consulted for additional information.

Duniway, Clyde A. "Slavery in California after 1848." In AMERICAN HISTORICAL ASSOCIATION: ANNUAL REPORT . . . FOR THE YEAR 1905, I, 241-48. Washington, D.C.: Government Printing Office, 1906.

> Good historical background.

Goode, Kenneth G. CALIFORNIA'S BLACK PIONEERS: A BRIEF HISTORICAL SURVEY. Santa Barbara, Calif.: McNally & Loftin, 1974.

> Provides good background material.

Lapp, Rudolph M. BLACKS IN GOLD RUSH CALIFORNIA. Yale Western Americana series, no. 29. New Haven, Conn.: Yale University Press, 1977.

> A fine resource for background material.

Thurman, Sue Bailey. PIONEERS OF NEGRO ORIGIN IN CALIFORNIA. San Francisco: Acme Publishing Co., 1952.

More biographical than the background studies of Goode and Lapp (above).

FEDERAL RECORDS

Mortality Schedules

1850-80 (C)

Population Schedules

1850-80 and 1900 (DNA); 1850-80 (CU, COG, C, CSfGS, CSmH, and many other public and college libraries)

Special Census—none

STATE AND COUNTY RECORDS

A very important source of information on black Californians is the State Archives located at Sacramento. A typed and indexed copy of the special California State Census of 1852, available at the archives, is available through the Genealogical Department Library in Salt Lake City and its nationwide network of branch libraries as well. In addition, a number of special censuses for cities and towns in California during the period 1897-1941 can be found at the archives with the names of persons in alphabetical order.

County records of Humbolt, Marin, Mendicino, Navada, Sacramento, San Diego, Sonoma, and Yuba are at the State Archives. For an excellent description and a comprehensive list of these county records see:

California. Historical Survey Commission. GUIDE TO THE COUNTY ARCHIVES OF CALIFORNIA. By Owen C. Coy. Sacramento: California State Printing, 1919.

Also available at most research libraries.

Vital statistics such as birth, marriage, and death records were not kept by the state until July 1, 1905. However, the State Archives in Sacramento has two groups of papers involving slavery which may be important for genealogical research:

California Supreme Court Papers (C-Ar)

Topics covered include status of black slaves, habeas corpus rights of blacks, criminal cases, and school segregation.

Sacramento District and County Court Papers (C-Ar)

Cases involving slavery and servitude.

One final group of county records is located at the Los Angeles County Museum of Natural History and Archives (CLCM):

Los Angeles Black Voters, 1892, 1896, 1898

Lists adult black males, with maps indicating voters' homes, and a card file index with occupational and residential changes for 1888, 1890, 1897, and 1905.

MISCELLANEOUS RECORDS

Cemetery Records, Church Records, Diaries

Availability not known.

Military Records

Grabill, Levi. Papers, 1861-92 (CSmH)

Grabill was captain of the 22d U.S. Colored Infantry. The collection includes pocket diaries, 1861 and 1865. MS 71-1060

Hooker, Joseph. Military Papers, 1861-64 (CSmH)

Includes information on freed slaves. MS 68-359

Shaffer, William Rufus. Papers, 1863-1904 (CSt)

Shaffer was commander of the 17th U.S. Colored Infantry. His papers include letters and broadsides about Spanish-American War activities in Cuba.

Civil War and Military Collection, 1851-69 (CSt)

Letters and diaries of several members of Colored Troops regiments.

Newspapers

ELEVATOR (San Francisco). April 6, 1865, to 1904? Weekly.

Holdings: 1865-98 (incomplete); CChiS, CLS, CSdS, CSS, CtY, CU, CU-B, DLC, InNd, IU, KHi, MB, MdBJ, NcU, WHi.

PACIFIC APPEAL (San Francisco). 1862-80. Weekly.

> Holdings: 1862-80; CSdS, CSfSt, CSmarP, CU, CU-B, DLC, FTaSU, KHi, LU-NO, MdBMC, MiKW, TNF, WHi.

Personal Papers and Slavery Records

Alexander Collection, 1848-1939 (CSmH)

> Papers of a freedman and his son (graduate of West Point). Included is a journal on an 1888 march with a cavalry troop.

Bullock, Rufus Brown. Papers, 1851-95 (CSmH)

> Correspondence between Bullock (governor of Georgia during Reconstruction) and his brother Freeman C. Bullock. MS 68-338

King, Martin Luther, Jr. Collection (CSf)

> Regional black newspapers, family papers, organizational files, and oral history recordings with San Francisco blacks.

James Abajian, 4801 17th Street, San Francisco, has for the past fifteen years been collecting primary source materials relating to blacks, particularly from California. He has census records, city directories, and over 90,000 other items. By making an appointment with him, you can examine his files. If that is not possible, send a self-addressed stamped envelope to request information. There is a nominal fee for photocopying his records.

Chapter 40
KANSAS (West)

Most blacks from Kansas will have to look elsewhere in search of their genealogical roots. For instance, many came with the westward movement from Kentucky, Tennessee, and Missouri, while others came as fugitive slaves to a free
state. Still others felt the expansiveness of the post-Civil War "emancipation"
and moved to Kansas after the war.

FEDERAL RECORDS

Mortality Schedules

    1860-80 (DNA, DNDAR, KHi)

Population Schedules

    1860-80* (DNA, KHi, and Wichita and Lawrence public libraries);
    1900 (DNA)

Special Census--none

*Two slaves are listed in the 1860 census for Anderson County. They are in-
cluded in the population schedules and are the only slaves reported in the entire state.

STATE AND COUNTY RECORDS

The Kansas State Historical Society in Topeka is a good place to begin research.
Besides the obvious primary sources of the historical society, the state and federal census records are housed there. Various state censuses are listed below:

    1855 Census--lists eligible voters with ages given by deciles.
    Some entries list names of family members; some give only the
    number of members.

1865 Census--Lists all in the household by name, and gives age, sex, race or color, state or country of birth, marital status, and military records, including company and regiment.

1875 Census--Same as 1865 with the additional information of last place of residence before coming to Kansas.

1885 Census--Same as 1875; in addition, the following is added to the military records: condition of discharge, state of enlistment, and name of prison, if confined in one.

1895, 1905, and 1915 Censuses--Same as 1885.

1925 Census--Same as 1885 with the addition of relationship to head of household, year of immigration to the United States, and year of naturalization, if applicable.

The state 1855 and federal 1860 censuses both have indexes, by names of those listed, for the entire state. All others are indexed and filed by county, township, and/or city. They are available from the Genealogical Department through its branch libraries.

MISCELLANEOUS RECORDS

Military Records

Cornish, Dudley Taylor. KANSAS NEGRO REGIMENTS IN THE CIVIL WAR. Topeka: State of Kansas Commission on Civil Rights, 1969.

Newspapers

AFRO-AMERICAN ADVOCATE (Coffeyville). September 2, 1891, to September 1, 1893. Weekly.

Holdings: 1891-93 (incomplete); CSdS, CtY, DLC, InNd, KHi, MB, MdBJ, MnU, NcU, NjP, TNF, WHi.

AMERICAN (Coffeyville). February 19, 1898, to 1899. Weekly.

Holdings: April 23, 1898, to April 1, 1899 (incomplete); CSdS, CtY, DLC, InNd, KHi, MB, MdBJ, MnU, NcU, NjP, TNF, WHi.

AMERICAN CITIZEN (Kansas City). July 26, 1889, to 1909? Weekly.

Holdings: 1889 to August 2, 1907 (incomplete); CSdS, CtY, CU, DLC, FTaSU, InNd, KHi, MB, MnU, NjP, TNF, WHi.

AMERICAN CITIZEN (Topeka). 1887 to July 19, 1889. Weekly.

Holdings: February 23, 1888, to July 19, 1889; CSdS, DLC, InNd, KHi, MB, MdBJ, NcU, NjP, TNF, WHi.

ATCHISON BLADE. July 23, 1892, to January 20? 1894. Weekly.

Holdings: July 23, 1892, to January 20? 1894; CSdS, CtY, DLC, FTaSU, InNd, KHi, MdBJ, MnU, NcU, NjP, TNF, WHi.

BENEVOLENT BANNER (Topeka). May 21? 1887, to ? Weekly.

Holdings: May 21 and October 22, 1887; CSdS, CSS, DLC, KHi, LU-NO, MdBMC, MiKW, TNF, WHi.

COLORED CITIZEN (Fort Scott). April 19 to July 5, 1878. Weekly.

Holdings: April 19 to July 5, 1878; CSdS, CtY, DLC, InNd, KHi, MB, MdBJ, MnU, NcU, NjP.

COLORED CITIZEN (Topeka). July 26, 1878, to 1880?; June 17, 1897, to 1900? Weekly.

See also the TOPEKA TRIBUNE (below).

Holdings: July 26, 1878, to December 27, 1879; June 17, 1897, to November 16, 1900 (incomplete); CSdS, CtY, DLC, InNd, KHi, MB, MdBJ, MnU, NcU, NjP, TNF, WHi.

COLORED PATRIOT (Topeka). 1882-? Weekly.

Holdings: April 29 to June 22, 1882; CSdS, CSS, CU, DLC, KHi, LU-NO, MdBMC, MiKW, TNF, WHi.

HERALD OF KANSAS (Topeka). January 30 to June 11, 1880? Weekly.

Holdings: January to June 1880; CSdS, CSS, CU, DLC, KHi, LU-NO, MdBMC, MiKW, TNF, WHi.

KANSAS STATE LEDGER (Topeka). July 22, 1892, to June 16? 1906. Weekly.

Title varies as STATE LEDGER.

Holdings: 1892-1906 (incomplete); CSdS, CtY, DLC, FTaSU, InNd, KHi, MB, MdBJ, MnU, NcU, NjP, TNF, WHi.

LEAVENWORTH ADVOCATE. 1888 to August 22, 1891. Weekly.

Continued by TIMES OBSERVER, Topeka.

Holdings: August 18, 1888, to 1891; CSdS, CtY, DLC, InNd, KHi, MB, MdBJ, MnU, NcU, NjP, TNF, WHi.

LEVENWORTH HERALD. 1894-1899? Weekly.

> Holdings: 1894-98 (incomplete); CSdS, CtY, DLC, KHi, MB, MdBJ, MnU, NcU, NjP, WHi.

PARSONS WEEKLY BLADE. August 20? 1892, to December 27, 1901? Weekly.

> Holdings: September 24, 1892, to 1900 (incomplete); CSdS, CtY, DLC, InNd, KHi, MB, MdBJ, MnU, NcU, NjP, TNF, WHi.

PITTSBURG PLAINDEALER. May 20? 1899, to May? 1900. Weekly.

> Continued by the WICHITA SEARCHLIGHT.

> Holdings: August 1899 to May 12, 1900 (incomplete); CSdS, CtY, DLC, InNd, KHi, MB, MdBJ, MnU, NcU, NjP, TNF, WHi.

TOPEKA TRIBUNE. 1880-1881? Weekly.

> Continues the COLORED CITIZEN, July 26, 1878, to 1880? (cited above).

> Holdings: June 24 to December 25, 1880; CSdS, CtY, CU, DLC, InNd, KHi, MB, MdBJ, MnU, NcU, NjP, TNF, WHi.

WEEKLEY CALL (Topeka). May 3? 1891, to 1898? Weekly.

> Title varies as TOPEKA CALL.

> Holdings: June 28, 1891, to October 29, 1898; CSdS, CtY, DLC, InNd, MB, MdBJ, MnU, NjP, TNF, WHi.

Personal Papers and Slavery Records

Freedmen's Relief Association Papers, 1879-81 (KHi)

> Activities and recipients of organizational help.

Marstella Family Papers, 1810-54 (KXSM)

> The collection contains indenture papers, lists of slaves, circuit court papers on runaway slaves, and records of the value and disposition of slaves.

Slave Papers, 1824-65 (KXSM)

> Eight bills of sale for slaves.

Chapter 41

OKLAHOMA (West)

The following two books are of relevance to a number of blacks whose ancestors migrated to Oklahoma:

Oklahoma. Department of Libraries. GUIDE TO OKLAHOMA MANUSCRIPTS, MAPS AND NEWSPAPERS ON MICROFILM IN THE OKLAHOMA DEPARTMENT OF LIBRARIES. Compiled and edited by Robert L. Clark, Jr. Oklahoma City: 1970.

Wright, Murial Hazel. A GUIDE TO THE INDIAN TRIBES OF OKLAHOMA. Civilization of the American Indian Series, no. 33. 1951. Reprint. Norman: University of Oklahoma Press, 1968.

> Some blacks have heard that an ancestor of theirs was Indian; if that is your case, you will want to understand something of the history of the numerous tribes who had strong relationships with blacks (see State and Miscellaneous Records below).

FEDERAL RECORDS

Mortality Schedules--none

Population Schedules
> 1860 and 1890 Territorial (DNA, OkHi); 1900 (DNA)

Special Census 1890 (DNA)

STATE AND MISCELLANEOUS RECORDS

A search in Oklahoma should begin at the Oklahoma Historical Society in Oklahoma City. They have the 1890 Territorial Census, as mentioned above, and some records of the Cherokee and Creek schools. County records are still held by the individual county courthouses.

Diaries

Brown, John, 1821-1865 (OkU)
Experiences of a lawyer and plantation owner in Arkansas.

Newspapers

LANGSTON CITY HERALD. May 2? 1891, to 1902? Weekly.
Holdings: 1891-93; January 27, 1900; CSdS, CSS, CtY, DLC, InNd, KHi, MB, MdBJ, MnU, NcU, NjP, OkHi, OkS, WHi.

OKLAHOMA GUIDE (Oklahoma City). 1898 to August 1903. Weekly, monthly.
Title varies as GUIDE.
Holdings: 1898-1903; CSdS, CtY, DLC, InNd, KHi, MB, MdBJ, MnU, NjP, TNF, WHi.

Slavery Records

Chickasaw Nation Records, 1866-1904 (OkU)
Papers relating to freed men. MS 62-693

Chicote, Samuel. Papers, 1867-68 (OkU)
Reports of problems with slaves freed by the Creek Nation.

Five Civilized Tribes. Papers, 1698-1904 (OkTG)
Includes papers of Cherokee, Chickasaw, Choctaw, Creek, and Seminole nations ownership of slaves. MS 67-125

Chapter 42

TEXAS (West)

Three beginnings for background into research on blacks in Texas are listed below:

Institute of Texan Cultures. THE AFRO-AMERICAN TEXANS. San Antonio, 1975.

Muir, Andrew Forest. "The Free Negro in Fort Bend County, Texas." JOURNAL OF NEGRO HISTORY 33 (1948): 79-85.

Rice, Lawrence D. THE NEGRO IN TEXAS, 1874-1900. Baton Rouge: Louisiana State University Press, 1971.

FEDERAL RECORDS

Mortality Schedules

1850-80 (DNA, Tx)

Population Schedules

1850-80 and 1900 (DNA); 1850-80 (Tx, public libraries in Houston, Dallas, Fort Worth, Temple, Amarillo, and numerous college and genealogical society libraries throughout the state)

Special Census 1890 (DNA, Tx, TxGR, and public libraries in Dallas, Fort Worth, Longview, and Temple)

Record Group 105 (DNA)

See chapter 4, p. 27, under Freedmen's Bureau, for a description of these records. Texas records contain school reports.

Record Group 56, "General Records of the Department of the Treasury" (DNA)

> Contains records of the Third Special Agency, including 1863-65 dealings of the Supervisory Special Agent in regard to freedmen before the Freedmen's Bureau was established.

STATE RECORDS

The Texas State Library Archives at Austin houses the records of all state agencies from the Civil War and Reconstruction periods. In addition, the following provides some county records related to blacks specifically:

Redwine, W.A. "History of Five Counties." CHRONICLES OF SMITH COUNTY 11 (Fall 1972): 13-68.

> This reprint of a 1901 book was reissued by the Smith County Historical Society and contains biographies and picture of several prominent blacks, mainly from the Smith and Rusk Counties in eastern Texas. Migration routes are indicated in addition to listing black property owners, their place of birth, age, value of property, etc.

MISCELLANEOUS RECORDS

Cemetery Records and Church Records

Availability not known.

Diaries

Groce, Jared E., 1866-67 (TxU)

> Transcript on care of slaves, including bills of sale. MS 64-756

Military Records

Circle M Collection (TxH)

> Civil War publications and official records.

DeGolyer Foundation Library Collection, Dallas

> Naval and western state regimental papers.

Fort Davis National Historic Site, El Paso

Military records, 1854-91 of "Buffalo Soldiers" and other black troops who served in the Indian wars.

Newspapers

FREE MAN'S PRESS (Austin). July 25 to October 17, 1868. Weekly.

Continues FREEDMAN'S PRESS.

Holdings: July 25 to October 17, 1868 (incomplete); CSdS, CSS, CU, DLC, IHi, KHi, LU-NO, MdBMC, MiKW, TNF, WHi.

Personal Papers and Slavery Records

Affleck, Thomas. Papers, 1847-66 (TxGR)

Records of the Glen Blythe Plantation near Brenham.

Ballinger, William Pitt. Papers, 1832-82 (TxGR)

Galveston lawyer's letters and documents; some pertain to slavery. MS 67-1994

Billingsley, James B. Account Book, 1856-94 (TxU)

Billingsley was a planter in Marlin. MS 62-4834

Borden, Gail. Papers, 1832-82 (TxGR)

Letters and papers dealing with slaves and Texas property. MS 67-1996

Bryan, Moses Austin. Papers, 1824-95 (TxU)

Peach Point Plantation in Brazoria County; includes slave sales.

Cartwright, Matthew. Papers, 1831-71 (TxU)

Slave sales and account book. MS 62-4018

Chambers, Thomas W. Papers, 1824-95 (TxU)

A Bastrop planter's personal and business letters, with slave sales. MS 62-4044

Darragh, John L. Papers, 1839-93 (TxGR)

A Galveston lawyer's slave-trading papers. MS 67-1999

Freedmen's Bureau Papers, 1865-68 (TxGR)

Includes payment and work of former slaves.

Fulmore, Zachary Taylor. Papers, 1735-1911 (TxU)

Fulmore was a lawyer, and secretary of the Colored Knights of Pythias. This is a large collection of personal material including letters on Texas history and genealogy (1880-1911). MS 64-748

Graham, Edwin S. Papers, 1825-1917 (TxU)

Contains diaries, bills of sale for slaves, indentures, and account books. MS 64-754

Green, Thomas Jefferson. Papers, 1789-1872 (TxU)

Deeds for slaves are included. MS 64-755

Kauffman, Julius. Papers, 1834-79 (TxGR)

Includes slave sale papers, 1859.

Lockhart, John Washington. Papers, 1830-1918 (TxGR)

A Galveston businessman and C.S.A. surgeon. Letters occasionally refer to slave trade.

Morgan, James. Papers, 1809-80 (TxGR)

Bills, receipts, and slave trade papers. MS 67-2011

Rosenberg, Henry. Papers, 1845-1907 (TxGR)

This collection includes Mrs. Mollie Rosenberg's papers on slaves.

Texas Southern University Library Heartmen Negro Collection

Includes personal recollections of blacks from as far back as the 1600s.

Thompson, Ishan. Papers, 1830-75 (TxGR)

Business letters, deeds, and bill of slave sales.

Chapter 43

WEST INDIES

In searching through ship manifest records, one fact becomes clear: most blacks brought to the United States were not brought directly from Africa, but rather had been previously enslaved in the West Indies. Consequently, tracing black roots to Africa, in many cases, requires a detour to the West Indies. In addition, many members of the black community are recent immigrants from the West Indies. The following are a few selected records available for those interested in West Indian ancestry.

Records for the West Indies—in particular, Barbados, Jamaica, Bermuda, St. Croix, and the Bahamas—can be found either on those islands (see below) or in the Colonial Office Records Room in London, England. The Colonial Office is located on Chancery Lane, Portugal Street, and Portchester Road in London. Search rooms are open Monday through Friday. A person wishing to inspect the records should complete an application form which can be obtained by writing the Colonial Office. Inquiries about the records available may also be addressed to the office.

For excellent guides to the Colonial Office collection, consult the following which can be found at the Public Records Office of large research libraries in the United States:

Andrews, Charles McLean. GUIDE TO THE MATERIAL FOR AMERICAN HISTORY, TO 1783, IN THE PUBLIC RECORD OFFICE OF GREAT BRITAIN. 2 vols. Carnegie Institution of Washington, Publication no. 90 A. Washington, D.C., 1912-14.

Bell, Herbert Clifford Francis, et al. GUIDE TO BRITISH WEST INDIAN ARCHIVE MATERIALS, IN LONDON AND THE ISLANDS, FOR THE HISTORY OF THE UNITED STATES. Carnegie Institution of Washington, Publication no. 372. 1926. Reprint. New York: Kraus Reprint Corp., 1966.

Crick, Bernard R., and Alman, Miriam, eds. GUIDE TO MANUSCRIPTS RELATING TO AMERICA IN GREAT BRITAIN AND IRELAND. London: Oxford

University Press, 1961.

Great Britain. Public Record Office. GUIDE TO THE CONTENTS OF THE PUBLIC RECORDS OFFICE. 3 vols. London: H.M. Stationery Office, 1963-68.

GUIDE TO MANUSCRIPT SOURCES FOR THE HISTORY OF LATIN AMERICA AND THE CARIBBEAN IN THE BRITISH ISLES. Edited by Peter Walne. London: Oxford University Press, 1973.

The following sample of records was extracted from Herbert Clifford Francis Bell and David W. Parker's guide. They illustrate the abundance of records available. Most records are grouped in volumes by date. This explains why materials which seem similar have different titles and dates, for instance, List of Negroes Imported 1707-26; Accounts of Negroes Imported October 14, 1746, to April 14, 1747; and Returns of Slaves Imported, 1747-51.

Barbados

    Accounts of Burials and Christenings and Slaves Imported, 1751-56 and 1756-59

    Accounts of Burials and Christenings and Slaves Imported, 1773

    Accounts of Negroes Imported, October 14, 1746, to April 14, 1747

    Census of Barbados by Parishes, 1783

    Christenings and Burials of Negroes, December 1, 1802, to December 1, 1803

    List of Negroes Imported, 1707-26

    Plantation Bonds and Certificates, January 6, 1777, to January 5, 1778

    Returns of Christenings and Burials of Negroes and Negroes Imported, August 11, 1772, to August 11, 1773

    Returns of Christenings and Burials of Negroes by Parishes, 1766

    Returns of Negroes, May 27, 1766, to May 27, 1767

        Shows number in each cargo received and number of consignees.

    Returns of Slaves Imported, 1747-51

    Revenue Accounts, May 1803 to May 1804

    Shipping Returns from 1680 to 1806 with Inward and Outward Records

Bermuda

Shipping Returns

Inward and Outward Returns for October 11, 1715, to October 20, 1720; July 9, 1738, to December 25, 1741; March 26, 1792; October 26, 1737; June 22, 1747, to June 24, 1751.

British Guiana

List of Vessels Entered with Slaves and Departures, November 13, 1764, to October 10, 1766

Jamaica

Assembly Journals, 1770

Has a list of slaves.

Jamaica Board of Trade Entry Books

Shipping Returns, 1683-1784

St. Croix

Various Shipping Returns Inward and Outward, 1684-1720

RECORDS IN THE ISLANDS

While records are available in several of the islands, the following is illustrative of Jamaica.

Jamaica

The Institute of Jamaica (IJ) on King Street in Kingston and the Island Records Office (IRO) have the following records:

Births, marriages, and deaths before 1815 (IRO)

Kingston Register of Slaves (manumitted) 1744-95 (IJ)

Manumission Records, 1747-1832 (66 vols. IRO)

Memorandum of Slaves sold at Kingston, 1738-43 (IJ)

Parochial Tax Rolls before 1815 (IJ)

Port Royal Sale of Slaves, 1783-94; 1800-1806 (IJ)

Slave Returns, 1817-32 (141 vols. IRO)

Slaves Sold in Kingston Toll Book, 1738-43 (IJ)

Wills and Inventories (IRO)

PARISH RECORDS

For all of the islands there are fairly complete parish records, kept in the British tradition. In the family ancestry class offered by the Ethnic Genealogy Center at Queens College, several students have been able to trace their families for five to six generations with one visit to the appropriate parish records offices.

The following records of baptisms, marriages, and burials indicate the year these records began in Jamaica. The consulate offices in the United States will be able to indicate what is available for each of the islands and where to find those records.

| | BEGINNING YEAR: | | |
PARISH	BAPTISMS	MARRIAGES	BURIALS
Clarendon	1690	1695	1769
Hanover	1725	1754	1727
Kingston	1722	1721	1722
Manchester	1816	1727	1818
Metcalf	1843	1843	1843
Portland	1804	1804	1808
Port Royal	1728	1727	1725
St. Andrew	1664	1668	1666
St. Ann	1768	1768	1768
St. Catherine	1668	1668	1671
St. David	1794	1794	1794
St. Dorothy	1693	1725	1706
St. Elizabeth	1708	1719	1722
St. George	1806	1801	1811
St. James	1770	1772	1774
St. John	1751	1751	1751
St. Mary	1752	1755	1767
St. Thomas the East	1709	1721	1708
St. Thomas the Vale	1816	1816	1816

PARISH	BAPTISMS	BEGINNING YEAR: MARRIAGES	BURIALS
Trelawny	1771	1771	1771
Vere	1696	1743	1733
Westmoreland	1740	1740	1741

MISCELLANEOUS RECORDS

There are numerous manuscripts and records in the United States which deal with some aspects of slavery in the West Indies. The DIRECTORY OF AFRO-AMERICAN RESOURCES described in chapter 2, pp. 16-17, lists many of these. The following is an example:

West Indies Records, 1680-1725 (MH)

   Documents related to slavery.

Chapter 44

CANADA

The exodus of slaves over the Underground Railroad provided the beginning of many black families north of the border. The following will be very helpful in Canadian research:

Drew, Benjamin. A NORTH-SIDE VIEW OF SLAVERY. THE REFUGEE; OR, THE NARRATIVES OF FUGITIVE SLAVES IN CANADA RELATED BY THEM-SELVES. WITH AN ACCOUNT OF THE HISTORY AND CONDITION OF THE COLORED POPULATION OF UPPER CANADA. New York: Johnson Reprint Corp., 1968.

Gregorovitch, Andrew. CANADIAN ETHNIC GROUPS BIBLIOGRAPHY. To-ronto: Department of the Provincial Secretary and Citizenship, 1972.

Lists forty-two items relating to black history in Ontario, some with applicability to genealogical research.

Howe, Samuel Gridley. REPORT TO THE FREEDMEN'S INQUIRY COMMIS-SION, 1864: THE REFUGEES FROM SLAVERY IN CANADA WEST. New York: Arno Press, 1969.

Materials on blacks in Ontario.

Jain, Sushil Kumar. THE NEGRO IN CANADA: A SELECT LIST OF PRIMARY AND SECONDARY SOURCES FOR THE STUDY OF THE NEGRO COMMUNITY IN CANADA FROM THE EARLIEST TIMES TO THE PRESENT. Unexplored Fields of Canadiana, vol. 3. Regina: Regina Campus Library, University of Saskatchewan, 1967.

Murray, Alexander Lovell. "Canada and the Anglo-American Anti-slavery Movement: A Study in International Philanthropy." Ph.D. dissertation, Uni-versity of Pennsylvania, 1960. Available from University Microfilms, Ann Arbor, Mich., order no. 60-03674.

Describes the abolitionist movement in Canada.

Parker, David W. GUIDE TO MATERIALS FOR UNITED STATES HISTORY IN CANADIAN ARCHIVES. Carnegie Institution of Washington, Publication no. 172. 1913. Reprint. New York: Kraus Reprint Corp., 1965.

> Excellent reference; indicates many black sources in Canada.

Rawlyk, George A. "The Guysborough Negroes: A Study in Isolation." DALHOUSIE REVIEW 40 (1961): 103-20.

> A study of the Loyalist Negroes who settled in Nova Scotia after the American Revolution.

Spray, W. THE BLACKS IN NEW BRUNSWICK. Fredericton, N.B.: Brunswick Press, 1972.

> Short history with some bibliographical references.

Taylor, Hugh A. NEW BRUNSWICK HISTORY: A CHECKLIST OF SECONDARY SOURCES. Fredericton: Provincial Archives of New Brunswick, Historical Resources Administration, 1971.

> Available at the Genealogical Department in Salt Lake City. Has several appropriate references, as does its supplement compiled by Eric L. Swainick and published in 1974.

MISCELLANEOUS RECORDS

Church Records

Halifax, Nova Scotia, Catholic Church, Parish Registers for Colored People, 1827-35 (US1GD) GD 872,001

> A microfilm copy of baptism, marriage, and burial records; includes an index.

APPENDIXES

Appendix A
LIBRARY SYMBOLS

A-Ar   ALABAMA DEPARTMENT OF ARCHIVES AND HISTORY, MONTGOMERY
Ar-Hi   ARKANSAS HISTORY COMMISSION, DEPARTMENT OF ARCHIVES AND HISTORY, LITTLE ROCK
ArU   UNIVERSITY OF ARKANSAS, FAYETTEVILLE
ATT   TUSKEGEE INSTITUTE, TUSKEGEE, ALA.
AU   UNIVERSITY OF ALABAMA, UNIVERSITY
Az   ARIZONA STATE DEPARTMENT OF LIBRARY AND ARCHIVES, PHOENIX
AzML   MESA BRANCH GENEALOGICAL LIBRARY, MESA, ARIZ.
AzTP   ARIZONA PIONEERS' HISTORICAL SOCIETY, TUCSON

C   CALIFORNIA STATE LIBRARY, SACRAMENTO
C-Ar   CALIFORNIA STATE ARCHIVES, SACRAMENTO
CChiS   CALIFORNIA STATE UNIVERSITY, CHICO
CFlS   CALIFORNIA STATE UNIVERSITY, FULLERTON
CFS   CALIFORNIA STATE UNIVERSITY, FRESNO
CLCM   LOS ANGELES COUNTY MUSEUM, LOS ANGELES
CLS   CALIFORNIA STATE UNIVERSITY, LOS ANGELES
CNoS   CALIFORNIA STATE UNIVERSITY, NORTHRIDGE
CoD   DENVER PUBLIC LIBRARY
CoFS   COLORADO STATE UNIVERSITY, FORT COLLINS
COG   OAKLAND BRANCH GENEALOGICAL LIBRARY, OAKLAND, CALIF.
CoHi   COLORADO STATE HISTORICAL SOCIETY, DENVER
CoU   UNIVERSITY OF COLORADO, BOULDER
CSdS   SAN DIEGO STATE UNIVERSITY
CSf   SAN FRANCISCO PUBLIC LIBRARY
CSfGS CALIFORNIA GENEALOGICAL SOCIETY, SAN FRANCISCO
CSfSt   SAN FRANCISCO STATE UNIVERSITY
CSmarP PALOMAR COLLEGE, SAN MARCOS, CALIF.
CSmH HENRY E. HUNTINGTON LIBRARY, SAN MARINO, CALIF.
CSS   CALIFORNIA STATE UNIVERSITY, SACRAMENTO
CSt   STANFORD UNIVERSITY, STANFORD, CALIF.
Ct   CONNECTICUT STATE LIBRARY, HARTFORD
CtD   WEST CONNECTICUT STATE COLLEGE, DANBURY

CtU	UNIVERSITY OF CONNECTICUT, STORRS
CtY	YALE UNIVERSITY, NEW HAVEN
CU	UNIVERSITY OF CALIFORNIA, BERKELEY
CU-B	UNIVERSITY OF CALIFORNIA, BANCROFT LIBRARY, BERKELEY
CU-Riv	UNIVERSITY OF CALIFORNIA, RIVERSIDE
De-Ar	DELAWARE PUBLIC ARCHIVES, DOVER
DeH	HISTORY SOCIETY OF DELAWARE, WILMINGTON
DeU	UNIVERSITY OF DELAWARE, NEWARK
DeWI	WILMINGTON INSTITUTE FREE LIBRARY, WILMINGTON, DEL.
DeWint	HENRY FRANCIS DUPONT WINTERTHUR MUSEUM, WINTERTHUR, DEL.
DHU	HOWARD UNIVERSITY, WASHINGTON, D.C.
DLC	U.S. LIBRARY OF CONGRESS, WASHINGTON, D.C.
DNA	U.S. NATIONAL ARCHIVES, WASHINGTON, D.C.
DNDAR	DAUGHTERS OF THE AMERICAN REVOLUTION, WASHINGTON, D.C.
FM	MIAMI PUBLIC LIBRARY, MIAMI, FLA.
FTaSU	FLORIDA STATE UNIVERSITY, TALLAHASSEE
FU	FLORIDA STATE UNIVERSITY, GAINESVILLE
G-Ar	GEORGIA STATE DEPARTMENT OF ARCHIVES AND HISTORY, ATLANTA
GAU	ATLANTA UNIVERSITY, ATLANTA
GEU	EMORY UNIVERSITY, ATLANTA
GHi	GEORGIA HISTORICAL SOCIETY, SAVANNAH
GSSC	SAVANNAH STATE COLLEGE, SAVANNAH
GStG	GEORGIA SOUTHERN COLLEGE, STATESBORO
GU	UNIVERSITY OF GEORGIA, ATHENS
HU	UNIVERSITY OF HAWAII, HONOLULU
IaCfT	UNIVERSITY OF NORTHERN IOWA, CEDAR RAPIDS
IaDH	HISTORICAL, MEMORIAL AND ART DEPARTMENT OF IOWA, DES MOINES
IaDM	DES MOINES PUBLIC LIBRARY, IOWA
IaHi	STATE HISTORICAL SOCIETY OF IOWA, IOWA CITY
IaMpl	IOWA WESLEYAN COLLEGE, MOUNT PLEASANT
I-Ar	ILLINOIS STATE ARCHIVES, SPRINGFIELD
IaU	UNIVERSITY OF IOWA, IOWA CITY
IC-Hi	CHICAGO PUBLIC LIBRARY, GEORGE CLEVELAND HALL BRANCH
ICHi	CHICAGO HISTORICAL SOCIETY
ICIU	UNIVERSITY OF ILLINOIS AT CHICAGO CIRCLE, CHICAGO
ICN	NEWBERRY LIBRARY, CHICAGO
ICU	UNIVERSITY OF CHICAGO
IdHi	IDAHO STATE HISTORICAL SOCIETY, BOISE
IHi	ILLINOIS STATE HISTORICAL LIBRARY, SPRINGFIELD
In	INDIANA STATE LIBRARY, INDIANAPOLIS

InFw	PUBLIC LIBRARY OF FORT WAYNE AND ALLEN COUNTY
InIB	BUTLER UNIVERSITY, INDIANAPOLIS
InMuB	BALL STATE UNIVERSITY, MUNCIE, IND.
InNd	UNIVERSITY OF NOTRE DAME, NOTRE DAME, IND.
InU	INDIANA UNIVERSITY, BLOOMINGTON
IU	UNIVERSITY OF ILLINOIS, URBANA
KH	KANSAS STATE HISTORICAL SOCIETY, TOPEKA
KU	UNIVERSITY OF KANSAS, LAWRENCE
KXSM	SAINT MARY COLLEGE, XAVIER, KANS.
KyBgW	WESTERN KENTUCKY STATE UNIVERSITY, BOWLING GREEN
KyHi	KENTUCKY HISTORICAL SOCIETY, FRANKFORT
KyLoF	FILSON CLUB, LOUISVILLE, KY.
KyLxT	TRANSYLVANIA COLLEGE, LEXINGTON, KY.
KyMoreU	MOREHEAD STATE UNIVERSITY, MOREHEAD, KY.
KyU	UNIVERSITY OF KENTUCKY, LEXINGTON
LN	NEW ORLEANS PUBLIC LIBRARY
LNT	TULANE UNIVERSITY, NEW ORLEANS
LU	LOUISIANA STATE UNIVERSITY, BATON ROUGE
LU-Ar	LOUISIANA STATE UNIVERSITY, DEPARTMENT OF ARCHIVES AND MANUSCRIPTS, BATON ROUGE
LU-NO	LOUISIANA STATE UNIVERSITY IN NEW ORLEANS
M-Ar	ARCHIVES DIVISION, SECRETARY OF STATE, BOSTON
MB	BOSTON PUBLIC LIBRARY
MBAt	BOSTON ATHENAEUM
MBU	BOSTON UNIVERSITY
McA	MICROFILMING CORPORATION OF AMERICA, 21 HARRISTOWN ROAD, GLEN ROCK, N.J. 07452
McP	MICRO PHOTO DIVISION, BELL AND HOWELL COMPANY, P.O. BOX 774, WOOSTER, OHIO 44691
MdAA	HALL OF RECORDS COMMISSION, ANNAPOLIS, MD.
MdBJ	JOHNS HOPKINS UNIVERSITY, BALTIMORE
MdBMC	MORGAN STATE COLLEGE, BALTIMORE
MdHi	MARYLAND HISTORICAL SOCIETY, BALTIMORE
MdPM	MARYLAND STATE COLLEGE, PRINCESS ANN
MeB	BOWDOIN COLLEGE, BRUNSWICK, MAINE
MeHi	MAINE HISTORICAL SOCIETY, PORTLAND
MeU	UNIVERSITY OF MAINE, ORONO
Me-Vs	MAINE OFFICE OF VITAL STATISTICS, AUGUSTA
MH	HARVARD UNIVERSITY, CAMBRIDGE, MASS.
MH-B	HARVARD UNIVERSITY, BAKER LIBRARY, CAMBRIDGE, MASS.
MHi	MASSACHUSETTS HISTORICAL SOCIETY, BOSTON
Mi	MICHIGAN STATE LIBRARY, LANSING
MiD	DETROIT PUBLIC LIBRARY
MiD-B	DETROIT PUBLIC LIBRARY, BURTON HISTORICAL COLLECTION
MiDW	WAYNE STATE UNIVERSITY, DETROIT
Mi-HC	MICHIGAN HISTORICAL COMMISSION, STATE ARCHIVES LIBRARY, LANSING

Mi-Hi	MICHIGAN HISTORICAL COMMISSION, LANSING
MiKW	WESTERN MICHIGAN UNIVERSITY, KALAMAZOO
MiMtpT	CENTRAL MICHIGAN UNIVERSITY, MOUNT PLEASANT
MiU	UNIVERSITY OF MICHIGAN, ANN ARBOR
MiU-C	UNIVERSITY OF MICHIGAN, WILLIAM L. CLEMENTS LIBRARY, ANN ARBOR
MiYEM	EASTERN MICHIGAN UNIVERSITY, YPSILANTI
MMeHi	MEDFORD HISTORICAL SOCIETY, MEDFORD, MASS.
Mn-Ar	MINNESOTA STATE ARCHIVES, ST. PAUL
MnHi	MINNESOTA HISTORICAL SOCIETY, ST. PAUL
MnU	UNIVERSITY OF MINNESOTA, MINNEAPOLIS
MoHi	MISSOURI STATE HISTORICAL SOCIETY, COLUMBIA
MoIG	GENEALOGICAL SERVICES, INDEPENDENCE, MO.
MoJcL	LINCOLN UNIVERSITY, JEFFERSON CITY, MO.
MoS	ST. LOUIS PUBLIC LIBRARY
MoSH	MISSOURI HISTORICAL SOCIETY, ST. LOUIS
MoSW	WASHINGTON UNIVERSITY, ST. LOUIS
MoU	UNIVERSITY OF MISSOURI, COLUMBIA
MSaE	ESSEX INSTITUTE, SALEM, MASS.
MSaP	PEABODY MUSEUM OF SALEM, MASS.
Ms-Ar	MISSISSIPPI DEPARTMENT OF ARCHIVES AND HISTORY, JACKSON
MsHaU	UNIVERSITY OF SOUTHERN MISSISSIPPI, HATTIESBURG
MsSM	MISSISSIPPI STATE UNIVERSITY, STATE COLLEGE
MsU	UNIVERSITY OF MISSISSIPPI, UNIVERSITY
MsVHi	VICKSBURG AND WARREN COUNTY HISTORICAL SOCIETY, VICKSBURG, MISS.
MtHi	MONTANA HISTORICAL SOCIETY, HELENA
MU	UNIVERSITY OF MASSACHUSETTS, AMHERST
MWA	AMERICAN ANTIQUARIAN SOCIETY, WORCESTER, MASS.
MWalAJ	AMERICAN JEWISH HISTORICAL SOCIETY, WALTHAM, MASS.
MWiW	WILLIAMS COLLEGE, WILLIAMSTON, MASS.
N	NEW YORK STATE LIBRARY, ALBANY
NAII	ALBANY INSTITUTE OF HISTORY AND ART
NbHi	NEBRASKA STATE HISTORICAL SOCIETY, LINCOLN
NbO	OMAHA PUBLIC LIBRARY
NbOU	UNIVERSITY OF NEBRASKA AT OMAHA
Nc-Ar	NORTH CAROLINA STATE DEPARTMENT OF ARCHIVES AND HISTORY, RALEIGH
NcD	DUKE UNIVERSITY, DURHAM, N.C.
NcGrE	EAST CAROLINA UNIVERSITY, GREENVILLE, N.C.
NcHiC	NORTH CAROLINA HISTORICAL COMMISSION, RALEIGH
NcU	UNIVERSITY OF NORTH CAROLINA, CHAPEL HILL
NcWsM	MORAVIAN ARCHIVES, WINSTON-SALEM, N.C.
NdHi	STATE HISTORICAL SOCIETY OF NORTH DAKOTA, BISMARCK
NdU	UNIVERSITY OF NORTH DAKOTA, GRAND FORKS
NGcA	ADELPHI COLLEGE--NASSAU COUNTY HISTORICAL AND GENEALOGICAL SOCIETY, GARDEN CITY, N.Y.
Nh	NEW HAMPSHIRE STATE LIBRARY, CONCORD
NhD	DARTMOUTH COLLEGE, HANOVER, N.H.

NhHi	NEW HAMPSHIRE HISTORICAL SOCIETY, CONCORD
NHi	NEW YORK HISTORICAL SOCIETY, NEW YORK
NIC	CORNELL UNIVERSITY, ITHACA, N.Y.
Nj	NEW JERSEY STATE LIBRARY, TRENTON
Nj-Ar	NEW JERSEY BUREAU OF ARCHIVES AND HISTORY, TRENTON
Nj-Hs	NEW JERSEY HISTORICAL SOCIETY, NEWARK
NjGbS	GLASSBORO STATE COLLEGE, GLASSBORO, N.J.
NjP	PRINCETON UNIVERSITY, PRINCETON, N.J.
NjR	RUTGERS, THE STATE UNIVERSITY, NEW BRUNSWICK, N.J.
NjRuF	FAIRLEIGH DICKINSON UNIVERSITY, RUTHERFORD, N.J.
NjT	TRENTON FREE PUBLIC LIBRARY, TRENTON, N.J.
NmU	UNIVERSITY OF NEW MEXICO, ALBUQUERQUE
NN	NEW YORK PUBLIC LIBRARY
NNC	COLUMBIA UNIVERSITY, NEW YORK
NNGB	NEW YORK GENEALOGICAL AND BIOGRAPHICAL SOCIETY, NEW YORK
NN-Sc	SCHOMBURG COLLECTION FOR BLACK CULTURE, NEW YORK
NRU	UNIVERSITY OF ROCHESTER, N.Y.
NSyU	SYRACUSE UNIVERSITY, SYRACUSE, N.Y.
NvHi	NEVADA STATE HISTORICAL SOCIETY, RENO
NvL	LAS VEGAS PUBLIC LIBRARY, LAS VEGAS, N. MEX.
NvU	UNIVERSITY OF NEVADA, RENO
OC	PUBLIC LIBRARY OF CINCINNATI AND HAMILTON COUNTY
OCHP	CINCINNATI HISTORICAL SOCIETY
OCl	CLEVELAND PUBLIC LIBRARY
OClWHi	WESTERN RESERVE HISTORICAL SOCIETY, CLEVELAND
OCX	XAVIER UNIVERSITY, CINCINNATI
OFH	RUTHERFORD B. HAYES LIBRARY, FREMONT, OHIO
OHi	OHIO STATE HISTORICAL SOCIETY, COLUMBUS
OKentU	KENT STATE UNIVERSITY, KENT, OHIO
OkHi	OKLAHOMA HISTORICAL SOCIETY, OKLAHOMA CITY
OkOkU	OKLAHOMA CITY UNIVERSITY
OkS	OKLAHOMA STATE UNIVERSITY, STILLWATER
OkTG	THOMAS GILCREASE FOUNDATION, TULSA
OkU	UNIVERSITY OF OKLAHOMA, NORMAN
OOxM	MIAMI UNIVERSITY, OXFORD, OHIO
Or-Ar	OREGON STATE ARCHIVES, SALEM
OrHi	OREGON HISTORICAL SOCIETY, PORTLAND
OrU	UNIVERSITY OF OREGON, EUGENE
OU	OHIO STATE UNIVERSITY, COLUMBUS
OWibfU	WILBERFORCE UNIVERSITY, WILBERFORCE, OHIO
P	PENNSYLVANIA STATE LIBRARY, HARRISBURG
PBL	LEHIGH UNIVERSITY, BETHLEHEM, PA.
PCC	CROZER THEOLOGICAL SEMINARY, CHESTER, PA.
PDoBHi	BUCKS COUNTY HISTORICAL SOCIETY, DOYLESTOWN, PA.
PEsS	EAST STROUDSBURG STATE COLLEGE, EAST STROUDSBURG, PA.
PHarH	PENNSYLVANIA HISTORICAL AND MUSEUM COMMISSION,

	HARRISBURG
PHC	HAVERFORD COLLEGE, HAVERFORD, PA.
PHi	HISTORICAL SOCIETY OF PENNSYLVANIA, PHILADELPHIA
PLuL	LINCOLN UNIVERSITY, LINCOLN UNIVERSITY, PA.
PP	FREE LIBRARY OF PHILADELPHIA
PPAmP	AMERICAN PHILOSOPHICAL SOCIETY, PHILADELPHIA
PPiD	DUQUESNE UNIVERSITY, PITTSBURGH
PPiU	UNIVERSITY OF PITTSBURGH
PPT	TEMPLE UNIVERSITY, PHILADELPHIA
PSC-Hi	SWARTHMORE COLLEGE, FRIENDS HISTORICAL LIBRARY, SWARTHMORE, PA.
PSt	PENNSYLVANIA STATE UNIVERSITY, UNIVERSITY PARK
PU	UNIVERSITY OF PENNSYLVANIA, PHILADELPHIA
PV	VILLANOVA UNIVERSITY, VILLANOVA, PA.
R	RHODE ISLAND STATE LIBRARY, PROVIDENCE
Readex	READEX MICROPRINT CORPORATION, 5 UNION SQUARE, NEW YORK, N.Y. 10003
RHi	RHODE ISLAND HISTORICAL SOCIETY, PROVIDENCE
RP	PROVIDENCE PUBLIC LIBRARY
RPB	BROWN UNIVERSITY, PROVIDENCE
RPPC	PROVIDENCE COLLEGE, PROVIDENCE
Sc-Ar	SOUTH CAROLINA DEPARTMENT OF ARCHIVES AND HISTORY, COLUMBIA
ScCC	COLLEGE OF CHARLESTON, CHARLESTON, S.C.
ScHi	SOUTH CAROLINA HISTORICAL SOCIETY, CHARLESTON
ScRhW	WINTHROP COLLEGE, ROCK HILL, S.C.
ScU	UNIVERSITY OF SOUTH CAROLINA, COLUMBIA
SdHi	SOUTH DAKOTA STATE HISTORICAL SOCIETY, PIERRE
T	TENNESSEE STATE LIBRARY, NASHVILLE
TC	CHATTANOOGA PUBLIC LIBRARY
TJoS	EAST TENNESSEE STATE UNIVERSITY, JOHNSON CITY
TKL	PUBLIC LIBRARY OF KNOXVILLE AND KNOX COUNTY
TNF	FISK UNIVERSITY, NASHVILLE
TNJ	JOINT UNIVERSITY LIBRARIES, NASHVILLE
TrC	TAYLOREED CORPORATION, 155 MURRAY STREET, ROCHESTER, N.Y. 14606
TU	UNIVERSITY OF TENNESSEE, KNOXVILLE
Tx	TEXAS STATE LIBRARY AND HISTORICAL COMMISSION, AUSTIN
TxF	FORT WORTH PUBLIC LIBRARY
TxFS	SOUTHWESTERN BAPTIST THEOLOGICAL SEMINARY, FORT WORTH
TxGR	ROSENBERG LIBRARY, GALVESTON, TEX.
TxH	HOUSTON PUBLIC LIBRARY
TxHR	RICE UNIVERSITY, HOUSTON
TxHTSU	TEXAS SOUTHERN UNIVERSITY, HOUSTON
TxU	UNIVERSITY OF TEXAS, AUSTIN

UL	CACHE COUNTY PUBLIC LIBRARY, LOGAN, UTAH
UPB	BRIGHAM YOUNG UNIVERSITY, PROVO, UTAH
USIGD	GENEALOGICAL DEPARTMENT OF THE CHURCH OF JESUS CHRIST OF LATTER-DAY SAINTS, SALT LAKE CITY
Vi	VIRGINIA STATE LIBRARY, RICHMOND
ViHal	HAMPTON INSTITUTE, HAMPTON, VA.
ViHi	VIRGINIA HISTORICAL SOCIETY, RICHMOND
ViU	UNIVERSITY OF VIRGINIA, CHARLOTTESVILLE
ViW	COLLEGE OF WILLIAM AND MARY, WILLIAMSBURG, VA.
ViWI	INSTITUTE OF EARLY AMERICAN HISTORY AND CULTURE, WILLIAMSBURG, VA.
Vt	VERMONT STATE LIBRARY, MONTPELIER
VtU	UNIVERSITY OF VERMONT AND STATE AGRICULTURAL COLLEGE, BURLINGTON
Wa	WASHINGTON STATE LIBRARY, OLYMPIA
WaBeW	WESTERN WASHINGTON STATE COLLEGE, BELLINGHAM
WaHi	WASHINGTON STATE HISTORICAL SOCIETY, TACOMA
WaOE	THE EVERGREEN COLLEGE, OLYMPIA, WASH.
WaSp	SPOKANE PUBLIC LIBRARY
WaSpG	GONZAGA UNIVERSITY, SPOKANE
WaU	UNIVERSITY OF WASHINGTON, SEATTLE
WHi	STATE HISTORICAL SOCIETY OF WISCONSIN, MADISON
WM	MILWAUKEE PUBLIC LIBRARY
WU	UNIVERSITY OF WISCONSIN, MADISON
Wv-Ar	WEST VIRGINIA DEPARTMENT OF ARCHIVES AND HISTORY, CHARLESTON
WvU	WEST VIRGINIA UNIVERSITY, MORGANTOWN
WvU-J	WEST VIRGINIA UNIVERSITY, SCHOOL OF JOURNALISM, MORGANTOWN
Wy-Ar	WYOMING STATE ARCHIVES AND HISTORY DEPARTMENT, CHEYENNE

Appendix B

BRANCH GENEALOGICAL LIBRARIES

The following is a list of the branch libraries of the Genealogical Department of the Church of Jesus Christ of Latter-day Saints. Any of these branches can order microfilm copies of the vast resources owned by the Genealogical Department in Salt Lake City. There is a nominal charge (approximately $.75) to use each film for a two-week period. Addresses listed are locations only, not mailing addresses.

ALABAMA

Huntsville Branch, 106 Sanders Drive, S.W., Huntsville

ALASKA

Anchorage Branch, 2501 Maplewood Street, Anchorage
Fairbanks Branch, 1500 Cowles Street, Fairbanks

ARIZONA

Flagstaff Branch, 625 East Cherry, Flagstaff
Globe Branch, 428 Sutherland, Globe
Holbrook Branch, 1600 North 2d Avenue, Holbrook
Mesa Branch, 464 East 1st Avenue, Mesa
Phoenix North Branch, 8602 North 31st Avenue, Phoenix
Phoenix West Branch, 3102 North 18th Avenue, Phoenix
Prescott Branch, 1001 Ruth Street, Prescott
Safford Branch, 501 Catalina Drive, Safford
Show Low Branch, across street from Show Low 1, 2, 3 Wards, Show Low
St. David Branch, St. David Stake Center, St. David
St. Johns Branch, 35 West Cleveland Street, St. Johns
Snowflake Branch, Hunt Avenue, Snowflake
Tucson Branch, 500 South Langley, Tucson
Yuma Branch, 6th Avenue and 17th Street, Yuma

ARKANSAS

Little Rock Branch, Highway 67, N., Jacksonville

AUSTRALIA

Adelaide Stake Branch, 120 Gage Street, Firle, South Australia
Melbourne Branch, 285 Heidelberg Road, Northcote, Victoria, Australia
Sydney Branch, 55 Greenwich Road, Greenwich, Sydney, Australia
Sydney South Branch, Sutherland Ward Chapel, 196 Bath Road, Kirrawee, NSW, Australia

CALIFORNIA

Anaheim Branch, 440 North Loara (Rear), Anaheim
Bakersfield Branch, 1903 Bernard Street, Bakersfield
Barstow Branch, 2571 Barstow Road, Barstow
Cerritos Branch, 17909 Bloomfield, Cerritos
Cerritos West Branch, 15311 South Pioneer Boulevard, Norwalk
Chico Branch, Stake Center, 1528 Esplanade, Chico
Covina Branch, 656 South Grand Avenue, Covina
Eureka Branch, 2734 Dolbeer, Eureka
Fresno Branch, 1838 Echo, Fresno
Gridley Branch, 348 Spruce Street, Gridley
LaCrescenta Branch, 4550 Raymond Avenue, LaCrescenta
Long Beach East Branch, Stake Center, 1140 Ximeno, Long Beach
Los Angeles Branch, 10741 Santa Monica Boulevard, Los Angeles
Los Angeles East Branch, 106 South Hillview Avenue, Los Angeles
Menlo Park Branch, Stake Center, 1105 Valparaiso Avenue, Menlo Park
Modesto Branch, 731 El Vista Avenue, Modesto
Monterey Branch, 1024 Noche Buena, Seaside
Oakland Branch, 4780 Lincoln Avenue, Oakland
Redding Branch, 3410 Churn Creek Road, Redding
Ridgecrest Branch, 501 Norma Street, Ridgecrest
Riverside Branch, 5900 Grand Avenue, Riverside
Riverside West Branch, 4375 Jackson Street, Riverside
Sacramento Branch, 2745 Eastern Avenue, Sacramento
San Bernardino Branch, 7000 Central Avenue, San Bernardino
San Diego Branch, 3705 10th Avenue, San Diego
San Jose Branch, 1336 Cherry Avenue, San Jose
San Luis Obispo Branch, 55 Casa Street, San Luis Obispo
Santa Barbara Branch, 478 Cambridge Drive, Goleta
Santa Clara Branch, 875 Quince Avenue, Santa Clara
Santa Maria Branch, 1312 West Prune Avenue, Lompoc
Santa Rosa Branch, 1725 Peterson Lane, Santa Rosa
Stockton Branch, 814 Brookside Road, Stockton
Upland Branch, Stake Center, 785 North San Antonio, Upland
Ventura Branch, 3501 Loma Vista Road, Ventura

CANADA

Calgary Alberta Branch, 2021 17th Avenue, S.W., Calgary, Alberta
Cardston Alberta Branch, 348 Third Street West, Cardston, Alberta
Edmonton Alberta Branch, 9010 85 Street, Edmonton, Alberta
Hamilton Ontario Branch, Stake Center, 701 Stonechurch Road, Hamilton, Ontario
Lethbridge Alberta Branch, Stake Center, 2410 28th Street S., Lethbridge, Alberta
Toronto Ontario Branch, 95 Melbert Street, Etobicoke, Ontario
Vancouver B.C. Branch, Stake Center, 5280 Kincaid Street, Burnaby, Vancouver, British Columbia
Vernon B.C. Branch, Kelowna Ward, Glenmore and Ivans Street, Kelowna, British Columbia

COLORADO

Arvada Branch, 7080 Independence, Arvada
Boulder Branch, 4655 Table Mesa Drive, Boulder
Colorado Springs Branch, 20 North Cascade, Colorado Springs
Denver Branch, Denver Stake Center, 2710 South Monaco Parkway, Denver
Denver North Branch, 100 East Malley Drive, Northglenn
Durango Stake Branch, 1800 East Empire Street, Cortez
Ft. Collins Branch, Stake Center, 600 East Swallow, Ft. Collins
Grand Junction Branch, Stake Center, 543 Melody Lane, Grand Junction
LaJara Branch, Stake Center, LaJara
Littleton Branch, 1939 East Easter Avenue, Littleton
Meeker Branch, 409 29th Street, Glenwood Springs

CONNECTICUT

Hartford Branch, 30 Woodside Avenue, Manchester

ENGLAND

Huddersfield Branch, Stake Center, 12 Halifax Road, Birchencliffe, Huddersfield, England
Sunderland Branch, Stake Center, Alexandra Road, Suderland, Tyne and Wear, England

FLORIDA

Jacksonville Branch, 4087 Hendricks Avenue, Jacksonville
Miami Branch, 1350 North West 95th Street, Miami
Orlando Branch, 45 East Par Avenue, Orlando
Pensacola Branch, 5673 North 9th Avenue, Pensacola
Tampa Branch, 4106 Fletcher Avenue, Tampa

GEORGIA

Macon Branch, 3006 14th Avenue, Columbus

Sandy Springs Branch, 1155 Mt. Vernon Highway, Dunwoody

HAWAII

Honolulu West Branch, Stake Center, 1733 Beckley Street, Honolulu
Kaneohe Branch, 46-117 Halaulani Street, Kaneohe
Laie Branch, BYU, Hawaii Library, Laie

IDAHO

Bear Lake Branch, Bear Lake County Library, 138 North 6th Street, Montpelier
Blackfoot West Branch, Stake Center, 6 miles northwest of Blackfoot on Pioneer Road, Blackfoot
Boise Branch, 325 West State Street, Boise
Burley Branch, 224 East 14th Street, Burley
Driggs Branch, Stake Center, 221 North 1st, E., Driggs
Idaho Falls Branch, 290 Chestnut Street, Idaho Falls
Iona Branch, Stake Center, Iona Road and Ririe Highway 26, Idaho Falls
Lewiston Branch, Stake Center, 9th and Preston, Lewiston
Malad Branch, 400 North 200 West, Malad
Moore Branch, Lost River Stake Center, Moore
Pocatello Branch, 156 1/2 South 6th Avenue, Pocatello
Salmon Branch, Salmon River Stake Center, Salmon
Twin Falls Branch, Maurice Street, N., Twin Falls
Upper Snake River Branch, Ricks College Library, Rexburg

ILLINOIS

Champaign Branch, 604 West Windsor Road, Champaign
Chicago Heights Branch, 402 Longwood Drive, Chicago Heights
Naperville Branch, 25 West 341 Chicago Avenue, Naperville
Wilmette Branch, 2801 Lake Avenue, Wilmette

INDIANA

Ft. Wayne Branch, 5401 St. Joe Road, Ft. Wayne
Indianapolis Branch, Stake Center, 900 East Stop 11 Road, Indianapolis

IOWA

Des Moines Branch, 3301 Ashworth Road, West Des Moines

KANSAS

Wichita Branch, 7011 East 13th Street, Wichita

KENTUCKY

Louisville Branch, 1000 Hurstborne Lane, Louisville

LOUISIANA
Baton Rouge Branch, 5686 Winbourne Avenue, Baton Rouge

MAINE
Augusta Branch, Hasson Street, Farmingdale

MARYLAND
Silver Spring Branch, 500 Randolph Road, Silver Spring

MASSACHUSETTS
Boston Branch, Brown Street and South Avenue, Weston

MEXICO
Colonia Juarez Branch, Colonia Juarez, Chihuahua, Mexico
Mexico City Branch, Churu Busco Stake Center, Mexico City, Mexico

MICHIGAN
Bloomfield Hills Branch, 425 North Woodward Avenue, Bloomfield Hills
Dearborn Branch, 20201 Rotunda Drive, Dearborn
Lansing Branch, Stake Center, 431 East Saginaw Street, East Lansing
Midland Branch, 1700 West Sugnut Road, Midland

MINNESOTA
Minneapolis Branch, 2801 Douglas Drive, N., Minneapolis

MISSOURI
Columbia Branch, Highway 63, S., Columbia
Kansas City Branch, 8144 Holmes, Kansas City
St. Louis Branch, 10445 Clayton Road, Frontenac,
Springfield Branch, 1322 South Campbell, Springfield

MISSISSIPPI
Hattiesburg Branch, Stake Center, U.S. 11, S., Hattiesburg

MONTANA
Billings Branch, 1711 6th Street, W., Billings
Butte Branch, Dillon Chapel, 715 East Bannock Street, Dillon
Great Falls Branch, 1401 9th Street, N.W., Great Falls
Helena Branch, 1610 East 6th Avenue, Helena
Kalispell Branch, Buffalo Hill, Kalispell
Missoula Branch, 3201 Bancroft Street, Missoula

NEBRASKA

Omaha Branch, 11027 Martha Street, Omaha

NEVADA

Ely Branch, Avenue E and 9th Street, Ely
Fallon Branch, 750 West Richards Street, Fallon
Las Vegas Branch, 509 South 9th Street, Las Vegas
Reno Branch, Washoe Public Library, 301 South Center, Reno

NEW JERSEY

Morristown Branch, 140 White Oak Ridge Road, Summit
East Brunswick Branch, 303 Dunham's Corner Road, East Brunswick

NEW MEXICO

Albuquerque Branch, 5709 Haines Avenue, N.E., Albuquerque
Farmington Branch, 400 West Apache, Farmington

NEW YORK

Albany Branch, 411 Loudon Road, Loudonville
Buffalo Branch, 1424 Maple Road, Buffalo
Ithaca Branch, 305 Murray Hill Road, Vestal
New York Branch, 2 Lincoln Square (3d Floor), Broadway at 65th Street, New York
Plainview Branch, 160 Washington Avenue, Plainview
Rochester Branch, 460 Kreag Road, Fairport

NEW ZEALAND

Auckland Branch, No. 2 Scotia Place, Auckland CI, New Zealand
Canterbury Branch, 25 Fendalton Road, Christchurch, New Zealand
Temple View Branch, Temple View, New Zealand
Wellington Branch, Wellington Chapel, 140 Moxham Avenue, Wellington, New Zealand

NORTH CAROLINA

Charlotte Branch, 3020 Hilliard Drive, Charlotte
Raleigh Branch, 5100 Six Forks Road, Raleigh

OHIO

Cincinnati Branch, 5505 Bosworth Place, Cincinnati
Cleveland Branch, 25000 Westwood Road, Westlake
Columbus Branch, 3646 Lieb Street, Columbus
Dayton Branch, 1500 Shiloh Springs Road, Dayton

OKLAHOMA

Oklahoma City Branch, 5020 Northwest 63d, Oklahoma City
Tulsa Branch, 12110 East 7th Street, Tulsa

OREGON

Beaverton Branch, 10425 Southwest Beaverton, Hillsdale Highway, Beaverton
Bend Branch, Stake Center, 1260 Thompson Drive, Bend
Coos Bay Branch, 3950 Sherman Avenue, North Bend
Corvallis Branch, 4141 Northwest Harrison, Corvallis
Eugene Branch, 3550 West 18th Street, Eugene
Gresham Branch, 3500 Southeast 182d, Gresham
LaGrande Branch, Old Welfare Building, 2504 North Fir, LaGrande
Medford Branch, 2980 Juanipero Way, Medford
Nyssa Branch, West Alberta Avenue, Nyssa
Portland Branch, 2931 Northeast Harrison, Portland
Portland East Branch, 2215 Northeast 106th, Portland
Salem Branch, 4550 Lone Oak, S.E., Salem

PENNSYLVANIA

Gettysburg Branch, 2100 Hollywood Drive, York
Philadelphia Branch, 721 Paxon Hollow Road, Broomall
State College Branch, Whitehall Road, State College

SOUTH AFRICA

Johannesburg Branch, 1 Hunter Street, Highlands, Johannesburg, South Africa

SOUTH CAROLINA

Columbia Branch, 4440 Ft. Jackson Boulevard, Columbia

TENNESSEE

Knoxville Branch, 400 Kendall Road, Knoxville
Memphis Branch, 4520 Winchester Road, Memphis
Tennessee South Branch, Old Shelbyville Highway, Tullahoma

TEXAS

Austin Branch, 2111 Parker Lane, Austin
Beaumont Branch, Williamson Ward Chapel, Vidor
Corpus Christi Branch, 505 North Mesquite Street, Corpus Christi
Dallas Branch, 616 West Keist Boulevard, Dallas
Dallas North Branch, 10701 Lake Highlands Drive, Dallas
El Paso Branch, 3651 Douglas Avenue, El Paso
Ft. Worth Branch, Stake Center, 4401 Northeast Loop 820, North Richland Hills
Houston Branch, 1101 Bering Drive, Houston
Houston East Branch, Stake Center, 3000 Broadway, Houston

Longview Branch, 1700 Blueridge Parkway, Longview
Odessa Branch, 2011 Washington, Odessa
San Antonio Branch, 2103 St. Cloud, San Antonio

UTAH

Beaver Branch, 15 North, 100 West, Beaver
Brigham City South Branch, 865 South 3d W., Brigham City
Cache Branch, 950 North Main, Logan
Cedar City Branch, 256 South, 900 West, Cedar City
Duchesne Branch, Stake Center, Duchesne
Fillmore Branch, Stake Center, 21 South, 300 West, Fillmore
Kanab Branch, Stake Center, Kanab
Monticello Branch, 225 East 2d, N., Blanding
Mt. Pleasant Branch, Mt. Pleasant Stake Center, Mt. Pleasant
Ogden Branch, 339 21st Street, Ogden
Price Branch, 85 East Fourth, N., Price
Richfield Branch, 91 South 2d, W., Richfield
Roosevelt Branch, 447 East Lagoon Street, Roosevelt
St. George Branch, 401 South, 400 East, St. George
Santaquin Branch, Stake Center, Santaquin
South Jordan Branch, 2450 West, 10400 South, South Jordan
Springville Branch, 245 South, 600 East, Springville
Uintah Basin Branch, 613 West 2d, S., Vernal
Utah Valley Branch, 405 HBL Library, BYU, Provo

VIRGINIA

Annandale Branch, 3900 Howard Street, Annandale
Norfolk Branch, 4760 Princess Anne Road, Virginia Beach
Oakton Branch, Hunter Mill Road, Oakton
Richmond Stake Branch, 5600 Monument Avenue, Richmond

'WALES

Merthyr Tydfil Branch, Top of Nantygwenith Street, Georgetown, Merthyr Tydfil, Wales

WASHINGTON

Bellevue Branch, 10675 Northeast 20th Street, Bellevue
Everett Branch, Everett Stake Center, Everett
Longview Branch, 1721 30th Avenue, Longview
Moses Lake Branch, 1515 Division, Moses Lake
Mt. Vernon Branch, 1700 Hazel, Mt. Vernon
Olympia Branch, Olympia Stake Center, Olympia
Pasco Branch, Stake Center, 2004 North 24th Street, Pasco
Quincy Branch, 1101 2d, S.E., Quincy
Richland Branch, 1720 Thayer Drive, Richland
Seattle North Branch, 5701 8th, N.E., Seattle

Branch Genealogical Libraries

Spokane Branch, North 919 Pines Road, Spokane
Tacoma Branch, South 12th and Pearl Streets, Tacoma
Vancouver Branch, Stake Center, 10509 Southeast 5th Street, Vancouver
Yakima Branch, 705 South 38th Avenue, Yakima

WISCONSIN

Appleton Branch, Lodge Hall, Main Street, Shawano
Milwaukee Branch, 9600 West Grange Avenue, Hales Corner

WYOMING

Afton Branch, 347 Jefferson Avenue, Afton
Casper Branch, 700 South Missouri, Casper
Cheyenne Branch, 2800 Central Avenue, Cheyenne
Cody Branch, Cody Ward Chapel, Cody
Evanston Branch, 1224 Morse Lee Street, Evanston
Lovell Branch, 50 West Main, Lovell

Appendix C
FEDERAL ARCHIVES AND RECORDS CENTERS

Most centers have extensive microfilm holdings of Federal Census Schedules for that region, in addition to regional materials. Each center prints a holdings list which can be obtained by mail or phone.

ATLANTA CENTER

1557 St. Joseph Avenue, East Point, GA 30344. Telephone 404-526-7577; hours 8 a.m. to 4:30 p.m., Monday through Friday. Serves Alabama, Florida, Georgia, Kentucky, Mississippi, North Carolina, South Carolina, and Tennessee.

BOSTON CENTER

380 Trapelo Road, Waltham, MA 02154. Telephone 617-223-2657; hours 8 a.m. to 4:30 p.m., Monday through Friday. Serves Connecticut, Maine, Massachusetts, New Hampshire, Rhode Island, and Vermont.

CHICAGO CENTER

7358 South Pulaski Road, Chicago, IL 60629. Telephone 312-353-8541; hours 8 a.m. to 4:30 p.m., Monday through Friday. Serves Illinois, Indiana, Michigan, Minnesota, Ohio, and Wisconsin.

DENVER CENTER

Building 48, Denver Federal Center, Denver, CO 80225. Telephone 303-234-3187; hours 7:30 a.m. to 4 p.m., Monday through Friday. Serves Colorado, Montana, North Dakota, Utah, and Wyoming.

FORT WORTH CENTER

4900 Hemphill Street, P.O. Box 6216, Fort Worth, TX 76115. Telephone 817-334-5515; hours 8 a.m. to 4:30 p.m., Monday through Friday. Serves Arkansas, Louisiana, New Mexico, Oklahoma, and Texas.

KANSAS CITY CENTER

2306 East Bannister Road, Kansas City, MO 64131. Telephone 816-926-7271; hours 8 a.m. to 4:30 p.m., Monday through Friday. Serves Iowa, Kansas, Missouri, and Nebraska.

LOS ANGELES CENTER

24000 Avila Road, Laguna Niguel, CA 90377. Telephone 714-831-4220; hours 8 a.m. to 4:30 p.m., Monday through Friday. Serves Arizona; the southern California counties of Imperial, Inyo, Kern, Los Angeles, Orange, Riverside, San Bernardino, San Diego, San Luis Obispo, Santa Barbara, and Ventura; and Clark County, Nevada.

NEW YORK CENTER

Building 22-MOT Bayonne, Bayonne, NJ 07002. Telephone 201-858-7164; hours 8:30 a.m. to 5 p.m., Monday through Friday. Serves New Jersey, New York, Puerto Rico, and the Virgin Islands.

PHILADELPHIA CENTER

5000 Wissahickon Avenue, Philadelphia, PA 19144. Telephone 215-438-5591; hours 8 a.m. to 4:30 p.m., Monday through Friday. Serves Delaware and Pennsylvania; for the loan of microfilm, it also serves the District of Columbia, Maryland, Virginia, and West Virginia.

SAN FRANCISCO CENTER

1000 Commodore Drive, San Bruno, CA 94066. Telephone 415-876-9001; hours 7:45 a.m. to 4:15 p.m., Monday through Friday. Serves California, except southern California; Hawaii; Nevada, except Clark County; and the Pacific Ocean area.

SEATTLE CENTER

6125 Sand Point Way, N.E., Seattle, WA 98115. Telephone 206-142-4502; hours 8 a.m. to 4:30 p.m., Monday through Friday. Serves Alaska, Idaho, Oregon, and Washington.

INDEXES

AUTHOR INDEX

This index includes authors, editors, compilers, translators, and other contributors to works cited in this text. Alphabetization is letter by letter.

A

Abajian, James de T. 19, 232
Affleck, Thomas 255
Alabama. Department of Archives and History 117
Alabama Genealogical Society 117
Alcorn, Governor James L. 141
Alexander Collection 246
Alilunas, Leo 222
Allen, Eliza A. 65
Allen, Eliza Harriet 64, 88
Allen, James Egert 165
Allinson, Samuel 162
Allinson, William 180
Allston, Robert Francis Withers 101
Alman, Miriam 257
Amann, William Frayne 32
American Antiquarian Society. Worcester, Mass. 155
American Society of Genealogists 11
Anderson, Edward Clifford 66
Andrews, Charles McLean 257
Applegate, Lisbon 219
Ardery, Julia Hope 133
Ardery, William E. 93
Ashtabula County Female Anti-Slavery Society Records 227
Atkins, James A. 235

B

Bacot, Peter Samuel 101
Bacote, Samuel William 13
Bacot-Huger Collection 101
Bailey, Everett Hoskins 213
Bailey, Frederic William 150, 155
Bailey, Rosalie Fellows 165
Bakken, Douglas A. 236
Ballinger, William Pitt 255
Bancroft, Frederic 35
Banner, Melvin E. 207
Barekman, June Beverly 201
Barrow, Bennet Hilliard 68
Barrow, Clara Elizabeth 64
Barrow, Col. David C. Renshaw 64
Batchelor, Albert A. 73
Bateman, Mary 73, 93
Baum, Willa K. 23
Beale, Edward 93
Beasley, Delilah Leontium 243
Bell, Herbert Clifford Francis 257, 258
Bell, Sir William 209
Bentley, George R. 14
Berlin, Ira 14
Berrien, John McPherson 66
Berry, William Wells 147
Betts, Edwin Morris 108
Bibliographical Society of America 19
Billingsley, James B. 255

Author Index

Author Index

Author Index

Author Index

Thurston, Charles Brown 192
Tiffany, P. Dexter 220
Tilghman, William 183
Tillery, Nannie M. 88
Tindall, George Brown 96
Torbert, James 121
Torrence, Clayton 109
Trapier, Paul 100
Trevor Arnett Library 52
Trexler, Harrison A. 215
Tucker, D.M. 221
Tucker, J.H. 221
Turnbull, Robert J. 96
Turner, Daniel 67
Turner, Edward Raymond 177

U

U.S. Bureau of the Census 17
U.S. Library of Congress. Catalog
  Publication Division 20
U.S. National Archives and Records
  Service 17, 30
U.S. Pension Bureau 17
U.S. War Department 18

V

Van Liew-Voorhees 163
Vick and Phelps Family Papers 143
Virginia Gazette 108
Virginia. General Assembly. Joint
  Committee on the State Library
  109
Virginia. University of 116

W

Wade, Walter 142
Walker, Timothy 228
Walne, Peter 258
Wamble, Gaston Hugh 216

Warmoth, Henry Clay 94
Warner, R.A. 150
Washington. State Library. Olympia
  241
Webb, Daniel Cannon 100
Welling, James Clarke 18
Wellman, Manly Wade 89
Welsch, Erwin K. 19
West, Earl H. 18
Westbrooks, Allie C. 148
Weston Family Papers 103
West Virginia University. West
  Virginia Collection 110
Wharton, Vernon Lane 138
White, John R. 221
Whiteman, Maxwell 13
William and Mary College. Earl
  Gregg Swem Library 110
Williams, E. Russ 138
Williamson, Joseph 191
Williamson Family Papers 148
Wilson, C.J. 222
Wilson, Clyde Norman, Jr. 16, 88
Wiltburger, Christian, Jr. 126
Wineman, Walter Ray 107
Wise, Jennings Cropper 105
Wood, Anna Wharton 183
Wood, Peter H. 97
Woodruff, William Edward 124
Woodson, Carter Godwin 18
Woodson, June Baber 207
Woodward, Carl Raymond 184
Work, Monroe Nathan 18
WPA Illinois Writers' Project 199
Wright, James Martin 78
Wright, Murial Hazel 251

Y

Yan, Paul D. 224
Yancey, B.C. 67
Yoshpe, Harry B. 167

TITLE INDEX

Index entries refer to page numbers. The titles listed in the index are alphabetized letter by letter and in some cases the titles have been shortened.

D

Descriptive Catalogue of the Documents Relating to the History of the United States in the Papeles Procedentes de Cuba Deposited in the Archivo General de Indias at Seville 68

Descriptive Inventory of the Archives of the City and County of Philadelphia 179

Diary of Colonel Landon Carter of Sabine Hall, 1752-1778, The 106, 111

Directory of Afro-American Resources 16, 17, 49, 125, 126, 129, 137, 199, 227

Directory of Historical Societies and Agencies in the United States and Canada 11

Documents Illustrative of the History of the Slave Trade in America 15

Documents Relative to the Colonial History of the State of New York 165

E

Early Connecticut Marriages as Found on Ancient Church Records, Prior to 1800 150

Early Massachusetts Marriages Prior to 1800 155

Essex County, Virginia, Wills, Bonds, Inventories, Etc., 1722-1730 107

Evidences of Progress 17

F

Federal Population and Mortality Census Schedules 1790-1890 in the National Archives and the States 26

1st Michigan Colored Infantry (102nd United States Colored Infantry). 209

First Michigan Infantry, Three Months and Three Years 209

Florida Plantation Records from the Papers of George Noble Jones 130

Forty-Third Regiment United States Colored Troops, The 32, 182

Fourteenth Regiment Rhode Island Heavy Artillery (Colored,) in the War to Preserve the Union, 1861-1865, The 31, 187

Freedoms Foundations 176

Free Negro Heads of Families in the United States in 1830 18

Free Negro in Ante-Bellum Georgia, The 51

Free Negro in Ante-Bellum Louisiana, The 70

Free Negro in Florida, 1565-1863, The 130

Free Negro in Maryland, 1634-1860, The 78

Free Negro in North Carolina, 1790-1860, The 88

Free Negro Labor and Property Holding in Virginia, 1830-1860 108

Free Negro Owners of Slaves in the United States in 1830, Together with Absentee Ownership of Slaves in the United States in 1830 18

Free Negroes in the District of Columbia, 1790-1846 125

Fugitive Slaves, 1619-1805 35

G

Genealogical Index, The 12

Genealogical Research Methods and Sources 11

Generations of Andrew Thompson and Silvey Williamson (the Story of the William Henry Lansdown Family) 216

Gouldtown 3

Gouldtown, a Very Remarkable Settlement of Ancient Date 160

Guide to British West Indian Archive Materials, in London and the Islands, for the History of the United States 257

Guide to Colorado Newspapers, 1859-1963 234

Guide to Genealogical and Biographical Sources for New York City, (Manhattan), 1783-1898 165

H

W

William Fitzhugh and His Chesapeake World, 1676–1701 107

Wills of Early New York Jews, 1704–1799 166

Where to Write for Birth and Death Records 4

Where to Write for Divorce Records 4

Where to Write for Marriage Records 4

Who's Who Among Colored Baptists of the United States 13

Y

Ye Kingdom of Accawmacke 105

SUBJECT INDEX

This index is alphabetized letter by letter and references are to page numbers. Unlined numbers refer to main areas within the subject. Some of the subjects are broken down geographically and can be found at the end of entry listing.

Subject Index

American Philosophical Society 177
Ancient Order of United Workmen 220
Anderson, Edward Clifford 66
Applegate, Lisbon 219
Appleton, John W.M. 157
Apprenticeship bonds. See Indentures
and bonds
Archivo General de Indias, Seville,
Spain 68-69
Ardrey, William E. 93
Arizona, records concerning blacks
233-34
Arizona Pioneers Historical Society
233
Arkansas, records concerning blacks
21, 122-26, 252
Arkansas. State Archives. History
Commission 123
Army records. See Military records
Arnold, J.N. 185
Arrest and conviction records 75
in newspapers 19
See also Freedmen, legal problems;
Slaves, legal problems
Artornish Plantation, Adams County,
Miss. 143
Ashtabula County (Ohio) Female Anti-
slavery Society 227
Association for the Benefit of Colored
Orphans 170
Associations, black. See Fraternal
orders, black
Atkins, James A. 235
Atlanta University. Trevor Arnett
Library 52
Auctions, slave. See Slave traders
and trading, records of
Aventine Plantation, Adams County,
Miss. 143
Ayers, James T. 197

B

Bacot, Peter Samuel 101
Bacot-Huger Collection. See South
Carolina Historical Society
Bahamas. See West Indies
Bailey, Everett Hoskins 213
Ball, John, Sr. 103
Ballinger, William Pitt 255

Bancker, Christopher 174
Bank of the United States 143
Baptismal records. See Church
records
Barbados. See West Indies
Barbary Coast, records of slavery in
181, 209
Barnwell Island Plantation, Tenn.
148
Barrow, Bennet H. 68
Barton family 148
Batchelor, Albert A. 73
Bateman, Mary 73, 93
Bates, William B. 158
Beale, Edward 93
Bell, William 209
Bell and Howell Corp. 226
Belmont Plantation, Claiborne County,
Miss. 143
Bermuda. See West Indies
Berrien, John McPherson 66
Berry, William Wells 147-48
Berwick, Beverly 67
Bibles as genealogical records 6, 32,
137
BIBLIOTHEQUE NATIONALE, Paris 70
Billingsley, James B. 255
Bills of sale, slave. See Plantation
records; Slave traders and
trading, records of
Birchard, Sardis 225
Birth records 14, 16, 17, 27, 38,
129
in business records 121
in church records 152
in city records 179
in county records 178
in federal records 4, 25, 26, 139
in military records 32, 111, 127,
188
in newspapers 19
in plantation records, diaries, and
papers 21, 51, 64, 95,
103, 108, 112, 121, 135,
142, 143, 220
in slavery records 114, 115, 149,
169
in township records 152, 156,
180, 185, 186
by geographical area

Subject Index

Divorce records 4. See also Marriage records
Dobbins, Archibald S. 123
Donnan, Elizabeth 154
Donnell, James Webb-Smith 121
Dorcey, James L. 87
Dover, Sally 214
Doyle (Doll) Benjamin 105
Duke University. Library 88, 107, 125
Dunlap, Hugh W. 148
Dunlap, John H. 148
Dupree, H.T.T. 143
Dutilh and Wachsmuth (slave traders) 183

E

Eakin, William 148
Earlham College Library. Quaker Archives 202
East Heritage Plantation, Argyle Island, Ga. 52
Education of blacks 213, 235, 244. See also School records
Eggleston, Dick Hardeway 141
Eliza, Allen A. 65
Elizafield Plantation, Glynn County, Ga. 51
Elliott, Newton G. 219
Emancipation records. See Manumission and emancipation records
Emigrant Aid Society 200
Emmons family 219
Employment. See Occupations and employment
Erwin, William 93
Executive Committee on Freedman 202

F

Family papers. See Diaries; Personal and family papers; Plantation records; names of people
Farmers, free blacks in federal censuses 27
Federal censuses. See Censuses
Federal records 24-28
  Alabama 118-19
  Alaska 233
  Arizona 233-34
  Arkansas 122-23
  California 244
  Colorado 234
  Connecticut 151
  Delaware 189
  Florida 130-31
  Georgia 53
  Idaho 235
  Illinois 196
  Indiana 201
  Iowa 204
  Kansas 247
  Kentucky 134
  Louisiana 71
  Maine 191
  Maryland 78-79
  Massachusetts 156
  Michigan 208
  Minnesota 212
  Mississippi 139
  Montana 236
  Nebraska 236
  Nevada 237-38
  New Hampshire 192
  New Jersey 161
  New Mexico 238
  New York 167-68
  North Carolina 89-90
  North Dakota 238-39
  Ohio 223
  Oklahoma 251
  Oregon 239
  Pennsylvania 177-78
  Rhode Island 184-85
  South Carolina 97
  South Dakota 238-39
  Tennessee 144-45
  Texas 253-54
  Utah 240
  Vermont 194
  Virginia 110-11
  Washington (state) 241
  Washington, D.C. 125-26
  Wisconsin 223
  Wyoming 242
  See also U.S. Federal Records Centers
Federal Writers Project. See U.S. Works Progress Administration

Subject Index

Hempstead, Joshua 7–8
Hempstead, Stephen 154, 220
Heyward Plantation, N.C. 89
Hickman–Bryan papers. See Missouri.
    University of
Hicks, Henry 231
Hicks, John 169
Hill, John 93
Hill, Jonathan 29
Hilliard, Isaac H. (Mrs.) 73, 141
Hill Plantation, Ala. 121
Hinson, Joseph Benjamin 104
Historical societies, directories of 11,
    17
Historical Society of Pennsylvania
    177, 182
Holley School for Blacks, Lottsburgh,
    Va. 113
Home Mission School for Negroes 146
Hooker, Joseph 245
Hooper, William 193
Hopeton Plantation, Glynn County,
    Ga. 64
Hord, William 135
Hospital records. See Medical records
Houston Public Library. Circle M
    Collection 254
Howard, Oliver Otis 191
Howard University 126, 192
    Library 125
Howth Plantation, Ala. 121
Hubbard family 95
Huntington (Henry E.) Library.
    Alexander Collection 246
Huston, Lee 104

I

Idaho, records concerning blacks 235
Illinois, records concerning blacks
    195–200
Illinois. State Historical Library 196
Illinois, University of, at Chicago
    Circle. Library. Slavery
    Collection 199
Indentures and bonds
    Arkansas 124
    Delaware 190
    Georgia 55, 59
    Illinois 196

Indiana 202
Kansas 250
Maryland 79, 80, 81, 84, 85,
    86, 87
Massachusetts 159
Mississippi 139
Missouri 220
New Jersey 162
New York 170
North Carolina 91
Pennsylvania 176, 180
South Carolina 99, 102, 104
Tennessee 145, 148
Texas 256
Virginia 105, 107, 114, 115
West Indies 258
Independent Order of Odd Fellows
    220
Indiana, records concerning blacks
    200–203
Indiana. State Library 203
Indiana Historical Society. Library
    203
Indians
    relationships with blacks 149,
      201, 251, 252
    as slaves 69
    Indian wars (western U.S.). See
      Military records
Indies. See West Indies
Insurance associations as sources of
    genealogical information
    17
Intermarriage between Indians and
    blacks 201
Interviewing. See Oral history
Inventories and estate records 42
    Kentucky 133, 135, 137
    Maryland 79, 80, 81, 82, 83,
      85, 86
    New York 164, 168
    Tennessee 149
    Virginia 107
    West Indies 260
    See also Wills
Iowa, records concerning blacks
    204–7
Iowa Historical Library. Department
    of Archives and History 204
Iowa Wesleyan College. Archives 204

Subject Index

J

Jackson, Andrew II 149
Jackson family 3, 8–9
Jacobs, Phillip 158
Jaeger (person) 111
Jamaica. See West Indies
Jay, John 174
Jefferson, Thomas 108
Jeffries family 102
Jenkins, John Carmichael 73
Jenks, Michael Hutchinson 182
Jermaine Memorial Library, Sag
        Harbor, N.Y. 174
Johnson, Anthony 105
Johnson, Thomas S. 182
Jones, Dorcus 174
Jones, George Noble 130, 154
Jones, J.J. 65
Jones, John L. 66
Jones, Morgan 181
Jones, S.A. 65
Jones, Samuel 175
Jones, William B. 66
Joyce, John 175
Justis, Horace Howard 93, 142

K

Kansas, records concerning blacks
        216, 247–49
Kansas State Historical Society 247
Kauffman, Julius 256
Keckley, Elizabeth 214
Kent State University 226
Kentucky, records concerning blacks
        21, 133–37
Kentucky Colonization Society 136
Kentucky Historical Society 134,
        135, 136, 137
King, Martin Luther, Jr. 246
King, Mary Rhinelander 63
King, Parrington 66
King, Richard Hugg 93
Knights and Daughters of Tabor 220

L

Ladies Aid Society 228
Land records 16
Alabama 119
Arkansas 124
Connecticut 151
Delaware 190
Florida 131
Georgia 66
Indiana 200
Kentucky 136
Maryland 79, 80, 81, 82, 83,
        84, 85, 86, 87
Missouri 219
Ohio 224
Pennsylvania 176
Rhode Island 185
South Carolina 96, 97
Tennessee 149
Virginia 105, 108, 113
See also Deeds
Lansdown family 3, 216
Lauch, B.M. 220
Laurens, Henry 101
Law, blacks and the
Arkansas 122
California 244
Iowa 204
Louisiana 68
Tennessee 144
Virginia 107
Law, Thomas Cassels 102
Lawton, Alexander James 94
Lawyers, black 78
Learmont Plantation, Woodville,
        Miss. 141
Learned Plantation, Hinds County,
        Miss. 143
Leases
South Carolina 102
Tennessee 145
Lewis, Ivery Foreman 121
Lewis, Junius R. 235
Lewis family 116
Liberia College 158
Libraries as sources of genealogical
        information 17, 20–21.
        See also names of libraries
Library Company of Philadelphia
        177
Library of Congress 107
Slave Narrative Collection 128–
        29

Subject Index

Maryland Historical Society 78
Maryland State Colonization Society
 87
Massachusetts, Commonwealth of.
 Archives 156
Massachusetts, records concerning
 blacks 32, 36, 37, 155-59,
 164
Massachusetts Anti-Slavery Society
 159
Massachusetts Colonization Society
 159
Massachusetts Historical Society 157
Massie, William 114
Mather, Joseph 74
Mather family 158
May, Samuel 113
Medical records 40
 Alabama 119
 Illinois 197
 Ohio 223
 Pennsylvania 179
 Virginia 111
Mexican War records. See Military
 records
Michigan. History Division. State
 Archives and Library 208
Michigan, records concerning blacks
 207-10
Mickley, Jeremiah Marion 182
Middleton, Nathaniel Russell 102
Middleton, Thomas 102
Midland Plantation, Ky. 136
Migratory patterns 34-36, 232
 to California 243
 to and from Georgia 52
 to Illinois 195
 to Indiana 200, 202
 to Iowa 204
 to Minnesota 211
 to Pennsylvania 176
 to Texas 254
 from the West Indies 257
 to Wisconsin 229
Military records 4, 6, 29-33
 of the Civil War 26-27, 31-33
  65, 99, 100-101, 111, 127,
  134, 147, 153, 157, 162,
  181-82, 187, 197-98, 205,
  209, 212-13, 215, 226-27

  230, 245, 248, 254
 of the French and Indian Wars
  184
 of the Indian Wars (western U.S.)
  6, 33, 255
 of the Mexican War 6, 226
 of the Revolutionary War 6, 29-
  30, 151, 187
 of the Spanish-American War 6,
  33, 157 198, 226, 245
 of the War of 1812 6, 31, 70,
  226
 of World War I 98, 226
 of World War II 98
 by geographical area
  Alabama 119, 120
  Arkansas 123
  California 245
  Connecticut 153
  Delaware 190
  Florida 132
  Georgia 62, 65
  Illinois 197-98
  Indiana 202
  Iowa 205
  Kansas 248
  Kentucky 134, 136
  Louisiana 70
  Maine 192
  Maryland 77, 87
  Massachusetts 157
  Michigan 207, 209
  Minnesota 212-13
  Mississippi 142
  Missouri 215, 218
  New Jersey 162
  New York 171
  North Carolina 94
  Ohio 225-26
  Pennsylvania 181-82
  Rhode Island 184, 187
  South Carolina 97, 98, 99,
   100-101
  Tennessee 147
  Texas 254-55
  Virginia 111, 112
  Washington, D.C. 127
  West Virginia 116
  Wisconsin 230
 See also Pension records, military

Subject Index

Subject Index

Plowden Weston Plantation, S.C. 103
Politicians, black 108
Poll tax records. See Tax records
Popular Grove Plantation, Scotts
 Hill, N.C. 95
Population schedules and enumerations.
 See Censuses
Porcher-Ford family 103
Porter, Nimrod 147
Pratt family 175
Preston (Davis) and Co. 114
Pringle, Elizabeth W. 94
Prison records. See Arrest and con-
 viction records; Freedmen,
 legal problems of; Slaves,
 legal problems of
Prostitutes, records of 180
Province Shelter for Colored Children
 188
Pryor, Jackson 148
Public Records Office, London. See
 Great Britain. Colonial
 Office. Records Room
Public School records. See School
 records
Putnam, Caroline F. 113

Q

Quakers. See Friends, Society of
Queens College. Ethnic Genealogy
 Center 7, 75, 89, 106,
 164, 198
 New York Historical Collection
 164

R

Rankin, John 228
Ransom, Reverdy Cassius 225
Raux, B. 74
Ravenel family 103
Records, genealogical. See Genealo-
 gical research; types of
 records, e.g. Church, Court;
 Marriage; Military
Reed, Seth 120, 147, 209
Reese, Ann 190
Regimental histories. See Military
 records

Remsen, Peter A. 231
Residence, records of 27
 in censuses 26
 in Freedmen's Bureau records 139
 in manumissions 167
 in voter registration lists 245
 in war records 29
 by geographical area
 California 245
 Connecticut 151
 Georgia 63
 Mississippi 139
 New Jersey 161
 New York 167
Revolutionary War records. See
 Military records
Rhode Island, records concerning
 blacks 31, 184-88
Rhode Island Historical Society 185,
 186, 188
Rice, Nannie Herndon 143
Richardson, Levin 87
Richardson-Nelson families 103
RIGHTS OF ALL (newspaper) 20
Risdon, Orlando Charles 226
Roberts, Jonathan 129
Rock County (Wis.) Historical
 Society 230
Rosedew Plantation, N.C. 94
Rosenberg, Henry 256
Ross, Isaac 143
Rowell, James 95
Royal Sons and Daughters of Douglass
 220
Rutgers University. Library 160

S

St. Croix. See West Indies
St. Francis College 169
St. George Plantation, Dorchester
 County, S.C. 101-2
St. Louis Public Library. Julia Davis
 Collection 216
Saint Mary College. Slave Papers
 250
St. Philips Negro Mission 93
Sams family 103
Sanders, Robert 169
Sanford, Henry Shelton 148

Subject Index

Saunders Colony, Calvin Township, Mich. 210
Sauters, Charles 142
Scanlan, Roger 5
Schoharie County (N.Y.) Historical Society 170
School records 6, 25, 27
  Arkansas 123
  Delaware 190
  Florida 131
  Georgia 53, 57, 59
  Kentucky 134
  Louisiana 71
  Massachusetts 158
  Mississippi 139
  Missouri 217
  New York 170
  Pennsylvania 183
  South Carolina 97, 99
  Tennessee 145
  Texas 254
  Washington, D.C. 126
  See also Education of blacks
Seale, H.M. 74
Seaman, Esther 169
Seminole Indians 252
Shaffer, J.J. 94
Shaffer, William Rufus 245
Shannon, Wesley 240
Shaw, John 181
Sheftall, Mordecai 159
Shepard, Charles 231
Sheperd family 115
Sherman, Adelbert C. 162
Ship's records 12, 14, 15, 37, 53, 67, 70, 71, 75, 114, 115, 127, 154, 159, 164, 186, 257, 258, 259
Shoemaker, Isaac 142
Siebert, Wilbur Henry 159, 228
Silk Hope Plantation 102
Simpson, Samuel 94
Sizer, Henry E. 143
Skinner, Tristin Lowther 94
Slave compensation papers, Kentucky 137
Slave owners, schedules of 6
  Alabama 118
  Florida 131
  Georgia 53, 61, 118

  Illinois 196
  Indiana 201
  Kentucky 133
  Louisiana 69, 70
  Maryland 78
  Mississippi 118
  New York 165–66, 169
  North Carolina 89
  Pennsylvania 178
  South Carolina 99
  Tennessee 144
  Virginia 108, 109, 114, 115
  See also Plantation records
Slave registers. See Names and lists of blacks
Slaves
  conspiracies and uprisings of 104, 166, 170, 181
  health conditions of 16, 73, 74, 142
  histories and narratives of 14, 15, 16, 158, 160
    California 243
    Connecticut 150
    Georgia 51
    Kentucky 133, 134
    Illinois 195, 198, 199
    Louisiana 71
    Massachusetts 156
    Michigan 209
    Mississippi 138
    Missouri 215, 216
    New York 165, 166
    Ohio 222
    Pennsylvania 176–77, 182
    South Carolina 97
    Tennessee 144
    Texas 256
    Utah 240
    Wisconsin 229
  legal problems of 54, 56, 57, 59, 60, 72, 86, 90, 126, 151, 152, 202, 245
  records of aid societies 6
  See also Blacks; Freedmen; Fugitive slaves; names of slave states; categories of statistics, e.g. Birth records
Slave ships. See Ship's records
Slave traders and trading 6, 15, 34–35, 49

322

Subject Index

New York 168-71
North Carolina 90-92
Ohio 223-24
Oklahoma 251-52
Pennsylvania 178-80
Rhode Island 185-87
South Carolina 98-100
Tennessee 145
Virginia 109
Vermont 194
Wisconsin 229-30
See also City and Township records;
    County and parish records
Steinmetz, Mary Owen 182
Still, Peter 163
Still, William 181
Stillwell, John Edwin 175
Stono slave revolt. See Slaves, con-
    spiracies and uprisings of
Strange, Agatha Jane (Rochester) 136
Strong, George W. 205
Sublette family 220

T

Tallcott, Joseph 183
Tax records 38
    Georgia 51, 60, 63
    Kentucky 134
    Louisiana 76
    Maryland 78, 79, 80, 81, 84,
        85, 86
    Mississippi 140
    Missouri 215, 219
    North Carolina 89, 95
    New York 164, 171
    Ohio 224
    Pennsylvania 176, 179, 180
    South Carolina 97, 104
    Virginia 105-6, 108, 109
    West Indies 259
Taylor, Francis 112, 136
Taylor, John 13
Taylor, William 74
Taylor family 148
Telfair Family Plantation, Ga. 67
Temple, Elizabeth Skyren 115
Tennessee, records concerning blacks
        21, 95, 144-49
Tennessee. State Library and Archives

119, 144, 145
Nichols-Britt Collection 149
Tennessee, University of 145
Tennessee Historical Society 145
Territories, slaves in the 18
Texas, records concerning blacks
        21, 253-56
Texas. State Library. Archives
        254
Texas Southern University. Library.
        Heartmen Negro Collection
        256
Thomas, Thomas 227
Thompson, Andrew 216
Thompson, Ishan 256
Thurston, Charles Brown 191
Tiffany, P. Dexter 220
Tilghman, William 183
Torbet, Charles 121
Torbet, James 121
Townsend, William 169
Township records. See City and
        township records
Trapier, Paul 100
Trials. See Blacks, legal problems;
        Court records; Slaves, legal
        problems
Tucker, D.M. 221
Tucker, J.H. 221
Tull, Isaac 66
Turner, Daniel 67
Tuskegee Institute. Library and
        Museum 119

U

Underground railroad. See Fugitive
        slaves
United Methodist Church. Iowa
        Conference Historical
        Society 205
U.S. Adjutant General's Office,
        records of 53, 79, 127,
        134
U.S. Bureau of Customs, records of
        53, 79, 127, 134
U.S. Bureau of the Census, records
        of. See Censuses
U.S. Department of the Interior,
        records of 53, 126

Subject Index